GOVERNMENT BEYOND THE CENTRE

SERIES EDITORS: GERRY STOKER AND DAVID WILSON

The world of sub-central governance and administration – including local authorities, quasi-governmental bodies and the agencies of public–private partnerships – has seen massive changes in the United Kingdom and other western democracies. The original aim of the **Government Beyond the Centre** series was to bring the study of this often-neglected world into the mainstream of social science research, applying the spotlight of critical analysis to what had traditionally been the preserve of institutional public administration approaches.

The replacement of traditional models of government by new models of governance has affected central government, too, with the contracting out of many traditional functions, the increasing importance of relationships with devolved and supranational authorities, and the emergence of new holistic models based on partnership and collaboration.

This series focuses on the agenda of change in governance both at sub-central level and in the new patterns of relationships surrounding the core executive. Its objective is to provide up-to-date and informative accounts of the new forms of management and administration and the structures of power and influence that are emerging, and of the economic, political and ideological forces that underlie them.

The series will be of interest to students and practitioners in central and local government, public management and social policy, and all those interested in the reshaping of the governmental institutions which have a daily and major impact on our lives.

Government Beyond the Centre
Series Standing Order
ISBN 0–333–71696–5 hardback
ISBN 0–333–69337–X paperback
(*outside North America only*)

You can receive future titles in this series as they are published by placing a standing order. Please contact your bookseller or, in the case of difficulty, write to us at the address below with your name and address, the title of the series and the ISBN quoted above.

Customer Services Department, Macmillan Distribution Ltd,
Houndmills, Basingstoke, Hampshire RG21 6XS, England

D0260282

GOVERNMENT BEYOND THE CENTRE

SERIES EDITORS: GERRY STOKER AND DAVID WILSON

Transforming Local Governance

From Thatcherism to New Labour

Gerry Stoker

First published 2004 by
PALGRAVE MACMILLAN
Houndmills, Basingstoke, Hampshire RG21 6XS and
175 Fifth Avenue, New York, N.Y. 10010
Companies and representatives throughout the world

PALGRAVE MACMILLAN is the global academic imprint of the Palgrave
Macmillan division of St. Martin's Press, LLC and of Palgrave Macmillan Ltd.
Macmillan® is a registered trademark in the United States, United Kingdom
and other countries. Palgrave is a registered trademark in the European
Union and other countries.

ISBN 0–333–80248–9 hardback
ISBN 0–333–80249–7 paperback

This book is printed on paper suitable for recycling and made from fully
managed and sustained forest sources.

A catalogue record for this book is available from the British Library.

Library of Congress Cataloging-in-Publication Data
Stoker, Gerry, 1955–
      Transforming local governance : from Thatcherism to New Labour /
Gerry Stoker.
        p. cm. – (Government beyond the centre)
      Includes bibliographical references and index.
      ISBN 0–333–80248–9
        1. Local government – England. 2. New Left – Great Britain.
      3. Conservatism – Great Britain. 4. Great Britain – Politics and government.
      I. Title. II. Series.

JS3111.S77 2003
320.8′0942—dc22   2003060863

10 9 8 7 6 5 4 3 2 1
13 12 11 10 09 08 07 06 05 04

Printed and bound in Great Britain by
Creative Print & Design (Ebbw Vale), Wales

To Deborah, Bethany, Robert and Benjamin
with lots of love

Contents

Contents

List of Tables, Figures and Boxes

Tables

Figure

Box

Acknowledgements

Very few books are written without a great deal of help from others. This book proves the truth of that observation. First and foremost there is my family, none of whom has the remotest interest in local governance or this book. This has proved healthy and supportive. They have had to put up with the many hours devoted by me to travelling and writing and they have done so with love and forbearance. It seemed logical to dedicate the book to them.

Second in line for acknowledgement are my many academic colleagues. There are my colleagues at Manchester and my past colleagues at Strathclyde, many of whom have helped me think through issues. A great contribution was made by all of the colleagues and researchers on the ESRC Local Governance Programme of which I was director between 1992 and 1997. Perri 6, with whom I co-wrote a book on holistic governance, proved to be an inspirational research colleague and the influence of his ideas are seen throughout the book. There are other research colleagues on whose joint work I have drawn – Neil McGarvey (Stratchclyde) Vivien Lowndes (De Montfort University, Leicester) and Lawrence Pratchett (De Montfort University, Leicester), Tony Travers (LSE), Francesca Gains (Manchester), Peter John (Birkbeck) and Nirmala Rao (Goldsmiths) – to whom I owe a considerable debt of gratitude. To be specific Chapter 5 includes material originally written with Neil McGarvey. Chapter 6 deals with issues that I have covered with Vivien Lowndes and Lawrence Pratchett. Chapter 7 draws on joint research with Francesca Gains, Peter John and Nirmala Rao. Chapter 8 covers material dealt with before in joint work with Perri b. Chapter 9 draws on earlier work with Tony Travers. I would like to give very special thanks to my series co-editor David Wilson at De Montfort University, Leicester, who has read earlier drafts of this book, made numerous helpful suggestions, and spurred me on to do more work to make this a better book. Others have helped in the last-minute preparation of the book, including Tessa Brannan, Karin Bottom and Stephen Greasley. The different parts of the book have benefited from presentations in many settings (including Australia, Norway, Denmark, Spain, Finland and Germany) and from the input of students on undergraduate courses at the University of Manchester. Steven Kennedy, as ever, has been a relentless but encouraging editor.

The third group that must be acknowledged are the policy-makers and practitioners who gave me access to their world. Local government councillors and officials have provided many insights, as have other players in the world of local governance. A whole set of people around the New Local Government Network (NLGN), of which I have been chair since its foundation in 1998, have contributed much to this book. The staff of NLGN have been, and continue to be, excellent colleagues. Geoff Filkin, John Williams and Dan Corry have all played key roles in NLGN and in shaping my thoughts. Government ministers, policy advisers and civil servants have been amazingly willing to tell me things and listen to what I have had to say. Hilary Armstrong, Nick Raynsford, Robert Hill, Darren Murphy and Paul Corrigan deserve my special thanks. I value the trust all these people have shown. Their openness, critical reflection and the fact that they care about getting policy right has made exchanges with them challenging and intellectually rewarding. A final mention should be given to Mike Emmerich, a former adviser in the Prime Minister's policy unit on local government and other matters, who in late 2002 joined me as a colleague and director of the Institute for Political and Economic Governance at the University of Manchester.

This book is not written by someone who is a neutral observer of reform. I have been an advocate of change. I cannot claim the sole authorship of any of New Labour's policies (which is some relief) but I cannot deny that I was involved in discussions about many of them. However, I do take full responsibility for the interpretation of the events of the last two decades offered here. This book represents my views and not necessarily the views of any of the people mentioned above.

GERRY STOKER

Introduction

A context of change

Local governance is in the throes of a struggle to transform its role in many countries. In the context of a changing welfare state and an increasingly globalised economy and society local government institutions in many western democracies have been changing their structures, systems of operation, political practice and modes of service delivery. The British experience of change stands out in part because of the scale of the reform that has been attempted since the late 1970s and in part because so much reform has come in the form of nationally imposed programmes. The issues addressed in the British reform process – about how to improve services, sustain local democracy, make multi-level governance work and fund local governance – are central to debates about the future of local governance in many other countries. The British reform process is a focus for international lesson-drawing, admittedly as much as for what not to follow, as to what to emulate.

This book has been given the title of 'transforming local governance' to capture the idea that we are not at the end of a process but rather in the middle of a dynamic of change that has not come to a final conclusion. Those interested in change and involved in the study of local politics and administration should concentrate their critical firepower on the emerging system of local governance and ask: what is the shape of the new system, how can we conceptualize its new form, what interests are to the fore and how can we assess the implications and impacts of the reforms that are taking place? Moreover we should address these questions with a degree of humility, recognizing that ideas held by those in the field during such a period of change often out strip those held by armchair observers. We should perhaps bear in mind that reform advocates and practitioners can soon tire of academics who point out that implementation has not gone smoothly or that some of the grander ambitions of the reformers have not yet come to fruition after a couple of years of practice. Most policy-makers and would be policy-influencers outside government I have met at local and national levels are naturally reflective and reflexive; in other words they expect things to foul up and to have to respond with further interventions. What interests them is where next to push

1

at the boundaries of the machine to see if it can be persuaded to take a few
more steps in what for them is the desired direction of change.

That said it seems to me that one of the defining characteristics of both
Thatcher's and New Labour's reform programmes are their relative inco-
herence. It took the Thatcher governments until the third term before the
emphasis moved way from a reactive concern to manage public spending to
a sustained drive to use market forms to drive efficiency and to some extent
quality gains into public services. There was also a journey in the
Conservative years in office from a focus on establishing powerful new
single purpose agencies outside local government to get things done to an
increasing emphasis on the virtues of partnership.

New Labour was clear that it did not buy the consensus reform agenda
developed by local government and its friends when Labour was in opposition. That programme involved restoring powers and funding to local councils, while allowing scope for them if they wished (but only if they wished)
to experiment with new political forms or new ways of delivering services.
The main planks of its policy towards local government emerged in the few
months before it was in office and in a series of policy debates that occurred
while was in office. It would be true to say that Labour's policy towards
local government is even now far from settled and not *per se* at the top of the
list in terms of political priority, in contrast to the broader objective of
improving public services. In many respects New Labour has deliberately
engineered its policy approach towards devolved governance in a manner
that has encouraged the sending out of conflicting and challenging messages.
What is notable about New Labour's programme is the way it has raised
a number of first principle arguments about the nature of local governance.
There is an assumption that local government needs to work in a new way.

The story so far in respect of the British case is that elected local government's role as a multi-purpose service provider in the context of a wider welfare state has been undermined. A form of local government that appeared to
be a permanent part of the landscape in the mid-1970s has, on the whole relatively easily, been sent to oblivion. Further although there have been substantial pockets of institutional resistance the great wave of change has
hardly elicited more than a murmur from the public. Many of those who represent or work for local government regret the truth in these observations and
it would also appear that some of those who study local government would
prefer it if the past model of local government was restored.

The study of local government has in some ways become wrapped up in
the reform process as academics try to make sense of the case for change

and the virtues of the emerging system. The challenge is made harder because it is not clear what new system will emerge. There has been a decisive attempt to switch in Britain from a system dominated by elected local government to a system of local governance in which a wider range of institutions and actors are involved in local politics and service delivery. It may be that elected local authorities are the weakest link in the chain of the new string of institutions of local governance and will eventually be asked to exit or it may be that they will discover a new role as the lead organization taking on the challenge of steering a complex set of managerial and democratic processes at the local level.

New forms of governance in many ways challenge traditional understandings of democracy, bureaucracy and service delivery. This is a strength but also a weakness, as there is a danger that the advantages of the old may be given away without sufficient benefits from the new. Moreover bringing new forms of governance into practice involves a struggle against past ideas and commitments and achieving change successfully is a considerable challenge. What direction for reform and how to reform are the key questions. To explain how the answers have unfolded at least in terms of local governance is the core subject matter of this book. It is worth now outlining the structure of the argument in the book.

The argument of the book

Understanding institutional change is a complex theoretical challenge. As Goodin (1996: 24–5) points out, there are three basic ways that social institutions might change over time: by accident, through evolution and directed by intentional intervention. It is the last type of change that is of key interest in this book. Change is viewed as 'the product of the deliberate interventions of purposive, goal-seeking agents' but the 'changes that ensue from their intentional interventions may or may not be exactly what was intended by any one (or by any subset) of them' (Goodin, 1996: 25). Change programmes under the Conservative and Labour governments since the late 1970s have certainly been intentional but equally have never delivered entirely what their advocates expected.

Using local governance reform as the basic raw material this book aims to shed light on the operation of intentional change programmes. It would seem necessary to understand such programmes to first explore the intentions of the reformers and their possibly competing recipes for change. It is important to understand not only their vision of what they wanted the reformed institution to look like but their understanding of how to achieve change. A second important element in understanding intentional change programmes is to be able to judge what the balance of forces have been and are likely to be between the champions of change and forces of resistance. The third issue that needs to be addressed is how the reform plans of the intentional reformers have worked out. The issue of evaluation must be essential in any examination of intentional reform. These themes are followed through in the book.

First, as to intentions, a key argument of the book is that the change process imposed on local government needs to be presented as the product of significant New Right and New Left political projects. Local government has been subject to deliberate re-design efforts. Since the late 1970s central–local relations have shifted from a period of relatively benign partnership to one where successive central governments have sought to impose their will on local government with an intensity that marks a significant break. This book explores the motivation and dynamic of reform and deliberately rejects the suggestion that local government is a random victim, picked on without purpose or reason. New Right and New Left ideas, which in turn represent an attempt to respond to changed conditions, have been played out in the arena of local government.

A shift in the pattern of governing at local and regional levels, almost stumbled into under successive Conservative governments elected from 1979, has been actively embraced and given a strong push under Labour governments elected from 1997. A quarter of a century of often centrally inspired change has had a substantial impact that has created a more complex and overlapping set of local institutions and actors. This general argument is explored in particular in Chapter 1 and examined further in Chapters 2 and 3, with the former concentrating on the Thatcher/Major years and the latter on New Labour. It is argued that New Labour had a distinctive approach to reform compared to that of the Conservatives. The book also provides more general insights into the objectives, strategies and perspectives of New Labour by examining the application of their ideas in the context of local government.

The second theme in understanding intentional change programmes is picked up in the central chapters of the book when the focus moves on to what happens to institutions under a sustained period of externally imposed change. We explore the dynamics of changes with key insights gleaned from institutional grid-group theory. The focus is the forces of promotion and resistance that characterize the implementation of reform programmes.

As suggested above the change process has been largely imposed, although there has been an active response from local government.

The book uses cultural grid-group theory not only to understand the direction of change but also its dynamic and reach. The utility of the grid-group framework is familiar to many in the guise offered by late political scientist Aaron Wildavsky and colleagues (Thompson *et al.*, 1990) as an analytical tool for exploring political and social life. Christopher Hood (2000) took the argument a stage further by showing how the grid-group framework reveals a range of forms of governing, a variety of ways of understanding the art of the state and its capacity for managing itself and its activities. The grid-group typology identifies ways of organizing our collective coexistence that take common and repeated forms in every institution we experience. Fatalism, hierarchy, communalism or entrepreneurial individualism provide world views, rules of thumb, common practices and rituals that can be traced through as ways of understanding and organizing our lives together. The tensions between them and the flaws in each provide a rich source of hypotheses that, in turn, when backed by appropriate evidence, can help to explain the way institutions change, the way they resist change and the way they 'muddle through' to a new resolution. Indeed the argument of this book is that grid-group theory offers an institutional analysis that goes beyond a useful heuristic device for thinking about patterns of social organization to provide powerful insights into strategies of change and how institutions respond to change.

The first discussion of grid-group work comes in Chapter 4 and is used to explore the nature of New Labour's reform strategy. It offers a rather strange conclusion, namely that New Labour's approach to the reform of local governance has many of the qualities of a lottery in which a complex variety of prizes have been offered to successful reformers but where the selection of winners reflects a mix of their capacity and chance. It would appear that a strategy driven by the principles of a lottery ties in with New Labour's fatalistic reading of its policy environment and has additional beneficial side effects in managing tensions within the administration and its relationship with various supporters.

The next four chapters explore the working out of New Labour's reform strategy in four areas. Chapter 5 deals with the drive to improve service delivery through Best Value strategies and the latter policy of comprehensive performance assessment. Chapter 6 examines the attempts that local authorities have undertaken, with New Labour's encouragement, to get more and a wider range of people involved in local politics and local decision-making. Chapter 7 tries to unravel the thinking behind the controversial policy of promoting directly elected mayors for local government and the reasons why the policy failed to deliver large numbers of mayoral authorities. Chapter 8 considers the rise of a huge variety of partnership arrangements at local and regional level in the context of New Labour's uncertain vision of how best to manage multi-level governance. Each of these chapters is focused on how the dynamic of change has progressed under a programme of intentional reform presented by New Labour.

The latter chapters of the book pick up the third theme in an investigation of intentional institutional change, namely what are the implications of the reform process. What has been achieved? How permanent is the settlement likely to be? What remains to be done? The conclusion of the book is that the shift away from a system dominated by elected local government is likely to be permanent but demands still more new thinking about and practice of local politics and service delivery. This theme is launched in the Chapter 9 with its discussion of the future of local finance and pursued in Chapters 10 and 11 in a more general way.

The issue of finance is the one that was famously subject to experiment by the Conservatives leading to the disaster of the poll tax (Butler *et al.*, 1994) and has been largely neglected by New Labour. Fundamental reforms have been attempted in service delivery and political practices but the finance system inherited from the Conservatives' ministrations has not been restructured except at the margins. Chapter 9 looks at the options if a new approach to finance is going to be developed to enable networked community governance to flourish.

Chapter 10 addresses the scale of the challenge of change taken on by the intentional reformers of local governance. Local governance reform has been constructed in a difficult environment where a lack of trust in public institutions and the legacies of past ways of doing things have proved a substantial drag on the unfolding of reform. New governing arrangements in turn raise complex and difficult issues about accountability and whether a more enabling form of state can emerge. Reformers have also had to learn hard lessons about how to steer reform and achieve change. Reforming any institution means recognizing the need to be reflective and flexible and that insight certainly applies in the case of the programmes of reform for local governance.

In Chapter 11 a set of conclusions about the reform of local governance under New Labour are presented. At best it is concluded that the job is only half done but the prize of a reformed system of networked local governance is of sufficient value to justify a continuing reform effort. The chapter takes up the theme of a New Localism to drive public policy in the early years of the new century.

As noted in the acknowledgements, this book is not written by a neutral observer but, rather, by an advocate of change. For me the goal of a reformed system of local governance is still achievable and it is a goal worth pursuing. Local government's job is to facilitate its community in achieving its objectives. Local government is there to influence the major social and economic dimensions of its locality even if it is not directly responsible for a particular service provision or policy issue. To deal with the issues that people care about – creating jobs, crime prevention, achieving quality education – requires leadership not only from government but from a variety of people in the community. Improving education calls for action from employers, headteachers, parents, teachers and students. Tackling crime requires the active commitment of not only the police but also insurance companies, those prone to the temptation of crime, and their potential victims. Local government's job is to help meet the fundamental challenge of achieving co-ordinated and effective collective action to deal with these and other issues that are central to its communities. Local government's job is not simply to provide more police or additional schools, although such provision may be part of the solution. The community leadership role involves local government's commitment to achieving outcomes desired by local people in co-operation with local stakeholders.

The new vision of networked community governance is premised in part on a critique of existing democratic politics and in part on a fuller recognition of the richness of democracy. A commonplace element in the political commentary of the last two or three decades of the twentieth century has been a recognition of the limits of government action. Mulgan (1994: 134) captures the spirit of much of the new thinking when he argues that 'government agencies are no longer deemed innocent until proven guilty or seen as essentially benign instruments of the public interest. Instead, a set of institutions that had come to seem a natural part of modern societies have found themselves open to a persistent challenge, charged with costing too much, with inflexibility and with neglect of the citizens they were meant to serve.' For New Labour the challenge is to redefine and reclaim a key role for the state. Governance implies a search for a new effective steering role for government. The commitment is to an enabling role for the state.

However, embracing governance also rests on a commitment to a richer understanding of democracy. Democracy in the twentieth century triumphed as an ideology because of two core virtues: democratic arrangements intrinsically treat all as free and equal (one person, one vote) and moreover they help protect the basic rights of citizens by insisting on the popular authorization of exercises of public power. However democracy put in practice through governance arrangements provides an additional benefit Democracy helps to solve problems by opening up the system to learning, ideas and the commitment of those who can offer solutions. The appeal of the new vision of local governance stretches beyond accountability to a focus on extending the effectiveness and capacity of governing arrangements.

1   The Emerging System of Local Governance

The established ways of doing local government are giving way to new, as yet not fully formed, governance alternatives. The use of governance captures an understanding that there has been for more than two decades a period of change in governing arrangements at the local level. Old has not entirely given way to a finally formed new but the obituaries for the old system can be written. However, our focus is on a period of intense transition that is under way. The search for a reformed local governance is a response to working in a post-industrial, post-bureaucratic and post-welfare state expansion period. Crouch (2000: 13) explains in abstract terms what is implied by 'post-X':

> Time period 1 is pre-X, and will have certain characteristics associated with the lack of X. Time period 2 is the high tide of X ... Time period 3 is post-X. This implies that something new has come into existence. However X will still have left its mark ... More interestingly the decline of X will mean that some things start to look rather like they did in time 1 again. Post periods should therefore be expected to be very complex.

It is the sense of moving from one phase to a yet not fully defined period – which in turn remains affected by historical legacies – that is captured by the use of prefix 'post'. The starting point for this book is that we have entered a post-elected local government era and are moving to a new era of local governance populated by a more diverse and varied set of institutions and processes. Moreover the period of transition is complex given that it is driven by reform programmes that are not entirely coherent and where new ways of working run alongside features of local governance that would have graced earlier periods.

The particular changes relating to local politics are framed within a wider set of changes in economy and society that have been variously entitled as post-modernity, post-industrialism or post-Fordism (see Stoker, 1989, 1990). From the early 1970s onwards the relatively settled pattern of post-war welfare states in the western democracies has been under challenge

(Stoker, 1999c). A key factor has undoubtedly been the financial crisis of the state, which has encouraged a reconsideration of its form and operation (Pierre and Peters, 2000: 52–5). The responses that are labelled as part of governance here are more than the acceptable face of spending cuts. They are a reaction, as Pierre and Peters (2000) argue, to globalization, the perceived failure of nation state to intervene effectively in tackling social and economic conditions and the sheer complexity of the governing challenges that now have to be confronted. At times the European Union, central government as well as local government have all pushed the search for new partnership solutions. Governance methods have also emerged as a result of social movements or campaigns such as those around the environment where arguments for more inclusive forms of action, which bring the public to the fore, have been aired. Several factors then explain the emergence of governance. Overall 'governance has become important due to changes in society ... and the new governance is a strategy to link the contemporary state to the contemporary society' (Pierre and Peters, 2000: 51–2).

This book argues that in Britain under New Labour the debate about public service reform at least at the local level has moved beyond the concerns of new public management to an emerging concept of networked community governance. The emerging system challenges central pillars of the world of local government that dominated in the immediate post-Second World War period. These arguments are explored further below. First, three models of how local government should be organized are outlined and associated with different eras from post-war, through the new public management of the 1980s and 90s to the changes that have taken place under New Labour at the start of a new century. The next two sections outline the changed governing institutions and processes associated with the emerging networked community governance.

Beyond new management: the emergence of networked local governance

Table 1.1 sets out in an abstract form three eras for the governing of local affairs. In the post-war period local government played its part in the establishment of the core services of the welfare state and along with that role in the welfare state went certain assumptions about how local services should be governed. A period in which local government adopted a traditional public administration form gave way under pressure from a New Public Management wave carried first by the local government reorganization in the early 1970s and given new impetus by the Conservative governments of

Table 1.1   *Eras of local governing*

	Elected local government in post-war setting	Local government under New Public Management	Networked community governance
Key objectives of the governance system	Managing inputs, delivering services in the context of a national welfare state	Managing inputs and outputs in a way that ensures economy and responsiveness to consumers	The overarching goal is greater effectiveness in tackling the problems that the public most care about
Dominant ideologies	Professionalism and party partisanship	Managerialism and consumerism	Managerialism and localism
Definition of public interest	By politicians / experts. Little in the way of public input	Aggregation of individual preferences, demonstrated by customer choice	Individual and public preferences produced through a complex process of interaction
Dominant model of accountability	Overhead democracy: voting in elections, mandated party politicians, tasks achieved through control over the bureaucracy	Separation of politics and management, politics to give direction but not hands on control, managers to manage, additional loop of consumer assessment built into the system	Elected leaders, managers and key stakeholders involved in search for solutions to community problems and effective delivery mechanisms. System in turn subject to challenge through elections, referendums, deliberative forums, scrutiny functions and shifts in public opinion
Preferred system for service delivery	Hierarchical department or self-regulating profession	Private sector or tightly defined arm's-length public agency	Menu of alternatives selected pragmatically
Approach to public service ethos	Public sector has monopoly on service ethos, and all public bodies have it	Sceptical of public sector ethos (leads to inefficiency and empire building) – favours customer service	No one sector has a monopoly on public service ethos. Maintaining relationships through shared values is seen as essential
Relationship with 'higher' tiers of government	Partnership relationship with central government departments involved in delivery	Upwards through performance contracts and delivery against key performance indicators	Complex and multiple: regional, national, European. Negotiated and flexible

Source: Developed from Kelly and Muers (2002).

the 1980s. The consequent model of enabling local governance on offer was driven by a different set of ideas about the way those public services should be governed, with efficiency and customer care as the watch words. We are moving in Britain at the beginning of the twenty-first century, under the impact of New Labour, towards another set of ideas about the governance of local public services. This is a vision of networked community governance that could provide the basis for a new role for local government. None of the models fits perfectly within the time frames as outlined. There is leakage and overlap. The first two models did become dominant ways of expressing an idealized statement of the role and core processes that were expected of local government. The third offers a vision of what may become the new common sense of what local government is there to deliver in the early years of the twenty-first century but it has not yet been realized.

These models represent different mixes of ideological forms that have for long been commonplace in local politics. Dunleavy (1980: 145) comments on 'the existence of ideological forms or stereotypes in local political institutions which ... may exert an extensive determining influence on individual actors or groups. By defining a series of options open to actors, and others which are foreclosed, such ideologies largely delimit the scope and direction of change, crucially influencing the "style" of local authority decision-making.' Writing in 1980 Dunleavy found professionalism and party partisanship to be the central ideological creeds of, respectively, officers and elected politicians. These are the creeds that dominated during the period in which traditional public administration understandings dominated elected local government.

Managerialism is the other main ideological creed identified by Dunleavy. A lesser role is also given to several other ideologies, of which one is particularly worthy of note, namely localism. Localism, Dunleavy defines as a policy focus on the concerns of the community served by the authority. These two ideologies were regarded by Dunleavy as marginal when he published his book in 1980. Managerialism was a cost-cutting creed espoused mostly by treasurers and localism the reserve of relatively powerless councillors with a ward or neighbourhood focus. Yet since 1980 professionalism and partisanship as the dominant legitimating ideologies of local government have come under considerable attack and both managerialism and localism have risen in prominence.

Under the traditional public administration model the key task for local government was delivering services as part of the welfare state. The assumption was that what was required was largely known. It was to build better schools, housing and roads, and provide better welfare and that we could rely on expert officers and politicians to define what was precisely needed in any one locality. This is the world of local government described in Ken Newton's (Newton, 1976) study of Birmingham or Jon Gower Davies's analysis of Newcastle (J. Davies, 1972) in the late 1960s and early 1970s. Within its role as provider of services in the welfare state, local government was a dominant and rather domineering player. It raised local rates and managed central government grants in order to deliver and develop services. It managed service delivery largely in-house and was confident that its actions were imbued with a special public sector ethos and mandated through the legitimacy provided by the operation of local elections. Professionalism and confident partisan politics were to the fore.

The first attack on this world view came from the New Public Management. The first expression was in the interest in corporate management in the late 1960s and 1970s (Dearlove, 1979; Cockburn, 1977) although that left few institutional traces other than a stronger role for chief executives (Gyford *et al.*, 1989: ch. 3). The second coming of New Public Management was more of the cost-cutting variety of managerialism recognized by Dunleavy (1980). Here the stress was on keeping down the cost of providing public services through stronger management disciplines such as across-the-board 'efficiency' savings, performance targets and the use of competition to select the cheapest service producer. The Conservative governments from the early 1980s onwards laid considerable stress on these New Public Management disciplines. In the 1990s, as part of a growing consumerist orientation in local government (Skelcher, 1992) central government began to call for responsiveness and choice in public services alongside the narrow focus on cost savings. Better management meant putting the customer first.

Managerialism, although in a somewhat broader form than the cost-cutting ideology identified by Dunleavy (1980), began in the 1980s and 90s to take an increasingly strong hold in local government in Britain (Stoker, 1999b). This ideology saw political leadership as important in setting direction but beyond that a potential source of inefficiency. Politicians were to set goals but should not dictate the means to achieve them. The key to managerialism is its emphasis on the rights of managers to manage against inappropriate interference from politicians, or, for that matter, the special pleading of professional groups. Managerialism focuses on running what is more effectively. The perspective of this era is that the welfare state is established but expensive and demanding in terms of taxpayers' money so the key challenge is to make service delivery more efficient. The idea of an exclusive public sector ethos to guide providers is rejected in favour of a more open competition between producers from a variety of sectors to keep down costs and in order to encourage responsiveness to users. In some formations a particular additional role is given to consumers in defining the purposes of public services and even more strongly in assessing whether public services have provided satisfaction. The key to good management is clear goals that meet consumer needs, solid contractual relations between service commissioners and service producers and effective monitoring of service delivery. It is at this final stage that including some measure of consumer satisfaction is seen as appropriate.

A third model of complex community governance began to take shape from the mid-1990s onwards (Sullivan, 2001). It takes its main inspiration from the ideology of localism, namely that the key task for local government is to meet the needs of its community either directly or indirectly. In that sense it places far more emphasis than either the post-war model or the New Public Management approaches on the search for what are the issues and what might be the solutions. Its reach is beyond the delivery of services. Its overarching goal is the meeting of community needs as defined by the community within the context of the demands of a complex system of multi-level governance (Stewart and Stoker, 1988). Its aim is to achieve not narrow efficiency but Public Value, defined as the achievement of favoured outcomes by the use of public resources in the most effective manner available (Moore, 1995; Goss, 2001). Given such a goal it is not surprising that no particular place is given to a public sector ethos but rather there is a broader commitment to maintaining system relationships in general. The choice of which sector or organization should be involved in provision is also a pragmatic one.

The model demands a complex set of relationships with 'higher' tier government, local organizations and stakeholders. The relationships are intertwined and the systems of accountability are multiple. The political process is about the search for identifying problems, designing solutions and assessesing their impact on the underlying problem. Beyond service delivery there is a focus on the purpose of services and their impact on the problems they are addressing. Success is not a simple matter of efficient service delivery but rather the complex challenge of whether an outcome favourable to the community has been achieved. The model retains a strong commitment to managerialism in order to join up and steer a complex set of processes. This is a managerialism that goes beyond a search for efficiency gains or a customer orientation to take on the challenge of working across boundaries (Sullivan and Skelcher, 2002) and to take up the goal of holistic working which is 'greater effectiveness in tackling the problems that the public most care about' (Perri 6 *et al.*, 2002: 46).

**Networked community governance: the
organizational and structural ingredients**

Beyond elected local government

In the early 1970s the elected local council with its committees and departments was the key institution of the local political environment. The 'Town' or 'County' Hall epitomized for many of the public their understanding of a bureaucratic organization: hierarchical, rule-driven and a permanent presence in their community. Reorganizations led to changes of name, and in the localities covered and functions held, but the basic organizational structure remained the same. Local government consisted of councillors elected to serve the governing body that supervised the operation of a range of departments each with its particular functions, bureau head and hierarchical tiers of permanent officials. In practice decision-making was concentrated in the joint elite of senior officers and councillors (Stoker, 1991: ch. 4). Chief officers, their deputies and committee chairs and vice-chairs jostled with one another over priorities and spending. Key additional influences came from ruling party group(s) and interdepartmental conflicts and intradepartmental arenas that engaged more junior officials. As in other institutions the local bureaucratic system appeared to give considerable openings for those in formally subordinate positions to gain influence (cf. Held, 1987: 161). The system was hierarchical but not entirely closed and scope remained for some interest groups and local interests to carve out decisions and measures to their liking (Stoker, 1991: ch. 5).

The governance account does not claim that the local bureaucratic machine, so dominant in the 1970s, has disappeared but rather argues its pre-eminence can no longer be taken for granted and that the organizational world has begun to look more complex. One key sign at the local level is the arrival of new organizations outside the formal span of control of the local council. There is virtually now no field of local decision-making where local government is able to operate on its own as Table 1.2 demonstrates. Whatever the function there are a mixed range of partners from freestanding agencies to various partnerships. Indeed the institutions listed in Table 1.2 are not a comprehensive or necessarily permanent set of institutional forms that make up local governance. Moreover some agencies were core to local government functions in the past, in terms of the role, for example, of water authorities or the nationalized providers of gas and electricity. But the range and variety of sectors from which key agencies are drawn means that at the beginning of the twenty-first century the challenge of networked community

Table 1.2   *Core functions of local governance and institutional complexity*

Community safety:	Employment and skills:	Education and early years:
• Police authorities • Fire authorities • Magistrate's courts • Crime and disorder partnerships • Drug action teams • Basic police command units • Neighbourhood wardens	• Learning and skills councils • Employment action zones • Colleges of further education • Universities	• School governing bodies • Education action zones • Learning partnerships • Early years development and child care partnerships

Housing and regeneration:		Health and well-being:
• Registered social landlords • Single regeneration budget • New deal for communities • Gas and electricity utilities	Local elected councils	• Primary Care Trusts • Health Action Zones • Sure Start partnerships • Children's Trusts • Strategic health authorities

Transport:	Environment and planning:	Leisure and arts:
• Passenger transport authorities • Highways authorities • Bus companies • Rail companies	• Environmental protection agency • Regional planning bodies • Regional development agencies • Water companies	• Sports councils • Arts councils

governance is characterized by a high level of complexity in the relationships between local councils and others local service agencies.

Beyond overhead representative democracy?

Post-war local government rested on the overhead democracy model. That model relied on two linkages: citizens control elected politicians (electoral accountability) and politicians control bureaucrats (bureaucratic accountability) (cf. B. Jones, 1995: 74). Accounts of local democracy in the 1970s to a large extent rested on this model but many commentators in the

1970s noted problems with both linkages in the overhead chain of account-ability. First, electoral accountability was threatened by the influence of national factors on voting so that as a test of local performance local elec-tions might be seen as inadequate (Newton, 1976: ch. 2). Some argued, however, that the electoral linkage remained in place notwithstanding such issues.

> Voters may cast their vote on the basis of all manner of motives – sensible, judicious, bigoted or capricious – what matters is that an elected body is produced that acts as if it is a representative of its constituents' interests. (Sharpe, 1970: 172)

The key issue was that the overseers of the system were elected and that guaranteed accountability.

In a similar manner problems with bureaucratic accountability are noted but judged by many to be not sufficient to undermine the thrust of the over-head model. The power of officials in controlling information and agendas is noted; so too are their claims of professional judgement to override polit-ical input. Yet the view of many commentators (Gyford, 1976) in the 1970s remained that if politicians were organized and committed they could con-trol their bureaucracies. Newton (1976: 164) comments, 'the relationship between elected representatives and appointed officials is rather more equal than (the) "dictatorship of the official" prophecy suggests'.

The community governance account does not dismiss the overhead model of democracy; although it might favour greater scepticism about how effectively electoral and bureaucratic accountability operates in the current period. Its key message is again that the complexity of the challenge has increased. New lines of accountability have been added to those identified by the overhead model.

The first challenge – and this was a force recognized in the 1970s – is the role of local pressure or interest groups (see Newton, 1976; Gyford, 1976). At the very least organized groups outside the council complicate the image of overhead democracy. In some versions of the argument they can lead to an alternative model of pluralist democracy in which factions of govern-ment and interested publics work together to make decisions and meet the challenges of their locality (cf. B. Jones, 1995: 75–6).

Accountability through local interest groups has been accompanied by the rise in accountability to service users through panels, committees, boards and discussion of forms of direct participation through citizen-initiated ballots or local authority or central government endorsed referendums. More broadly there is a considerable emphasis on and growth in schemes for public participation and consultation that potentially cut across the simplistic linkages of the overhead democracy model. Processes of consultation and user involvement that were observable in the 1980s in British local politics (Gyford, 1986; Gyford *et al.*, 1989) have become an established part of local government operations in the late 1990s (see Lowndes *et al.*, 2001a and b). Accountability directly to stakeholders involved in using services or based in particular communities of interest or geography is a much more accepted, indeed expected, part of local politics at the beginning of the twenty-first century than it was in the late 1960s and 1970s.

Administrative accountability has also been strengthened through the establishment of the local ombudsman in 1974 as well as more developed rights to information and mechanisms to bolster complaints procedures. The local ombudsman system in England handled some 20,000 cases a year by the late 1990s although in less than 1 per cent of cases is a maladministration with injustice finding made (Wilson and Game, 2002: 153–5). There has also been a wider use of judicial review. In 1974 leave for review was sought 160 times. In 1995 this had grown to 4400 cases (Wilson and Game, 2002: 153). The final wave of accountability has a managerial character and involves increased use of auditors and inspectors for achieving value for money and effective service performance. This enhanced form of regulation within government is discussed in more detail in Chapters 3 and 5. Both Conservative and Labour governments since 1979 have encouraged increased use of this form of accountability.

The governance perspective brings into focus forms of accountability that stretch beyond the overhead model. In doing so it recognizes how changes in the last few decades 'challenge the traditional role of members and officer-professionals to shape the organization of the service and even to determine appropriate standards of performance' (Loughlin, 1996: 50). Whether these new forms of accountability have brought benefits that outweigh any costs is, of course, open to doubt. By rendering the local government system to much greater external accountability by consumers, taxpayers, review agencies and central departments a profound shift has occurred with substantial implications for the constitutional position of elected local government (Loughlin, 1996). The governance account brings this fundamental break from the overhead democracy model to our attention.

The rise of multi-level governance

The governance account shifts attention beyond the two-way relationship between central and local government to recognize not only the complexity of intergovernmental networks of various forms but also more generally the rise of multi-level governance. Again the underlying message is of increased complexity. The issue of central–local relations remains a matter for discussion but is placed in the context of a wider web of intergovernmental relations.

In the 1970s the key intergovernmental issue was about the relationship between central and local government. The Layfield Committee (1976), for example, debated long and hard about the constitutional implications for central–local relations of the financing of a new range of local public services. Given the centre's increased contribution to funding local services, could scope for local government and decision-making remain, asked Layfield. This concern about the way that local services are financed from central government grants or local sources has not gone away but it has been deflected by a recognition of a more complex reality.

At the beginning of the twenty-first century local authority total spending in Britain constitutes only about a quarter of all public spending in localities. Admittedly a considerable proportion of that other public spending comes from the health and social security sectors in as much as it would have done in the 1970s. Nevertheless a wide range of appointed bodies, partnerships and agencies have over the last three decades become an important part of the local government scene, joining various benefits and health bodies. As noted earlier the emergence of local quangos – a term used to capture here the range of appointed bodes, partnerships and self-governing agencies – is a key empirical development for the governance perspective.

Alongside an array of semi-independent or autonomous agencies operating at the local level there has been a recognition following the studies of Dunleavy (1980) and especially Rhodes (1988) of the wider organizational networks and influence of intergovernmental relations.

> The term 'central–local government relationship' can be misleading if it encourages a narrow focus on the interaction between central departments and local authorities. In practice a range of other organisations cut across the relationship, including the local authority associations, professional organisations, party institutions, quasi-government organisations and trades unions. (Stoker, 1991: 146)

The wider world of the national local government system has an enormous impact.

Still further institutional complexity is added by recognition of the increased significance of bodies operating at spatial scales other than that of the local authority. Devolved political institutions in Scotland, Wales and Northern Ireland operate alongside weak unelected regional assemblies in England. The European Union has emerged as an actor of substance in local affairs through its regulation and funding regimes (Benington and Harvey, 1999). It might also be added that the Labour Government elected in 1997 has encouraged the establishment of neighbourhood and other partnership organizations governing institutions under the New Deal for Communities and other programmes. In short, institutional actors at neighbourhood, regional and supranational levels have complicated the experience of inter-governmental relations.

The overall result of these various institutional factors – quangos, network organizations and multi-tier spatial political institutions combined with central and local government – has been characterized as the arrival of multi-level governance. 'Governing Britain to-day – and indeed any other advanced western democratic state – has thus become a matter of multi-level governance' (Pierre and Stoker, 2000: 29). To understand the challenge of governing requires a recognition that decision-making has multiple locations – spatial and sectoral – and is driven by a complex interplay of forces across these multiple locations. The governance account takes it as axiomatic that to study local governance the richness and complexity of its organizational and spatial settings needs to be recognized. The new starting point needs to be multi-level governance which, in turn, means 'no pre-judgements about the hierarchical order of institutions: global patterns of governance can hook up with local institutions just as local or regional coalitions of actors can bypass the nation-state level and pursue their interests in international arenas' (Pierre and Stoker, 2000: 30).

The search for fiscal fudges and value for money

As noted at the start of the chapter, financial constraints provide an important element in background to the rise of governance. Governance solutions, in part, represent an attempt to cope with the fiscal tension created by an increasing demand for public services and at the very least a certain ambiguity about the willingness of all sections of the public to pay the taxes necessary to cover increased expenditure. The governance account places a central concern on the management of this fiscal tension.

In some ways because tensions over holding back public spending have been part of the policy of Britain and many other western democracies for the last twenty years – certainly for all my working life! – it is easy to forget that at least for a period during the 1950s and 60s it was not such a prominent issue. Between 1955 and 1975 local authority current expenditure tripled in size at constant prices (Stoker, 1991: 7). Assumptions of continued growth were deeply ingrained. According to Sharpe (1970: 173) 'rising demand is likely to be a permanent feature' of a large number of local services. He identified three factors that were likely to sustain the push for higher spending.

The first is the growth in the numbers of those age groups that consume the lion's share of these services, the young and the old. Second, there is the rise in expectations generated by rising living standards; and third, on the supply side, rising standards generated by the services themselves. This last one may be the most decisive of the three and broadly takes the form of last year's most advanced increment to standards becoming next year's basic need (Sharpe, 1970: 172). Sharpe's analysis over the factors driving forward spending is perceptive. Demographic pressures, rising expectations and producer-sponsored pressure for improvements have all played a part in the push for higher spending. What is conspicuous by its absence is recognition that countervailing forces might exist.

There are two general countervailing forces to consider (Pierre and Peters, 2000: 52–5). The first is that the economic growth that for many states had delivered growing tax revenues became slow or uncertain. The second is the stalling of the political platform for tax revenues. By the 1970s taxes in many countries had reached a level beyond which they could not be raised further. Growing political protest, increasing incentives for tax evasion and impaired economic growth all seemed to prohibit further tax increases (Pierre and Peters, 2000: 53). In Britain the 1970s saw protest votes for ratepayer groups in a few areas and in 1976 the establishment of the Layfield Committee in part as a response to a concern about how to fund local finance. The election of a Conservative government in 1979 began a period of considerable struggle over local finance which delivered (eventually) central control over local spending to an overwhelming degree.

The governance account takes as a central theme the tension between increased demand for public spending and a strong sense of limitation on the taxpayers' willingness to pay. The focus of governance is, in part, about the search for solutions to manage the tension.

Solutions involve the search for 'value for money'. New methods of working – contracting, partnering, regulatory provisions – may deliver that elusive 'more for less' and help, therefore, to ease the fiscal tension. They can also be more about fiscal fudge through dressing services in private clothing to give them greater public appeal or an appearance of efficiency.

Some private finance deals that appear to delay but not reduce taxpayer funding for the service might fall into this category (Kelly, 2000). The contribution of public–private partnerships is in a key question for researchers inter-ested in the development of governance. More generally a focus on managing financial constraints is a defining characteristic of the governance perspective.

Towards new governing processes

Governing is concerned with the processes that create the conditions for ordered rule and collective action within the political realm. What is it that enables complex tasks to be managed, priorities set and decisions made? How in a complex environment with a vast range of actors can a sense of order and direction be established? How in the context of conflict over goal definitions and the practice of implementation is some capacity to act collectively maintained?

These challenges are issues central to governing in any time period and the Weberian paradigm – so long dominant in public administration – has provided a particular set of solutions to the challenges posed. In Weber's political thought three institutions are seen as essential to coping with the complexity of modernity and for delivering order to the governance process. They are political leadership, party and bureaucracy (Held, 1987: 148–60).

Weber was not opposed to the idea of direct democracy but felt it was unlikely to be a viable option for most decision-making within a mass democracy. A representative form of democracy, in contrast, is seen as having the flexibility to balance different interests and develop policies to meet shifting circumstances. However, Weber placed modest expectations on the representative body of elected politicians. It allowed for discussion and debate but was primarily there to provide a pool of potential political leaders. Elections, in turn, provide the crucial mechanism for popular endorsement or otherwise of political leadership. Competing political leaders lies at the heart of the democratic process. Weber assumed that the public was largely uninterested in wider political engagement and participation. This concept of elite democracy was a central plank in western political thought for much of the twentieth century.

Parties – with tight discipline – are the key institution for both mobilizing support in a mass democracy and in organizing the practice of government by holding representatives to a shared collective line. Career politicians emerge who owe their advances to political parties and the parties in turn become key vehicles for fighting and winning elections. Parties get out the vote and organize government. Modern democracy was unthinkable save in terms of political parties (Dalton and Wattenberg, 2000). Bureaucracy forms the third arm for organizing the modern state. Mass citizenship leads to increased demands on the state – in areas such as education and health – which can only be managed by standardization and routinization of administrative tasks. Moreover modern economic systems demand the stability and predictability provided by bureaucracy. From a Weberian perspective bureaucracy delivers organizational effectiveness through four features (Beetham, 1987). The first is the placing of officials in a defined hierarchical division of labour.

The central feature of bureaucracy is the systematic division of labour, whereby complex administrative problems are broken down into manageable and repetitive tasks, each the province of a particular office (Beetham, 1987: 15). A second core feature is that officials are employed within a full-time career structure in which continuity and long-term advancement is emphasized. Third, the work of bureaucrats is conducted according to prescribed rules without arbitrariness or favouritism and preferably with a written record. Finally, officials are appointed on merit. Indeed they become expert by training for their function and in turn control access to information and knowledge in their defined area of responsibility.

The dominance and influence of the Weberian model on what constitutes government in the western democratic tradition of thought is substantial. It finds reflection in the Westminster model, a dominant paradigm in British politics (Gamble, 1990). This model characterized the British political system as a unitary state led through strong cabinet government, parliamentary sovereignty, an impartial civil service and accountability through regular elections. At the local level Weberian assumptions underlie a large part of what John Stewart (2000: ch. 4) calls the 'inherited world of local government': the committee system, the departmental base, the bureaucratic habit and the influence of professionals. More generally assumptions about the role of party, the passivity of the public and the overriding legitimacy that comes from election are deeply ingrained in much of the thinking of both local government practitioners and observers.

From the arguments made in the first section of this chapter it is clear that the Weberian governance paradigm is under severe pressure. The reduction of politics to a competition between leaders is seen as too limiting in the new world of governance. Overhead democracy is not enough. The role of political parties is the key instrument of political organization and representation is subject to challenge by other forms of participation and accountability.

The view that the bureaucratic form of provision delivers the greatest organizational effectiveness is widely questioned.

So the world has changed but here a more general argument is developed; namely that while the Weberian perspective rested on viewing governing as a tight cluster of connected institutions, the networked community governance perspective offers a contrasting organizing framework of wider, looser organizations joined through a complex mix of interdependencies. Advocates of networked community governance make a virtue out of these features. In this book, for the present, it is simply suggested that in order to develop a better understanding of local politics and service delivery we need to make these governance features a focus of analysis.

Networked community governance frames issues by recognizing the complex architecture of government. In practice there are many centres and diverse links between many agencies of government at neighbourhood, local, regional and national and supranational levels. In turn each level has a diverse range of horizontal relationships with other government agencies, privatized utilities, private companies, voluntary organizations and interest groups. There is nothing to suggest that networked community governance should be any less susceptible to conflict regarding goal definitions and defining priorities than the traditional views of governing. Governance does not wish away conflict but it does recognize that there are a variety of ways in which it can be managed other than through a tight core of institutions such as bureaucracy and political party and a limited elite form of democracy.

Moreover, whereas the Weberian model offers one solution to the co-ordination challenge in a complex setting the governance perspective recognizes there are at least four governing mechanisms beyond direct provision through a bureaucracy. The bureaucratic form solves the problem of organizing in a complex world by dividing tasks into manageable parts and then connecting the actors responsible for individual tasks through a hierarchical structure of command. From the community governance perspective co-ordination through bureaucracy is joined by co-ordination through regulation, market, interest articulation and networks of trust.

Governing by regulation is of course compatible with the Weberian perspective if it is seen as government laying down and monitoring rules for private firms or individuals to follow. What the governance perspective calls attention to is regulation *within* the public sector. Hood and his colleagues (1998: 8–13) outline three dimensions to regulation inside government:

1. One public organization aims to shape the activities of another.
2. Oversight is at arm's length, in that there is not a direct action or command relationship.

3. The regulator has some kind of official mandate to scrutinize the behaviour of the regulatee and to seek to change it.

Regulation within government operates, then, not through a Weberian hierarchical chain of command, although it does rely on the regulator having the authority to oversee the operation of other agencies. Their behaviour is checked through inspection, which in turn may lead to intervention ranging from advice to termination, if the organization undergoing regulation fails to meet the regulatory challenge. A second co-ordinating mechanism is provided by the market (see Savas, 2000). The co-ordination task of achieving a complex activity is achieved through the invisible hand of appropriate incentives being provided to individuals so that their self-interested behaviour contributes to collective goals. Market or quasi-market mechanisms provide a common way of achieving the appropriate incentives. A government agency under such a mechanism retains the role of arranger but the responsibility for producing the service rests within another agency that 'earns' the right to do so through competition. Introducing competition is vital and requires a conscious governance strategy to create the conditions in favour of a market-like system. Options may take a wide variety of forms from the familiar contract with a private or voluntary sector producer to 'market-like' competition between public sector producers. The government agency achieves effective co-ordination through the specification of the service, the selection of the best producer and by monitoring and oversight of their performance. The presence of competition both keeps the performance of producers up to scratch and encourages innovation among producers as they seek to sustain or enhance their position in the market. As Hirschman (1970) has shown, it is the capacity of the purchaser or arranger of the service to 'exit' to another supplier that gives the market its power as a governance mechanism.

A third co-ordinating mechanism is that provided by interest articulation. By expressing concern, and taking action to change an undesired state of affairs, or achieve a desired one, then individuals can achieve collective benefits. The governance process at work here is what Hirschman calls 'voice':

> Voice is here defined as any attempt at all to change, rather than to escape from, an objectionable state of affairs, whether through individual or collective petition to the management directly in charge, through appeal to a higher authority with the intention of forcing a change in management, or through various types of actions and protests, including those that are meant to mobilize public opinion. (Hirschman, 1970: 30)

Voice requires the expression of an interest and then a process of adjustment between interests leading to a new compromise. In contrast to the public apathy assumed as part of the Weberian model the voice mechanism recognizes the role that active political participation can play in determining state action, priorities and forms of service provision.

A fourth governance mechanism can be identified. It is labelled as 'loyalty' by Hirschman (1970). Loyalty is a problematic term and its use by Hirschman has come in for some criticism (Barry, 1974; Birch, 1975; Laver, 1976). Reading Hirschman carefully it is clear that his concern with loyalty is not with the political behaviour of the committed activist or that of the follower who has blind faith but rather with behaviour driven by a willingness to give an organization or an individual the benefit of the doubt. In short it is what might better be termed as trust. Its effectiveness in the realm of governance is explained by Fukuyama (1999: 16, 49):

> If members of the group come to expect that others will behave reliably and honestly, then they will come to trust one another. Trust is like a lubricant that makes the running of any group or organisation more efficient … If people can be counted on to keep commitments, honor norms of reciprocity and avoid opportunistic behaviour, then groups will form more readily, and those that do form will be able to achieve common purposes more efficiently.

Trust helps to bind actors together and in doing so 'solves' collective action problems.

The governance perspective offers an alternative organizing framework to that of the Weberian world view. Complex tasks of co-operation do not necessarily always require the imposition of a hierarchical chain of command in an integrated organization. There are other options: regulation at arm's length, contracting through the market, responding to interest articulation and developing bonds of loyalty or trust. Recognition of this wider array of governance mechanism enables the processes of networked community governance to be better understood.

Conclusions

Networked community governance is the end goal. It marks a break from traditional public administration and New Public Management in its vision of the role of local government and its understanding of the context for governing and the core processes of governance. However, it is a vision that has not yet been realized. Not only is there much evidence of the continuing impact of traditional local government forms and thinking, so too New Public Management approaches have had a major impact and continue to drive some reforms. To repeat the focus of this book is on a period of transition. This chapter has merely sought to establish some elements of the direction of travel and the potential dominant local government form of the future. As the subsequent chapters will show, the road of reform has been neither straightforward nor easily travelled.

2 The Legacy of the Conservatives: Governance by Default

When the Conservatives were elected in 1979 the initial rhetoric was one of deregulation and decentralization. In practice the next eighteen years saw a host of interventions aimed at local government that transformed its institutional structures and practices, encouraged initiatives in introducing market forms into public service delivery and facilitated a degree of regulation of local public service providers that surpassed anything that had been previously seen.

The key issue for the Conservatives was initially to try and hold back the public spending undertaken by local government. From the mid-1980s onwards a second theme was more strongly developed around the issue of improving service delivery. This challenge led some, in turn, to articulate a radical challenge to the whole idea of the significance of elected local government. William Waldegrave, a government minister under the Conservatives, captures the heart of the challenge. For him the core question about service delivery was 'not whether those who run our public services are elected, but whether they are producer-responsive or consumer-responsive'. The reform process was about 'making our public services directly accountable to customers'. This was to be achieved by 'giving the public choices, or by instituting mechanisms which build in publicly-approved standards, and redress when they are not attained' (Waldegrave, 1993).

On the back of such thinking the Conservatives created a governance system by default that in practice undermined the position occupied by elected local government for most of the post-war period. There was a shift in the institutional structure of governing with a range of local appointed bodies or quangos gaining greater responsibility and prominence. Second, there was a change in the pattern of governing, a blurring of responsibilities with appointed bodies and partnerships, and organizations working alongside elected local authorities. Elected politicians and full-time local government bureaucrats found themselves joined by a range of other actors. There were major roles for users, interested citizens and the private sector in this complex interplay of local actors. In short, the Conservatives created the environment for a shift from local government to local governance. This chapter explores the legacy created by the Conservatives' years in office. First, the changes in institutional arrangements are examined. Next, attention is directed towards the use of market-like forms in the management of public services. The chapter then deals with the increased use of regulation during the period of Conservative rule. The remainder of the chapter is devoted to an assessment of the impact of the Conservatives' reforms on the quality of services, the complexities of governance and the practice of local democracy. Finally, the key argument of the critics of the Conservatives' period in office is examined, namely that from 1979 onwards the Conservatives systematically enfeebled elected local government.

A changed institutional framework: making new governance structures

The institutional structure of local governance changed substantially during the long period of national Conservative government between 1979 and 1997 (see Stewart and Stoker, 1995). The basic structure of local government shifted from a largely two-tier to a unitary structure. Central control over local finance became far tighter and more detailed. The functions and responsibilities of elected local authorities were squeezed and restructured. Alongside elected councils there emerged new or reshaped local appointed bodies or quangos that came to play a prominent role in the governance of localities.

A reorganised local government

The two-tier system of local authorities, established following the reorganizations of the 1960s and 70s, did not stand the test of time. There has been a general shift towards a 'unitary' or single-tier system of local government. It was argued that such a system minimized the levels of wasteful bureaucracy and was easier for the public to understand. The process of reform began in the metropolitan areas of England in 1986 with the abolition of the Greater London Council and the six metropolitan counties. This reform, in effect, created a unitary system of local government in the main urban conurbations. However, not all functions were taken on by the London boroughs and metropolitan districts so that a number of joint boards and committees – which group authorities together – had to be established.

The abolition of the metropolitan counties led to the creation of a series of joint boards covering police, fire, public transport and waste disposal. These boards consisted of councillors appointed by the constituent authorities but they had their own identity and legal status. The abolition of the Greater London Council led to the creation of a joint board for fire, while London Transport had been removed from the control of the Greater London Council prior to abolition. In other fields of London government concerning land-use planning and roads, central government gained significantly greater powers than elsewhere. The governance of London, of course, changed again in May 2000 with the establishment of a directly elected mayor and assembly under the New Labour reforms.

The pattern of organizational restructuring was further promoted by the process of local government reorganization launched in the early 1990s for non-metropolitan areas (Stoker, 1993; Leach and Stoker, 1997; Chisholm, 2002). In Wales and Scotland the Government took direct responsibility for drawing up reform plans and created single-tier systems of local authorities. In England the reform was in the hands of a semi-independent Local Government Commission. The Government's original purpose was widely believed to be the establishment of a single tier of unitary authorities throughout non-metropolitan England but many county councils fought a successful campaign against change. The first round of the Commission's investigations eventually produced the abolition of four county councils and the establishment of fourteen new unitary councils. The second round of deliberations led to the setting up of a further range of unitary authorities. In broad terms the review of structures in non-metropolitan areas delivered unitary local government in most major towns, cities and urban areas in England.

At the end of the Conservatives' period in government the basic structure of elected local authorities in Britain was as outlined in Table 2.1. The total number of authorities in Britain was reduced from 520 in 1976 to 441 in 1998. The unitary authorities remained responsible for a wide range of services including education, social welfare, housing, environmental protection, planning and economic development. In the two-tier structure the county councils retained their position as the dominant spenders taking responsibility for major services with the districts' main functions remaining housing and leisure services. The areas and populations covered by many county councils, however, had been reduced given that in many cases the major county town or city gained unitary status.

Table 2.1 *The structure of elected local government in Britain, 1997/1998*

Single-tier (unitary)	Two-tier (functions split between levels)
46 English unitary councils	34 English county councils
36 English metropolitan districts	238 English non-metropolitan authorities
32 London boroughs (plus City of London Corporation)	
22 Welsh councils	
32 Scottish councils	

A tight financial regime

During their period in office the Conservatives introduced numerous changes to the financial system. By 1997 local taxation (the council tax) accounted for at best only a quarter of total local authority income. The remainder of local authority income came from central government and other nationally distributed sources. The crucial shift occurred in the financial year 1990–91 when the Government removed the non-domestic or business rate from local authority control (Butler *et al.*, 1994). In the mid-1980s a combination of local rates and the business rates meant that local government raised about half its own income. The heavy reliance on non-local revenue established in the early 1990s created a substantial opportunity for central government to dictate the level of local spending in aggregate terms. In addition it was able to influence the spending decisions of individual authorities through defining what needed to be spent by way of an annual Standard Spending Assessment (SSA) and by holding capping powers over local budgets to ensure that they did not rise above government approved levels.

These Draconian measures produced an increasing degree of control over local spending. Indeed some authorities had to make drastic cuts. Others protected programmes through various measures and engaged in what is referred to as 'creative accounting'. They became expert in juggling the books so that the figures for spending matched government targets but resources continued to flow to local services. However, over time the scope for creative accountancy was reduced through new controls and through the costs imposed by the past use of that practice. Local government in 1997 operated in a highly controlled financial climate yet still it consumed about a quarter of all public spending.

The rise of local quangos

There was a growth in the number of appointed bodies or quangos at the local level (see Skelcher, 1998; Stoker, 1999a). Training and Enterprise Councils took over local authorities' responsibilities in further education for training towards the end of the 1980s. Institutions of further education, along with sixth form colleges, were also removed from local authority control and constituted as corporate bodies in their own right, following the previous removal of what were then polytechnics and are now universities. In specific areas, urban development corporations, housing action trusts, housing associations and more broadly various partnership organizations assumed, with the support of central government funds, responsibilities for renewal and development. In Scotland, Local Enterprise Companies had a broad role in training and regeneration. For other functions local authorities were required to set up companies to take over responsibilities in public transport, airports and waste disposal, sometimes as a means towards privatization. In England and Wales, water was handed over to the control of private companies. In Scotland responsibility for water provision was given to appointed boards. Provisions for opting out of the control of local authorities and health authorities led to the creation of grant-maintained schools and hospital trusts as freestanding institutions. Freestanding police authorities were established in 1995. The Conservatives' original intention was to change the composition of police authorities so that there would be no majority of councillors. As a result of intervention by the House of Lords a bare majority was available to appointed councillors in most authorities but the intended weakening of local authority control occurred.

A variety of factors explain why local quangos and non-elected bodies gained an increased role under the Conservatives. Each quango has its own history and particular reasons why it was established but it is possible to see a number of shared elements in the story of the growth of quangos.

One significant factor was undoubtedly the desire to bypass local government. Distrust of local authorities was evident from the early years of the Conservative Government but it became more pronounced as the Conservatives lost political control at the local level. By the mid-1980s Labour controlled more councils than the Conservatives, and by the 1990s the Conservatives had been reduced to running just under two dozen local authorities (i.e., about 5 per cent of the total). Parties that control national government expect to lose seats at the local level. However, for the Conservatives local government, especially in urban areas, become virtually a 'no-go' area. In such circumstances bypassing elected authorities appeared particularly attractive.

A second factor behind the growth of local quangos was the desire to bring new participants into the process of local governance. The electoral system and its demands, it was argued, discouraged many with relevant skills and experience from being involved. Bringing business skills, knowledge and interest to local governance was a key theme for the Conservatives but there was also recognition of the value of enabling user representatives, volunteers and active citizens to become involved in local decision-making. ✗ Finally, there was a view that quangos would help to develop more businesslike management of public services in tune with the ideas and arguments of the 'New Pubic Management'. By developing more slimline and focused management teams to run organizations and by encouraging competition between these organizations to attract users and/or public funds it would be possible to stimulate efficiencies and greater effectiveness through quasi-market incentives. Moreover, because it controlled the purse strings more directly the centre would be able to dictate not only aggregate spending levels but also priorities in these organizations.

New Public Management

In both local authorities and the major local quangos a shift in the pattern of internal management occurred, encouraged by 'New Public Management' ideas, and legislation generated by the Conservative Government (Stoker, 1999b). The 'New Public Management' presents a complex set of ideas, which have evolved and developed different themes. The version most clearly embraced by the Conservatives provided a critique of existing forms of service provision and a prescription for improvement based on introducing market-like disciplines.

Public service organizations, so the argument had it, were dominated by producer interests (the bureaucrats and the various ranks of other employees). Unlike in private sector organizations the power of the producer was not held in check by market incentives and demands. As a result public service organizations tended to be neither efficient in terms of saving public money nor responsive to consumer needs. The solution was to fragment 'monopolistic' public service structures and develop quasi-market forces to govern the way that they operated. Key reforms included the introduction of a purchaser–provider divide within organizations and the development of performance targets and incentives. The aim was to create an organizational 'home' for the client–consumer voice within the system in order to challenge the power of producers. Consumers or their surrogate representatives as regulators or commissioners would have the power to purchase the services they required and measure performance.

A key driver of change was the introduction of compulsory competitive tendering which started with a focus on the main 'blue collar' services of building, cleaning, and refuse collection but towards the end of the Conservatives' tenure began to be directed towards 'white collar' services. Tendering led to some services being undertaken by private sector providers under time-limited contracts but most work remained 'in-house'. Only in building cleaning and construction were over half of all contracts won by the private sector. In leisure services, housing and legal services the private sector won less than a quarter of all contracts (Wilson and Game, 2002: 330). However, although 'in-house' service providers remained connected to the local authority a fundamental shift in organizational arrangements occurred.

The purchaser part of the organization developed a client role to both specify the form of service required and monitor the performance of the contractor. The contractor, which took direct responsibility for service delivery even when an 'in-house' direct service organization (DSO), had to operate within its own finance and accounting provisions. There was also a tendency for such DSOs to demand a degree of flexibility in their management of personnel and in the development of their own business plans. Moreover, rather than pay set or long-established overheads for central services such as salary management, financial information and computer support many DSOs negotiated service level agreements with the central departments responsible for these provisions (Stewart and Stoker, 1995).

Competitive tendering provisions applied to local authorities and some other appointed bodies. In education the introduction of devolved management responsibilities to schools created similar pressures for a more contract-oriented form of management. In social services a separation was introduced between the assessments of need for the provision of services, which created a similar client–contractor dimension in the operation of these services.

What emerged with the introduction of 'New Public Management' reforms was a more differentiated system of internal management. Local authorities and to some extent other institutions in the world of local governance found themselves divided into a series of separate units with relationships conducted through contractual or semi-contractual arrangements.

The regulation of public services

Regulation within government, broadly defined as the use of public authority to set and apply rules inside government, has increased in complexity and intensity over the last two decades (Day and Klein, 1990; Hood *et al.*, 1998). The experience of regulation varies considerably from sector to sector. Hood *et al.* (1998) argue that local government has over the last twenty years felt the impact of a 'double whammy' of more demanding and intense regulation aimed at ensuring compliance with detailed rules but also focused on achieving set performance levels:

> Finding reduced scope for a prominent role in high politics, central government had found a new role in low politics. Ruling colonies in the Empire was replaced by regulation of Britain's internal colonies – its counties, towns and cities. Central government was now regulating not only how local authorities should carry out their functions (process controls) but also in many cases the level and nature of the services they should provide (output controls). Apart from a few services (like leisure) in which it had little interest, central government pursued a strategy of increasing regulation, mixing heightened oversight with new elements of competition. (Hood *et al.*, 1998: 98)

The years between 1976 and 1995 saw the number of regulatory bodies directed at local government grow from 57 to 67, with an estimated more than doubling of expenditure on audit, inspection and regulation (Hood *et al.*, 1998). Local government of all institutions attracted the greatest degree of regulatory concern.

As can be seen from Table 2.2 several new bodies were established during the Conservative period in government. Some of these bodies took over the functions of other previous regulators but each developed its activities in a more intense manner. In addition existing inspectorates stepped up the intensity of their regulation and intervention. The key inspectorates here were those aimed at the fire service and police. Finally, local quangos were also subject to greater regulation, with notably the Housing Corporation being given increased powers to oversee the work of housing associations.

Local government of all institutions attracted the greatest degree of regulatory concern.

Central government has for most of this century had general powers of supervision over local government but in the Conservatives' period in office legislation, and associated regulators, became more directive. Not surprisingly those powers and their operation were perceived differently depending on the position of the observer:

> At the centre many see regulations as designed to encourage self-regulation and self-management, yet from the regulatees' perspective the various regulators often seem an external intrusive pressure seeking to enforce uniformity. (Hood *et al.*, 1998: 115)

Table 2.2   *Key new regulators of local public bodies created by the Conservatives, 1979–97*

Organization (Year)	Main Task	Accountability
Audit Commission for local authorities and the NHS in England and Wales (1982)	Appoints auditors to local authorities and health bodies, undertakes value for money studies, publishes key performance indicators	Reports to central government, particularly Department for the Environment
Magistrates' Court Inspectorate (1994)	Inspects the administration and management of the Magistrates' Courts	Lord Chancellor's Office
Office of HM Chief Inspector of Schools (Office for Standards in Education) (1992)	Reports on every state school at least once every four years	Secretary of State for Education
Social Services Inspectorate (1985)	To manage national inspection of services to carers and users in the social services sector	Secretary of State for Health

Source: Information taken from Hood *et al.* (1998) Appendix III.

Some regulators tend to be quite close to the bodies they oversee and may share professional values and norms. This feature can be observed in the case of the regulation of police and fire services. Generally, the relationships between local authorities and central regulators, 'were far from universally antagonistic' (Hood *et al.*, 1998: 107). However, there was a general drift towards a more formal oversight and deterrence model in contrast to the more mutuality based approach of the earlier era. Table 2.3 captures the difference in styles.

The Conservatives introduced regulation as a key mechanism to challenge local public bureaucracies to get them to change their behaviour. Although some of the pressure to change stemmed from the use of inspectors' reports to put information in the public domain to, in turn, allow members of the public to make a judgement about their local providers, much of the pressure was intergovernmental or created space for challenge within organizations. A critical report from inspectors meant that politicians or managers inside the system were given the ammunition to launch reform programmes.

Table 2.3   *Control and compliance: two approaches*

	Oversight	*Mutuality*
Detection of problems	By regular checking	Reliance on networks and information channels to throw up issues
Setting standards	Defined by official norms	Defined competitively by various agencies.
Achieving compliance Control	Authority backed by sanctions Defined group of inspectors	Manipulated self-policing Variable location and operatives throughout the system
Recipe for 'stepping up control'	Strengthen authority and sanctions, expand inspectors, tighten up procedures	Re-think system to provide stronger incentives and greater efficiency in self-policing

Source: Adapted and developed from Hood (1986b: 768).

The impact of the Conservative reforms on services

The quasi-market reforms of the Conservatives had a considerable impact on public services in the UK. Managers of public service organizations claimed to have become more customer-oriented (K. Young and Mills, 1993; Talbot, 1994). Pollitt (1996) confirms that 'accumulated evidence of many managers is that changes can be achieved and benefits in terms of increased efficiency and sometimes improved service quality have been won'. Survey and case study evidence of organizational change, innovations in service delivery and improvements in performance can also be found (K. Young and Mills, 1993; Leach *et al.*, 1994; Pollitt *et al.*, 1998). Using the somewhat crude measures provided by opinion surveys there is evidence of increased satisfaction with particular services. Table 2.4 presents some evidence in relation to local government services.

Yet as Pollitt (1995) points out, the judgement about what has improved and why is very difficult. The evidence of managers that service performance has improved is significant and so is evidence of increased satisfaction among the public. In general, as Pollitt *et al.* (1999: 54) comment, there 'was plenty of evidence that activity intensified – that more service users had

Table 2.4   *Satisfaction with specific council services,*
1986, 1991 and 1995

Service	% Very/Fairly satisfied		
	1986	*1991*	*1995*
Environmental:			
refuse collection	85	81	91
street lighting	80	77	81
footpaths/street cleaning	44	41	53
road maintenance	29	30	43
Leisure:			
libraries	78	68	70
swimming pools and sports facilities	61	55	55
parks, playgrounds and open spaces	63	55	54
Education:			
primary schools – all	43	43	44
child 5–10 yrs in household	76	70	81
secondary schools – all	34	37	46
child 11–14 yrs in household	60	60	78

Source: From data collected by the National Consumer Council.

been processed more quickly and/or with lower unit resources'. But the judgement of managers needs to be treated with caution and that of the public may reflect satisfaction with services against very low or negative expectations. Judging what leads to improvement is beset by three types of problem (Politt, 1995; Pollitt *et al.*, 1999: 84–5). First, there is the issue of deciding what constitutes better performance. There is a choice, at least, to be made between efficiency and quality. A second problem is that very little reliable information is available about service performance over a continuous time series. Finally, identifying the cause of any improvement that is observed is difficult because a variety of factors could often have been seen as affecting the outcome.

It is helpful to think of the Conservatives' reforms in terms of the exit and voice mechanisms, outlined in Chapter 1. Bearing in mind difficulties in measuring performance improvement, it nevertheless seems plausible to argue that the crucial driving force behind change in public services has not been exit by customers directly. Users have not been the key choosers. Rather, externally imposed demands from central government via regulation, and the extensive internalization of the mechanisms of the new managerialism among the officials running public services, appear to have driven the search for change. The threat of exit in the hands of managers encouraged a sustained search for efficient and responsive provision. The example of public or socially rented housing, education and a range of services affected by competitive tendering would appear to fit this pattern. What gave the market principle its cutting edge was the internal establishment of a range of internal challenge agents. The purchaser–provider divide created a focus for change and new thinking (Stoker, 1999b: 12–13). Managers, acting as surrogate purchasers, used their new-found power to negotiate at the margins shifts in service provision and priority.

Market-like mechanisms also provided new opportunities for voice, even if in a somewhat weak version. Complaints and grievance procedures were extended and enhanced. More information than ever before was made available through a range of performance indicators, providing the active citizen-customer or their surrogates with the ammunition to hold service providers to account. It was increasingly commonplace for managers in public services to 'play the user card' – that is claim user support for their position – in internal debates about priority-setting and resource allocation (Barnes *et al.*, 1999: 119).

The exit mechanism might not be as full-blooded and stark as that facing private companies in a perfectly competitive market but it did have an impact on public service providers. The voice mechanism, encouraged by the Conservatives, was not as strong and as rich as the ideal envisaged by Hirschman (1970) but it was nevertheless present, even though it was, in a somewhat thin and manipulated form. The market form introduced the sense of challenge or even crisis that is a key starting element in achieving organizational change. Getting local authority staff to recognize that there were alternative providers that could be called upon and requiring their managers to justify service performance in public were byproducts of the market-like rhetoric and they had an effect. Local authorities felt challenged and as a result were more willing to consider change options that previously would have been thought unthinkable (Stoker, 1999b: 14). The rhetoric about choice and competition placed new weapons in the hands of managers as commissioners of service or as overseers of the workforce and that power was used by managers to wring changes out of local public service organizations. The impact was variable and reflected various local conditions and circumstances (Lowndes, 1999a) but there is evidence to suggest it was a driver of change.

A range of unintended problems also accompanied the Conservatives' reforms of local public services. The ESRC Local Governance research programme (Stoker, 1999b: 9–12) revealed a host of these difficulties. They stretched from a general fragmentation and loss of coherence in the system to opportunistic behaviour in which schools, for example, creamed off the best students and dumped the worst to enhance their performance. Some providers focused on their targets, even at the expense of service improvement wanted by their communities. Crime prevention and community intervention initiatives from the police lost priority against the pressing need to deliver on targets for arrests or clear-ups (Benyon and Edwards, 1999). Moreover the reform process, especially the compulsory nature of the tendering process imposed on local government, created a deal of provocation that in turn led to resistance and latent non-co-operation. Local authorities and trade unions in several areas reacted to the perceived unfairness of imposed reform by developing counter-measures to protect in-house workforces (Doogan, 1999). Researchers also identified examples of placation, where changes were nothing more than organizational musical chairs in which the illusion of success and going forward left real problems untouched.

It would be possible tentatively to conclude that the Conservatives' programme of reform did lead to some positive improvements in service performance but also had some adverse side-effects. The use of exit mechanisms did provide new incentives for managers. Voice – in terms of user empowerment – was enhanced but only in a marginal way. Trust and loyalty, both for those inside and external to the system of local governance, were compromised. The Conservatives appeared to create a system that no one had any faith in any more, as the next section will explore.

The problems of the world of governance created by the Conservatives

The scorecard for the Conservatives' reforms is more clear-cut when it comes to the overall system of local governance institutions that it created. First, the complexity and blurred responsibilities of the system raised some doubts about the legitimacy of governance arrangements. Second, questions were raised about standards of probity in public affairs. There was a concern that the system had lost a capacity for overall coherence and steering. Finally, there were issues about the strength of accountability in the system.

Introducing new forms of governance can create a divorce between the formal constitutional understanding of governing arrangements and the way they work in practice (see Stoker, 1998). The emergence of single-purpose bodies as such was nothing new. Throughout all of the post-war period local authorities were not the only governmental actors in localities. The health authorities, public utilities and other agencies had a substantial impact on service provision and the physical shaping of localities in that period. However, the increased intensity and prominence given to non-elected agencies and privatized utilities (Stoker, 1997b) under the Conservatives between 1979 and 1997, and the associated downgrading of the role of elected local authorities, created a system that appeared to lack strong legitimacy. The divorce between the normative codes used to explain and justify government and the reality of the decision-making in the system created tensions. The issue is more than there being a 'cultural lag' while public attitudes catch up with the new reality of public services. The public and more specifically the media lacked a legitimating framework in which to place the emerging system of governance.

The exercise of power needs to be legitimate. This argument is more than a normative assertion. It rests also on the pragmatic grounds that to be effective in the long run power-holders must be seen to be legitimate (Beetham, 1991). A legitimation deficit undermines public support and commitment to programmes of change and ultimately undermines the ability of power-holders to mobilize resources and promote co-operation and partnership.

The new arrangements, driven by the New Public Management concerns of the Conservatives, may through their concern with performance have improved managerial efficiency but in the minds of many members of the public and indeed some policy-makers there was a blurring of overarching responsibility and clarity about who was responsible for what. It no longer seemed so self-evident that it was the 'council' (town hall or county hall) that was responsible. The Conservatives stood accused of creating a system that was more difficult to understand and as a result appeared more difficult to influence (or perhaps even more out of control).

Second, there was a raft of concerns about the standards of appointed agencies in the conduct of their business (see Stoker, 1999a; Skelcher, 1998). People were appointed to the boards of quangos not on the basis of merit or as a reflection of their expertise but because of political sympathies, it was claimed. In some instances, having failed to win public office by election, people were appointed through the 'back door' to public positions. The management and decision-making of many quangos established by the Conservatives, it was argued, were shrouded in secrecy and there was a lack of openness in the conduct of their affairs compared to that of elected local authorities. A further criticism was that appropriate standards in declaring interests or ensuring probity in the management of public finances were not always in place or observed. All in all the issue of probity in public affairs became more prominent in the era of the Conservatives' reforms.

Third, there was a view that although quangos may be effective in their narrow area of operation the existence of a diverse and complex range of such agencies exacerbated the problem of joined-up governance – the bringing of the parts together (for a review of these arguments see Perri 6 *et al.*, 2002: 19–20). The increasing differentiation, along with the weakening of the relative position of local authorities, represented a fragmentation within the overall system. Differentiation has the strength of specialization and focus. Organizations have a clear if bounded task and bring relevant expertise to that task. But a balanced system of governance has to have a capacity for integration as well as differentiation. The relative weakening of the position of local authorities in the system may have reduced the capacity for integration through a multi-purpose if not an all-purpose authority. Many of the new agencies of local governance were subject to direct influence from central government through the appointment of their controlling boards or because their funding was coming directly or indirectly from the centre. Central government, however, could not readily provide integrative mechanisms at the local level. The integrative mechanisms of central government, which have themselves often been criticised, focused on the central government departments, the Cabinet and its committees, and processes of consultation. They did not, however, provide the necessary integrative mechanisms at the local level.

The fourth batch of criticisms about quangos was focused on the issue of accountability. Quangos were subject to strict financial and managerial accountability in many instances but what they lacked was political accountability. The key point was that these other forms of accountability could not replace the need for collective accountability for the policy and resource allocations of these bodies. The framework of democratic control through Parliament does not meet the requirements of that further and more general accountability. The effective control that can be exercised over so complex a machinery of bodies through this central route was inherently limited. Further, there was the issue as to whether in any event public accountability at national level was appropriate for appointed bodies at local level. If there are local choices to be made by appointed bodies about priorities or the setting of policy, even though these choices may take place within a framework of national policy and funding for such agencies, the argument was that where there is local choice there should be an opportunity for local voice (Skelcher, 1998: 164–9).

The Conservatives' neglect of local politics

A further charge against the Conservatives was that because they concentrated on a largely consumerist and managerial agenda they largely neglected the political organization of local government and the fabric of local democracy. In practice the Conservatives had a rather anti-politics agenda and left local politics to wither. The Conservative Government in the mid-1980s did launch the Widdicombe Committee (1986) to examine how politics was changing at the local level. The brief to the Committee took a relatively negative outlook on local politics, seeing it as a potential source of corruption and inappropriate interference in the running of local services (Stewart, 1995). The evidence and research presented to the Committee captured key elements of the changing world and presented a relatively positive view of the world of local politics. The Government ignored much of its analysis and went ahead with some minor tinkering reforms of local political practice in the Local Government and Housing Act 1989.

Following the removal of Prime Minister Thatcher from office, Michael Heseltine returned to take charge of local government policy in late 1990, again as Secretary of State for the Environment. Along with a range of other possible reforms he floated the idea of strengthening local leadership through the introduction of elected mayors. A consultation paper (Department of the Environment, 1991) was developed by the Government that made a rather broad brush argument for radical change but the paper and in particular the idea of elected mayors appeared to quickly run out of steam and by 1992 academic observers (Stoker and Wolman, 1992) were confidently concluding that the mayoral option would be unlikely to take off in Britain because of the range of established interests ranged against reform. In 1993 a joint working party of government and local authority officials produced a set of suggestions about how incremental and evolutionary changes in the established system could be encouraged by allowing for experiments that stepped outside the existing legislative framework. Overall in 1995 Stewart (1995) argues that while in many areas the Government was happy to intervene and impose legislative solutions it appeared reluctant to do so in this field. The report of the working party was, in effect, left without any response.

The independent Commission for Local Democracy (CLD) published a series of research reports, which laid bare the problems of existing local democracy, and in its final report in 1995 it made radical proposals for change that took up two broad themes: the need to revive local politics and democracy and the need to restore powers to local decision-makers and local government (see Pratchett and Wilson, 1996; Commission for Local Democracy, 1995). On the former front the Commission recommended sweeping changes in the organization of local government, including the idea of directly elected executive mayors held in check by an assembly of councillors elected under a proportional representation system. On the latter front it proposed giving local authorities greater constitutional and financial freedoms.

The sense that something was fundamentally wrong with local democracy in practice was a theme pursued by a House of Lords Select Committee chaired by Lord Hunt (House of Lords, 1996). The Commission for Local Democracy and the Hunt Committee shared some of the same analysis and a general vision of the way forward, although their detailed prescriptions varied. The Conservatives did not newly create the problems of local democracy in their period of national government, both the CLD and Hunt reports recognized, but a number of weaknesses were exacerbated. The most obvious weakness was the low turnout in local elections. Participation in local elections declined especially from 1990 onwards. Between 1990 and 1999 the numbers of voters turning out as a proportion of those registered averaged 36 per cent, compared to 43 per cent between 1973 and 1978. In short, turnout in local elections that was never high got worse towards the end of the Conservatives' long years of central rule; placing Britain at the bottom of the league in terms of European Union local government systems (Rallings and Thrasher, 2000).

Ending local government: the Conservatives stand accused

Above all the Conservatives have been criticised for creating a system of governance that limited local discretion to an excessive degree and placed an over-reliance on the role of the centre. By concentrating accountability on the centre the Conservatives ran the risk of making all other institutions superfluous. Simon Jenkins argued in *Accountable to None* (1995) that the result of Tory centralization was a public service system battered and reformed but not noticeably any better at doing what it was supposed to do, i.e., serve the public. In effect the Conservatives were accused of undermining the very existence of local government and towards the end of their years in office many from the local government community and beyond began to call for measures to redress the balance in central–local relationships and restore a positive role to local government.

The view of many commentators on British local government was that the institution had suffered grievously and unfairly under successive Conservative governments. On the one hand it had seen a loss of powers and responsibilities and on the other it had seen the rise of a range of unelected appointed bodies or local quangos. Martin Loughlin (1996: 56) captures the broad view of many:

> The recent reforms have altered the basic character of local government. The tradition of the self-sufficient, corporate authority which was vested with broad discretion to raise revenue and provide services has been directly challenged ... Local councils have been stripped of governmental responsibility for certain services which continue to be public services but which are now provided by agencies, which are funded directly from the centre.

Both local quangos and local authorities were subject to extensive central direction, which limits the scope for local discretion.

Many viewed the shift in the system of governance in negative terms. Vernon Bogdanor, for example, refers to a process of 'steady attrition' leading to an outcome in which elected local authorities become 'merely residuary bodies ... the repository of those public services that no one else can be bothered to provide' (quoted in House of Lords, 1996: 36). Above all the centralization of the last two decades was seen as threatening, indeed undermining, the checks and balances that are essential to the British political system. To quote Martin Loughlin (1996: 58) again:

> The recent reforms thus reflect on the constitutional status of local government precisely because they affect the distribution of political authority, the

character of our democracy and, ultimately, our conceptions of politics. The reforms pose a serious challenge to the traditional view that it is only by the combination of local representative institutions with the central institutions of Parliament, Ministers and Departments, that a genuine national democracy can be sustained.

Thatcher, in particular, was seen as having led governments (1979–90) that broke the constitutional understandings of the British system and local government was one of her main targets.

The House of Lords Report of July 1996 comments that an argument 'put forward by many witnesses' to them was that 'over a long period local authorities have lost powers, whether to central government or to quangos, not to conform to some over-arching philosophy but in a way which has incrementally soured relations, weakened local democracy and blurred accountability' (House of Lords, 1996: 5). The Committee demurs from endorsing that analysis but it does note that although the Major years (1990–7) saw steps forward in central–local relations there was still much room for improvement. The Committee goes on to make a range of recommendations to rebuild local government and to 'mark the respect and status owed to a system of local government enjoying a democratic mandate'.

The House of Lords Report captured many of the elements of a widely held reform agenda aimed at restoring power and status to elected local government. The *de facto* arrival of governance in the sense of service agencies other than the local authority was accepted. What was demanded was that local authorities, because of their elected status and multi-purpose character, guide and co-ordinate the world of local governance. Drawing on their Lordship's proposals and those of a range of other commentators and academics (see, for example, Chisholm *et al.*, 1997; Carter, 1986) a shared local government reform agenda can be identified. It included:

- the provision of increased tax-raising power at the local level, most straightforwardly by the return of the business rate to local control.
- the granting of a power of local competence to overcome the constraining influence of *ultra vires* and provide a more positive legal framework for local authority action.
- provision to make local quangos responsible to elected local government through information sharing at one end of the spectrum and supervision or control at the other.
- legislation to allow local authorities to choose if they wish to experiment with new forms of political management or service provision.

We shall see that although the New Labour Government accepted that local government had been undermined by the Conservatives it was not inclined to simply adopt this reform agenda favoured by local government advocates.

Conclusions

The Conservatives in their eighteen years in government, in effect, brought to an end a particular form of local government. A sustained drive based on financial controls and constraints; regulation of service provision; compulsory competitive tendering for key services; and new managerial reforms terminated the post-war regime of local authorities as semi-autonomous, pre-eminent and large-scale service providers for the welfare state. The Conservatives blurred the boundaries of the system by creating new roles for existing non-elected agencies and new local quangos, alongside a complex array of partnership arrangements.

Local government reorganization in first metropolitan and then the remainder of Britain enhanced the appearance of change in the system and yet led to fundamental questions about what, if anything, the Conservatives wanted local government to do. Neither of the reorganizations appeared to have a clear strategic vision behind it and instead reorganization plans appeared to be determined by short-term tactical considerations and the vagaries and happenstance of wider political developments. There appeared to have been very little interest in local government as a political institution in Conservatives' thinking, little respect for any tradition of local discretion and choice and no clear sense of what particular role democratic local authorities could play. Under the Conservative national governments between 1989 and 1997 local government lost an empire and emerged with no coherent role. It is possible to argue that some improvements in service delivery and improvement did occur and that local government became more consumer-friendly but such gains were achieved with rather too heavy a price in the judgement of many.

3 New Labour: Embracing Local Governance?

The aim of this chapter is to capture New Labour's approach to local governance. First, it is necessary to examine New Labour's broad approach to domestic policy issues. 'Modernization' is the key rhetorical commitment but it is necessary to look more at the actions and detailed practice of New Labour in order to understand what its aims and purposes have been. It is argued that in domestic policy terms it is possible to identify three overarching New Labour projects that were launched in its first term and it is important to place local governance policies in the context of these broader projects. However, to develop a deeper understanding it is necessary to explore the reasoning behind Labour's rejection of the consensus view about how to revive local government and its own vision of the future of local governance.

This chapter claims that there is a distinctiveness to New Labour's approach to local governance. It has a vision of local governance that marks it out from the predecessor Conservative governments and which, at the same time, challenges many of the cherished views of the local government community of academics and practitioners. As Tony Blair puts it: the solution to the problems experienced by local government in recent years 'does not lie in local authorities gathering again unto themselves all the functions and roles they once had ... a flawed model is not the answer to to-day's problems' (Blair, 1998b: 12). New Labour demands, 'a new – a different – local government' (Blair, 1998b: 13) to contribute to the task of modernizing Britain.

New Labour is convinced that local government needs to change. Unlike the Conservatives it has developed a new vision of the future of local government that embraces the idea of governance and has given it a particular normative spin. Its programme for local governance has been less narrowly focused on service delivery and more broadly based. Regulation, in order to achieve improvements in service performance, is still to the fore, although applied in a different manner at least to some degree. Crucially, New Labour has sought to make politics work again at the local level. There is also a greater emphasis on the need to build 'joined-up' networks of governance agencies. These three themes of performance management, democratic renewal and 'joined-up' partnership working are the key elements in New Labour's agenda. In the language introduced in Chapter 1 New Labour is less interested in using exit as a mechanism of governance and more committed to the use of voice and trust-based systems.

The three projects of New Labour: beyond the rhetoric of modernization

In terms of domestic policy the watchword for New Labour is 'modernization'. According to Perri 6 and Ed Peck (2003):

> A search on 'modernisation' using the Webcat search engine on the (now superseded) official http://www.open.gov.uk site on 13th July 2001 produced 5,399 government documents currently available in which the word appeared on the first page. Examination of the first hundred of these showed that nearly all featured the word in the title.

The word 'modernization' is used in a wide variety of ways but, as the authors go on to note, the key significance of modernization is two-fold. The first is that it expresses the idea that New Labour is committed to the new and the cutting edge, and not therefore able to be criticised as an outdated centre-left party. The second is that New Labour is committed to changing and improving institutions involved in governance and public services. Modernization signals a general challenge to past practices and a commitment to a reform process to improve performance.

It would be unwise to build too much analysis on the back of New Labour's rhetoric and its liberal, even promiscuous, use of the term modernization. Taking New Labour's language too seriously ignores the key point about its politics, which is that although it has values and a general sense of direction it does not have a worked through ideology that tells it what to do. The judgement about what to do is driven by evidence, contingency and political circumstance. New Labour is a self-confessed pragmatic political force. The key challenge for its leaders is not finding the right statement of principle but rather to develop an understanding of what works or what delivers (Temple, 2002).

Beyond modernization New Labour has played with other overarching definitions of its approach from the short-lived stakeholder society to the most long lasting, namely the Third Way debate (Giddens, 1998; Giddens, 2000).

New Labour does share some of the general themes of Third Way politics. These include: a recognition that there is no alternative to the market economy; a celebration of the contribution of civil society; and a commitment to a continuing, if different, role for the state. But for New Labour the Third Way is not a programme but rather a way of drawing a boundary around a debate about the future of progressive politics that they are keen to encourage. The Third Way debate stretches beyond Britain to provide a new global perspective on progressive politics. There remains the challenge of explaining the particular nature of New Labour's programme.

Concepts such as the Third Way are not the key to understanding New Labour. It came to power quite deliberately without a great strategic plan about what it was going to do. In part this was to avoid providing any ammunition during the campaign period when they were elected and in part reflected a sheer lack of capacity given the long years in opposition. There were broad objectives that were established, using words such as modernization. There were ministers with particular plans and agendas; in local government's case the crucial player in the first term was Hilary Armstrong, the Minister for Local Government. However, to understand New Labour it is necessary to look not at its general policy statements but rather its practice.

If the focus is on domestic policy it is possible to identify at least three distinctive projects within New Labour's programme. It is assumed here that New Labour shares with previous Labour governments a concern to manage the economy effectively and public finances competently. The difference is that thus far New Labour has proved more adept at these tasks than some of its predecessors. The discussion below develops arguments in Stoker (2000a) and identifies the distinctive features of New Labour's programme.

The first project is to make Labour a successful party in elections in the short run and ultimately the natural party of government for the twenty-first century. There are various strands to this project, including the mixture of media management, campaigning techniques and sensitivity to public opinion that emanates from Labour's media headquarters and the Prime Minister's office in No. 10 Downing Street. There is a recognition that New Labour had to construct a new electoral coalition stretching beyond its traditional working-class base. This project is, in one sense, an entirely pragmatic reaction to new circumstances, in particular changes in the employment conditions and class base of British society. But the project does have a larger, even a moral, dimension in that Labour, it is argued, should represent a wider coalition including the aspiring working and middle classes, women and ethnic minorities and not let a male, manual working-class image restrict its appeal and constituencies. Labour has always looked to build electoral coalitions beyond the manual working class. New Labour is different in the extent and breadth of its coalition building and in its claim to see more than political expediency driving the spread of its representative claims.

It is worth emphasizing the scale of what is involved in the electoral project. While short-term management of the media, the party and political issues is to the fore the underlying ambition is a long-term attempt to construct a progressive coalition to dominate British politics in the twenty-first century to match the ascendancy of the Conservatives in ruling the country during the twentieth century. It is also not necessarily the case that the political project is restricted to political management. It is compatible with a strategy of devolution to Scotland, Wales and the English regions and the progressive introduction of proportional representation (PR) into elections. The argument here is that by establishing a range of devolved institutions and by using PR in elections it should be possible to prevent the Conservatives from dominating national or subnational politics again. The goal is to open up the way for varieties of progressive coalitions to construct a hegemony over political debate and control over political institutions for an extended number of decades.

The second project is captured by the phrase 'entrepreneurial welfarism'. Its home base is the Treasury under Gordon Brown but it is widely shared within New Labour circles. The core policy objective is set by a critique of the way that the post-war welfare state acted to create dependency among its clients rather than provide them with the means to take responsibility for their own lives. It is a politics of redistribution not simply of income but rather of life chances or opportunities. Policies are assessed on the basis of whether they bring benefits and incentives to a social strata stretching from the lower middle class to the unemployed working class. The key challenge is to give people in this strata greater opportunities and stronger material incentives to succeed. In addition there is a particular emphasis on providing support to poor families with children.

A second strand of entrepreneurial welfarism emphasizes less the provision of opportunities and more the demand for civic responsibility. Policies on the minimum wage, child support measures and private pension plans seek to achieve their goals by the state's requiring the individual or a third party to take action to ensure that a need is meet. There is no assumption that the state will pay but rather the state uses its legal authority to ensure that someone takes responsibility for meeting welfare needs (White, 1998).

The themes of entrepreneurial welfarism have a number of dimensions. On the one hand there is an emphasis on opportunity, on enabling individuals to realize their potential. On the other hand there is a concern with civic responsibility; a recognition that individuals, as well as rights, have obligations to their fellow citizens. These values are, of course, capable of being interpreted in a variety of ways. There is a connection with the issue of civic responsibility. For those of a more liberal disposition the range of areas where the state or the community can demand civic responsibility will be more narrowly defined than those of a more communitarian outlook that might favour a wider range of areas where 'responsible' behaviour is demanded. Within the terrain of the Third Way debate, as White (1998: 26) points out, 'there is a plausible range of consensus on what these responsibilities include: the responsibility to work (in return for a share of the social product) and to make an effort to acquire relevant skills for work; the responsibility to be a good parent ... the responsibility to pay a fair share of taxes; the responsibility to respect the environment.' However, it is clear that there are some areas where disagreements begin to arise, such as the cases of family values, drugs policy and the methods (such as curfews) used to enforce 'good' behaviour.

The third project can be summarized as the attempt to restore state capacity. New Labour believes in government but a reformed government that is flexible, uses new technology, works across its boundary with partners and which, above all, is responsive to citizens. Constitutional change, education reforms, modernizing government and the commitment to 'joining-up' reflect a view that state capacity can be restored only if reform is radical and effective.

The commitment to rebuild state capacity reflects a determination to move beyond the New Right's anti-government rhetoric and to reassert the argument that government action can be effective and deliver valued social and economic outcomes. Indeed there is much emphasis on increasing the capacity to deliver in education, health, transport and a host of other policy areas. Another strong strand is a commitment to re-engineer state bureaucracies using new information and communication technologies, organizational and staffing reforms and public–private partnerships to introduce greater flexibility, speed of access and relevance to the services provided to the public. A further element in the building of state capacity is the search for 'joined-up' solutions to complex problems so that the various parts of government work more effectively with each other and with partners in the private and voluntary sectors. A final element of the programme, which can be identified, is the most obviously political, in that it seeks to establish the basis for a devolution of power within the state. The key policies here are the creation of a Scottish Parliament, an Assembly for Wales, a Northern

Ireland Assembly, a revitalized and more accountable local government and possibly a range of regional governments in England.

The rebuilding of state capacity, then, stretches from a simple determination to make the government machine (and its agencies) work more effectively, through an interest in a longer-term re-engineering of public bureaucracies and the means of service delivery, to a political commitment to a decentralized politics.

There have been clear tensions in New Labour's implementation of the three projects. The short-term thinking associated with some elements of the electoral project counts against the long-term playing out of the strategy to build state capacity. The benefits of the latter are delivered too slowly from the perspective on the former. Achieving perceivable or eye-catching change on the ground can seem a higher priority than creating the conditions for a new politics or a sustainable new set of institutional arrangements. New Labour appeared to spend half its first term boasting how public servants were delivering its agenda and the other half telling them they were no good and needed to be more open to change. The commitment to protecting the New Labour brand, that is seen as essential to the electoral project, sits uneasily alongside the new politics of devolution being created in an attempt to restore state capacity: as the embarrassment over the selection of Labour candidates for the post of mayor of London or leader of the Welsh Assembly showed. The attempt to impose candidates against those favoured in the local areas went against the grain of a commitment to decentralized politics. In London Ken Livingstone might not be seen as a champion of New Labour ideas but he was a popular choice as mayoral candidate among many Labour party supporters in the capital. The blocking of his candidature in the late 1990s was a low point in New Labour politics. More generally, what was successful image and personnel management when in opposition too often appeared as 'control freakery' when New Labour found itself in government.

The redistributive politics of entrepreneurial welfarism are partly downplayed or denied for fear of electoral backlash and so Labour faces the accusation of 'stealth taxes'. The general message that New Labour gave out over its attitude to taxes was in the first term confused. In fairness it can be noted that the saying, derived from Edmund Burke, that it is not given to governments to tax and to please is not without substance. New Labour in its first term offered the public the traditional pose of a government which plays up its public spending on essential services and plays down its tax-collecting activities. All of which is understandable because British public opinion appears to favour US-level taxes and continental European quality in its public services, in the words of Tony Travers, the LSE public finance expert. The second term, with its extensive commitments to public expenditure and tax measures to match, represents a stronger and a clearer commitment to a fairly traditional social democratic faith in the ability of the state to deliver quality services that are life-improving for its citizens (see Blair, 2002).

The core of New Labour may not be as tightly defined as Thatcherism or so straightforwardly captured in the views and position of one person but there is no reason to assume it is not sustainable. Thatcherism, of course, had several themes (perhaps even projects) captured in Andrew Gamble's summary, 'free economy, strong state' (Gamble, 1984). Tensions existed within Thatcherism, in particular between its liberal approach to economics and its illiberal approach to politics.

A more substantial area of difficulty for New Labour is that some leading figures in the Labour Government, some parts of the parliamentary party and considerable elements of the active party membership in local government and in the constituencies do not sign up to all of New Labour's programme. Electoral success is wanted but there is resentment at the so-called neglect of the traditional 'heartlands' because of the efforts made to appeal to new voters and interests. The welfare agenda is given some support but when tough decisions are required that support can evaporate, and the bottom-line is that many just want to raise taxes and spend more. The rebuilding of state capacity is embraced in a patchy and half-hearted way.

The problem, then, facing New Labour is that compared to Thatcherism its programme is more diverse and its support base within its own party is weaker. Thatcherism echoed themes that were close to the hearts of many of its supporters and that is why the legacy lives on. New Labour is attempting to construct an agenda which is challenging to many of its traditional activists. Like the New Democrats in the United States, New Labour has what Corera (1998) calls 'shallow roots'. An elite group around Brown and Blair (and in the early years Mandelson) hold ownership of New Labour. But a key to understanding New Labour is recognizing its sense of isolation and its lack of an activist base. The implications of this argument are considered further in Chapter 4.

New Labour's critique of elected local government

At the heart of New Labour's ambiguous, even at times hostile, response to the consensus case for reinvigorating elected local government – outlined at the end of Chapter 2 – is a critique of the way that local government works. 'It is what works that matters' is apparently one of the Prime Minister's favourite phrases and from the point of view of New Labour elected local government does not work well enough. The inadequacies of local government are seen as a part of a wider failure to innovate and change within public services. Local government also displays a particular political failure to attract public interest and legitimacy. Neither in its management of public services nor style of politics is elected local government adequate to the tasks it faces.

As part of a general critique of public services the Labour government believes that 'because institutions tend to look after their own interests, public services can be organised too much around the structure of the providers rather than the users' (HM Government, 1999: 11). There are echoes here of the previous Conservative administration's preference for a public choice-inspired critique of public bureaucracies (see Stoker, 1991). Labour's view, however, is that at the local level at least the producer culture was not broken by the Conservatives and, if anything, was reinforced by their primary instrument of reform: compulsory competitive tendering (CCT). Forced to put a wider range of services out to tender, many local authorities became more and more skilled at deterring external bidders. As the architect of Labour's Best Value policy Lord Filkin comments:

> Many councils saw CCT as being about defending the in-house organisation from losing the work to an external bidder. The private sector organisation was seen in hostile terms and the aim was to make it as unlikely as possible for them to win work. (Filkin, 1999: 5)

Moreover the Conservatives' narrow insistence on efficiency led to a focus on inputs (in particular costs) but neglected outputs. More broadly in public bodies there is too much effort devoted to 'maximising funding rather than considering what difference they can make in the form of actual results or outcomes' (HM Government, 1999: 11). Local authorities are seen as particularly prone to argue with great tenacity, and with the consumption of considerable effort, about their grant settlement (or SSA) or their capital spend allocation. At the same time they appear not always willing to ask hard questions about what they are achieving with their spending. As the Government's White Paper *Modern Local Government*, puts it:

> Too often within a council the members and officers take the paternalistic view that it is for them to decide what services are to be provided, on

the basis of what suits the council as a service provider. The interests of the public come a poor second best. The culture is still one where more spending and more taxes are seen as the simple solution rather than exploring how to get more out of the available resources. (DETR, 1998: 14)

Labour takes the view that while many public servants are 'hard-working and dedicated' their organizations including those at the local level are slow to respond to demands for change. As the White Paper, *Modernising Government* argues:

> Although the public can express its dissatisfaction with its public service through the ballot box, this can be a blunt instrument, removing whole local or central governments intermittently and often not addressing the underlying reasons why things are wrong. The risk is that particular parts of the public sector can therefore be left to fail for too long. (HM Government, 1999: 11)

The view that public services lack mechanisms to ensure that they are responsive is a theme that finds echoes in the arguments of the previous Conservative administration, although Labour's proposals for addressing the issue take a somewhat different course it will be argued later. More broadly public services are seen as risk averse and slow to take advantage of new opportunities.

A final theme in the critique of existing public services, although one where local government is seen as better placed than many, revolves around Labour's view that services are not sufficiently 'joined-up'. Too little attention has been paid to ensuring that services meet people's various and mixed needs in a holistic manner and where necessary by working across institutional barriers. Governance needs to be experienced in a way that meets people's needs rather than as a fragmented and confusing institutional jungle (see HM Government, 1999: ch. 3).

The local political system is seen by new Labour as in need of radical reform. The quality of local democracy as expressed through elected local government is seen as fundamentally inadequate. Put more abstractly, in the language introduced in Chapter 1, voice as an option for controlling public bureaucracies is not able to work sufficiently well and effectively at the local level. The first set of problems rests around the role and quality of elected representatives. In private conversations ministers and their advisers make comparisons between the lively, ethnically diverse and gender-balanced representation on some local quangos and police authorities and the dull, middle-aged or elderly men that dominate the politics of many elected local authorities. Indeed, they argue, appointments to local quangos open up opportunities for involvement to a whole variety of people that would not stand in local elections.

A key problem from New Labour's viewpoint is that being a councillor is not a position for which there is a great deal of competition. The status and standing of the councillor has been low and the time demanded of a councillor, for modest allowances and minimal expenses, has meant for many people it is a position incompatible with a career and family demands. The formal virtues of directly elected representatives are not delivered in practice and in the context of the experience of the rise of broader non-elected governance arrangements it is not clear that councillors as a body ensure that public bodies are more responsive. There are many dedicated and talented councillors, the Government is always quick to concede in public, but there were great private doubts expressed by many ministers about precisely what was the 'value-added' of most councillors.

A second set of problems identified by the New Labour Government revolves around the indifference of the public to local politics. Elections attract little public interest and the decision-making structures of local government are inadequate and invisible to the public. There is a recognition that the stuff of local politics is not always going to attract the highest level of interest and engagement at a great emotional or moral level but there is a clear view that improvement in electoral turnout is vital and, more broadly, participation in local politics is an issue that cannot be left to decline further. The low visibility and lack of capacity of elected representatives and public disinterest in local politics present obstacles to any strong claim to exercise local leadership by local government. Thus the Prime Minister comments:

> The way that local government currently operates is inefficient and opaque. It is not fit for its modern role. Councillors are very diligent and spend many hours on civic business. But the heart of the problem is that local government needs recognised leaders if it is to fulfil the community leadership role. People and outside organisations need to know who is politically responsible for running the council. The shifting sands of committee membership and chairs fails to foster leaders and leadership. (Blair, 1998b: 16)

The community leadership role is not an automatic right of elected local government. It needs to develop a political capacity to deliver it, which in much of local government is absent.

In the organization of public services and in the operation of its politics New Labour sees elected local authorities as in need of considerable improvement. In effect the bargain on offer to local government is reform and the Government will reward you. As one author has argued, local government's view is that it should be trusted as a partner by virtue of its elected and broader constitutional status (Lowndes, 1999b). The Government's reply is that trust depends on performance. A 1996 publication of the think-tank DEMOS makes clear that local government must earn back powers:

> Local self-government is neither a viable nor a desirable goal: councils cannot escape from all accountability to the centre. Therefore, we need, not general blueprints or schemes of unfettered fiscal freedom, but schemes that reward competence and popular support with incrementally rolling fiscal devolution, subject to continuing pressure from the centre on competence, quality, innovation in holistic budgeting, partnership and strategic purchasing. Local authorities can once again become local government, but they must expect to earn that right, and earn it individually, and service by service. They must not be permitted to assume that it is theirs by inheritance. (Mulgan and Perri 6, 1996: 9)

Given that one of the authors of this argument went to work initially in Blair's policy unit and in 2003 heads up the Strategy Unit of the Cabinet Office and the PM's Policy Unit, and the other is a regular adviser to the Government, it would seem fair to conclude that a key feature of New Labour's policy is its distrust of existing local government but its willingness to empower elected local authorities that demonstrate competence and popular support. The idea of earned autonomy is a distinctive feature of New Labour's managerial style (Perri 6 and Peck, 2003).

New Labour came to power with a fairly jaundiced view of local government as prone to producer domination in the delivery of services and lacking a strong consumer focus, as weak in terms of political standing and value, and as an institution not to be fully trusted but rather put on trial to see if it could be made to work better.

Labour's vision of local governance

New Labour's vision for the local political system involves a positive embracing of governance rather than a reluctant accommodation with it.

Governance implies an acceptance of the limits of state action and the considerable scope for contributions to solving societal problems from the voluntary and business sectors and individual citizens. Governance suggests an end to the tradition of direct, in-house service provision and a more open-minded approach to procurement. Governance involves processes of negotiation and bargaining which give recognition to the legitimacy of many stakeholders or participants. Governance encourages the search for active consent from the public not restricted to elective democracy. Governance suggests a key role for government as a facilitative leader. The qualities and characteristics of governance as they have emerged over the last two decades have been reshaped and reformulated by New Labour to provide its vision for the good local polity.

Labour's modernizing commitment stems from a view that fundamental societal changes demand a radical rethink about state provision and practice. An important element in the Third Way debate is to construct a less ideological and more pragmatic approach to issues of public service management and politics – and make a virtue out of it (Blair, 1998a). Old certainties are rejected and the selection of policy choice is not driven by a fixed ideological position but by attempting to find the best way to achieve a desired end. Overarching values still have a role to play but effective policy-making demands a pragmatic, evidence-driven approach.

There is a strong sense in New Labour's thinking that old certainties have been challenged. People – or at least significant sections of them – are not so reliant on public services except in certain core areas such as health and education. The information revolution and the emergence of the knowledge society suggest that the democratization of society is outstripping the capacity of the state to respond. The reality of multi-level governance – with the emergence of European Union and regional level government – suggests that governing has become a more complex task. Changes in the form of production and consumption in the private sector – in particular the use of new information and communication technology – presents a challenge to the public sector if it is not going to be left behind.

Labour's response to these new 'realities' is to embrace governance by first recognizing the limits to state action on its own. The key issue is to design local institutions so that they can best explore the contribution of private, business and voluntary sector contributions to the achieving of social outcomes. To some extent the emphasis is on finding new ways of working, a new set of tools and partners for government. However, although that is part of the vision there is also a suggestion of a shift in the purpose or justification of state intervention. Providing services is no longer an adequate rationale for state intervention funded by citizens – whether those services are provided directly or commissioned. The key issue is what contribution such provision makes to the achievement of outcomes.

In contrast to the Conservatives' emphasis on efficiency, Labour has put effectiveness at the forefront of the public service agenda. Searching for effectiveness implies clarity about intentions, hence the concern with outcomes. Boldly stated, the ambition to focus on outcomes can appear glib (see Stoker, 1999d). Yet as Mark Moore argues the underlying philosophy of public managers (whether politicians or officials) should be to create public value. The issue that needs to be addressed is whether the public intervention which they are directing is achieving positive social and economic outcomes. The focus on generating public value brings in its wake some implications which carry considerable bite.

> Public managers create public value. The problem is that they cannot know for sure what that is. Even if they could be sure to-day, they would have to doubt tomorrow, for by then the political aspirations and public needs that give point to their efforts might well have changed ... It is not enough, then, that managers simply maintain the continuity of their organizations, or even that the organizations become efficient in current tasks. It is also important that the enterprise be adaptable to new purposes and that it be innovative and experimental ... It is not enough to say that public managers create results that are valued; they must be able to show that the results obtained are worth the cost of private consumption and unrestrained liberty forgone in producing the desirable results. Only then can we be sure that some public value has been created. (Moore, 1995: 57, 55, 29)

Providing services is no longer a sufficient justification for state intervention funded by citizens – whether those services are provided directly or commissioned. The question that has to be answered is: does the service advance valued social or economic outcomes? A constant readiness to think again about what is being achieved is also necessary. Modernizers expect public managers to not assume that the solution to any problem is the input of more resources. There is a need to consider what more could be achieved with the resources and assets at your disposal. There is no prejudice against public spending but equally there is no automatic endorsement of it. The rationale for governmental intervention is driven by the contribution it can make – together with the forces of the non-state sectors – to achieving social and economic goals.

Governance is also embraced in Labour's open-minded approach to procurement. The *Modernising Government* White Paper comments:

> We will review all central and local government department services and activities – by consulting widely with users, by benchmarking and by open competition – to identify the best suppliers in each case. The focus will be on end results and service standards, rather than simply on processes. The aim will be to secure the best quality and value for money for the taxpayer. (HM Government, 1999: 41)

Effective procurement – without any particular preference for either direct or commissioned services providers – lies at the heart of New Labour's approach to service provision. The assumption is that while in-house provision may be appropriate in some circumstances in many others the advantages of private or voluntary sector provision will be greater (Filkin, 1999).

Governance for New Labour is about recognizing that other stakeholders have the right to be involved in policy debates and decisions (Goss, 2001). They are not to be incorporated because to ignore them would be problematic or because they can bring resources to the process of implementation. They are there as partners not as interlopers. Local politicians and their officials have a particular legitimacy given that local government is elected but within a network of governance there are other valid claims to legitimacy. Sue Goss explains the different bases of legitimacy:

> People have to have the right knowledge, and this underpins the legitimacy of both professionals and public managers. But it also increasingly applies to individual service users and local communities, since their self-knowledge makes it important to engage them in governance ... There is also the legitimacy that derives from leadership or the capacity to mobilise followers – that of the community leader, the charismatic priest, the campaigner. There is a legitimacy that goes with a function performed on behalf of a wider community – the role of the police officer, the judge, the director of finance, and the auditor. And finally there is a legitimacy that derives from the capacity to build consent, to find a solution with which everyone agrees. Because all these legitimacies are real, they cannot be simply disregarded or 'trumped' by political legitimacy. (Goss, 2001: 23)

As well as a positive challenge to embrace stakeholders, the recognition of multiple sources of legitimacy is a challenge to the more narrow concept of party democracy that has been a feature of, particular, Labour debates and practice (see Game and Leach, 1996). The Prime Minister comments that 'councils need to avoid getting trapped in the secret world of caucus and the party group' (Blair, 1998b: 15). There is no outright rejection of party politics in local government from New Labour but there is the characteristic Blairite suggestion that there is a need to step beyond party group and loyalties.

Labour embraces governance in the search for the active consent of the public for policy measures and service prescriptions. Consent needs to be sought through and beyond the ballot box by way of methods of public consultation and deliberation. The commitment is not only about better approaches to public participation at the local level – although these are seen as vital (see Lowndes *et al.*, 1998a,b) – it is also about recognizing that effective policy outcomes often require changing the public's behaviour. Challenging people to change their driving habits or take up waste recycling requires some mechanisms of intensive dialogue and high levels of public trust in order to change cultures and go beyond more regulation or shifting patterns of rewards and penalties.

Finally, governance demands of elected local government a new role as a community leader rather than a service provider. The Prime Minister's local government pamphlet (Blair, 1998b) emphasizes that at the heart of local government's new role is leadership. However, the style of leadership is to be facilitative rather than commanding. It is about developing a shared vision, building partnerships to achieve social outcomes and seeking to support others to achieve valued social and economic objectives. The challenge for elected government at the local level is to actively steer processes of co-ordination and collective action across public, private and voluntary boundaries using a wide range of tools (see Stoker, 1999d).

The reform agenda

The White Paper – *Modern Local Government: In Touch with the People* (DETR, 1998) – provides the most comprehensive statement of Labour's agenda. A second White Paper was published in December 2001 but this should be seen as a document confirming the broad thrust of the policy but indicating a few changes in style and modest movement with respect to substance. In particular there is a strong theme in the second White Paper about giving local authorities more freedoms and flexibilities to deliver on the Government's agenda. There were many more warm words about local government but little in the way of radical new measures. There is a clear commitment to interfere less and allow greater freedoms for all councils but especially those that are high performing. They are to be encouraged to get on and make changes that they deem appropriate on the ground. The New Localism, that we shall consider further in Chapter 11, is in 2003 stronger in terms of rhetoric than new policy levers (Corry and Stoker, 2002). There was reassurance that the radical political reforms of the first term would be given time to 'bed in' rather than being replaced by further radical new measures or interventions. Fundamentally no great new set of goals were outlined but a rather different implementation strategy was indicated. The draft Local Government Bill that was published in June 2002, picking up on some of the issues in the December 2001 White Paper, confirmed that no major new agenda was planned in the second term. This judgement is confirmed by the House of Commons Select Committee investigation into the draft bill (House of Commons, 2002b).

New Labour's programme for local governance has four main elements. The first is a system for performance management of service delivery that puts the emphasis on local authority self-improvement matched by a national system of regulation and inspection. The second is the theme of democratic renewal, providing councils with better political leadership, more effective electoral processes, more accountable decision-making and a greater capacity for consulting the public on key issues. A third theme is the focus on councils as leaders in a complex system of multi-level governance, working in partnership with a whole series of other agencies and institutions. Finally, there is a sustained cautious note on local finances. More money has been provided but not necessarily more freedoms to councils.

The most developed proposals in the 1998 White Paper relate to the disciplines associated with Best Value, New Labour's first attempt to provide new performance management arrangements for local government. Legislation containing these measures was enacted in mid-1999. Compulsory competitive tendering was scrapped and in its place a framework designed to encourage, for all local councils, clarity about service standards, targets for continuous improvement, greater involvement for service users and independent audit and inspection procedures. The Government has also taken powers to intervene in a 'flexible and constructive' way if service and performance failure is persistent or serious. The 'Best Value' regime combined with the existing regulatory regimes covering other services provided New Labour with a comprehensive performance management system to cover all the services provided by local government and several other agencies in the wider world of local governance.

The initial Best Value regime has been joined by three other performance management measures. The first is the designation of councils with 'beacon' status in respect of certain services. Councils can apply to have their achievements in particular areas recognized against a priority list set out by central government. The award of beacon status carries with it a certain amount of prestige and a commitment on the part of the council to provide its experience of best practice to others (Rashman and Hartley, 2002). The second was an initiative from the Treasury to establish local public spending agreements with individual local authorities, similar to those it has developed for central government departments and agencies. In effect, for agreeing to a negotiated set of challenging targets in service delivery the local authority receives a promise of additional funding from the Treasury if the targets are met.

Further, the 2001 White Paper (DTLR, 2001: 23) proposed the introduction of what is described as a 'national framework of standards and accountability' in service delivery. Specifically it is proposed to grade all councils in terms of a comprehensive performance assessment system and to make those grades available to local communities and use them as a guide to the degree of additional freedoms and flexibilities to be provided to a council or the level of support that a council may need to improve. The proposal for an overall assessment of performance will be based on the collection of data from a variety of sources on a council's service-specific and general corporate capacity, resulting in an allocation into one of four initially proposed categories, allowing for a designation stretching from high- to poor-performing councils. A package of performance support will be tailored to authorities in each of the categories. With more freedoms and less regulation being aimed at high-performing councils but less freedoms and more targeted support, and ultimately forced intervention, aimed at poorer performers (ODPM, 2002a). The system was piloted by the Audit Commission in the spring and developed in the summer of 2002 and results for the primary tier of local government were announced at the end of that year.

Beyond the focus on service delivery there have been a number of measures aimed at democratic renewal within local authorities and in the wider system of local governance. First, councils are expected to adopt new political structures. A number of options were laid out – a directly elected mayor with a cabinet, a cabinet with a leader, and what in effect is a hybrid form of mayor and council manager system. In the passage of the legislation a so-called fourth option – a revised committee system – was introduced for small shire district councils with very few functions and serving populations below 85,000. In addition local people were to be given the right to trigger a referendum on the directly elected mayor option. Legislation to enable these measures was published in draft form in mid-1999 and became law in mid-2000. Even before legislation is in place authorities have been encouraged to make changes by developing new-style committee arrangements or informal executive arrangements. The process of implementation – in terms of moves to new structure – was completed in the Autumn of 2002 when the second phase of mayoral elections was held.

Alongside these reforms New Labour provided a great push behind the practice and promotion of consultation by local authorities. The Government has published at least three guidance documents on how to undertake consultation in general (Lowndes *et al.*, 1998b), with respect to political management changes (Copus *et al.*, 2000) and finally in dealing with council tax raising (Stoker *et al.*, 2002). It has also made demonstrated capacity for consultation a key demand in relation to a whole series of issues stretching from the implementation of Best Value reviews to the provision of new forms of neighbourhood renewal funding. The emphasis is on enhancing the accessibility and legitimacy of local government through 'higher participation in elections and close and regular contact between a council and local people between elections' (DETR, 1998: 38).

Legislation to enable pilots or experiments with electronic voting, the location of polling stations, postal voting and the timing of elections was passed in time to enable a number of experiments in the May 2000 local elections. They have followed a series of other schemes in May 2002 and 2003. The most positive effect on turnout was achieved by those experiments that encouraged wider use of postal votes.

The third strong theme in New Labour's plan for local governance is based on a commitment to enhancing the overall coherence and integration of the system. The language is about the virtue of developing 'joined-up' or 'holistic' approaches to tackling service provision and social and economic problems. Local government with its range of responsibilities and leadership role has a particular contribution to make in this area (see Perri 6 *et al.*, 1999, 2002). There are two aspects to joining up. The first focuses on the delivery of services to individual clients in a way that enables them to gain access to the appropriate mixture of provision to their circumstances. Here the key from the government's point of view is the more effective development of electronic systems of service delivery and easy access systems to a whole range of services. The other is more concerned with the way the community tackles certain difficult issues – such as crime prevention, health promotion or urban regeneration – that require action from a variety of agencies and indeed voluntary and business sectors to take action.

The building of networks and partnerships is seen as crucial to the delivery of the capacity to achieve both forms of joining up.

To give expression to the commitment to partnership and joint working under the leadership of local councils the government has committed itself to trying to ensure that the legal framework in which local authorities operate has sufficient flexibility within it to enable innovative and imaginative schemes to be put together. There are the powers of well-being under the 2000 Local Government Act to engage in activities for the benefit of your community and the specific provisions to modify enactments concerning plans, etc. as well as a power to ask for amendment or the repeal of enactments that are unnecessarily restricting to local councils. Other legislation gives councils powers to form partnerships, to trade within certain limits and other freedoms and flexibilities. The 2001 White Paper suggests a willingness to work up other freedoms if they are needed. Along with this responsibility has come a duty on the council to provide a community strategy for its area (DETR, 1998: 80) and in 2000 the Government proposed that all local authorities establish local strategic partnerships in their area. The extent and nature of community leadership function provided to local authorities is not very tightly defined but there is a broad commitment to local government having a key role in guiding a range of partnerships and activities in their area.

On the financial side the Government has adopted a cautious but generous approach in comparison with Conservative years. During its first term Labour sustained a commitment to financial constraint for the first two years of its period in office but since then it has provided substantially more money to local authorities (ODPM, 2003). Indeed between 1997/98 and 2000/1 the average annual real terms (that is allowing inflation) increase in local spend for the education and social services has been around 5–6 per cent. During the same period the average annual real-term increases for other services has been much lower, at between 1 and 2 per cent. Further spending increases have followed up to 2003/4. The increase in spending has been swallowed by additional demand for services, rising expectations about service standards and a cost base that has increased faster than the standard rate of inflation. The cost of the extra spending has been met by substantial rises in the amount of central grant provided and council tax raised. The capping of budgets has been kept but only as a reserve power. This is despite real-term increases in the average payment of council tax from about the mid-£300 mark when Labour came into office in 1997 to an amount close to £500 for 2003/4.

On the capital side the broad aim is to give local councils more flexibility in their use of capital allocations, the disposal of assets and use of reserves.

Considerable encouragement has also been given to local public–private partnership and private finance arrangements but these remain a relatively modest part of the overall structure of local finance.

Other policies of the Labour Government have reduced further the discretion available on local spending decisions notwithstanding the removal of universal capping (indeed capping was only used in Labour's first year in office). The main explanation is that Labour has increased the proportion of funding provided by special grants (from 5 per cent to 14 per cent as a proportion of revenue support funding by the end of 2002/3). This has been accompanied by *de facto* ring fencing through the 'pass porting' of education funds and through the requirements to find match funding for monies provided through special measures, such as the schools standards fund. The arguments for these measures are driven by the commitment to improve education and welfare standards.

The proposals in the 2001 White Paper suggested that a cautious policy line was set to continue throughout Labour's second term but there were a number of significant moves proposed and the prospect was held out for a more radical change in local finance. The system for allocating central grant was changed in 2003/4 and given a new name of formula grant. The effects were notable for some individual authorities but the underlying principles of allocation remain the same. The aim is to equalize to a substantial degree the spending capacity of local authorities reflecting both their need to spend money and their abilities to raise monies. The Government has proposed that by 2005/6 the amount of ring-fenced funding will be substantially scaled back but these grants will remain a way of allocating specific funds to specific local authority services. The White Paper also puts forward a number of changes on the revenue, giving local councils greater freedom over the collection of council tax and the raising of charges for a wide range of discretionary services. There are also a mix of proposals to increase the revenue-raising options for local authorities from a variety of sources including through business improvement districts, congestion charging and other measures. On the capital side the White Paper proposes a move to a prudential system of borrowing where it will be up to local councils to decide how much they want to borrow. As the White Paper (DTLR, 2001: 83) comments:

> The local prudential regime is about self-regulation. It will require individual authorities to decide how much they can prudently borrow. They must set limits on the total amount of debt that they can take on. Having set these limits, the authority will be required to adhere to them.

Local authorities are going to receive a substantial increase in the amount of capital support delivered through a single capital pot, rather than through a range of service discrete allocations. How far these various measures offer a real advance and a base for a radical step forward will be examined in Chapter 9. Certainly the prospect of radical change cannot be ruled out with the establishment of the Balance of Funding Review by the ODPM in April 2003. The Review team has drawn on representatives from the Government, local government, various stakeholder organizations and academics (including the author) and is due to report in mid- to late 2004. Its brief is to examine whether a major overhaul of the system of local finance is required.

Conclusions

This chapter has set out to establish New Labour's policy agenda and in particular its provisions in relation to local governance. As a result two simplistic ideas can be dismissed. First, New Labour is not different to the predecessor Conservative governments, but just doing more of the same. New Labour's policy agenda is plainly different in that it is broader and more explicitly welcoming of the opportunities created in an era of governance. Although it does share some of the concerns, methods and tools that the Conservatives adopted, New Labour's agenda is substantially different. The second is that New Labour has betrayed a commitment to local government by not delivering on an agenda of reforms favoured by local government and many of its academic friends in the mid-1990s. That it has not delivered on that agenda is undeniable; that it neither intended to nor offered to deliver on that agenda is also clear.

4 Understanding New Labour's Reform Strategy

This chapter adds to our understanding of New Labour's approach to local governance by looking behind the substance of its policy agenda to consider the underlying motivation and dynamic of its reform strategy. It offers a rather strange conclusion, namely that New Labour's approach to the reform of local governance has many of the qualities of a lottery in which a complex variety of prizes have been offered to successful reformers but where the selection of winners reflects a complex mix of their capacity and chance. This may seem an odd view yet it would appear that a strategy driven by the principles of a lottery ties in with New Labour's fatalistic reading of its policy environment and has additional beneficial side-effects in managing tensions within the administration and its relationship with various supporters. The interpretation offered here draws heavily on insights from institutional grid-group theory and this chapter provides an introduction to that theory, which in turn is used in the remainder of the book to inform the analysis of New Labour's reforms of local governance.

The aim is not to add to the literature on the inevitability of unclear objectives or unintended consequences undermining grand reforms: the stock in trade of much political science analysis of policy reforms (Rhodes, 1997a; and with respect to New Labour in particular see Seldon, 2001; Ludlam and Smith, 2001). The point of the interpretation offered here is not that New Labour's programme is incoherent but rather that up to a point it is incoherent with reason, and for a purpose. New Labour's policies are in part deliberately designed to be a muddle in order both to search for the right reform formula and to create a dynamic for change by creating instability but also space for innovation. At first glance it is of course ironic to think that any plausible perspective on strategic change could have the qualities of a lottery and doubly ironic that it might be associated with a New Labour that, as noted in Chapter 3, often describes itself as calculated and technocratic in its approach (Blair, 1998a,b; Boyne *et al.*, 2001; Temple, 2000).

The aim of this chapter is to explore the idea that New Labour has chosen to build into its reform approach to local governance premised on the principles of a lottery. It develops the arguments in an article published in *Public*

Administration (Stoker, 2002a). The chapter is divided into four parts. The first introduces the broader grid-group theory that provides the inspiration for the explanation offered here and analysis provided elsewhere in the book. It argues that certain forms of social organization are regularly repeated in human societies and can be divided into the nostrums of hierarchy, individualism, network egalitarianism and fatalism. These social forms or tropes provide guides for people about the way that institutions should work and relationships should be constructed. The second section argues that New Labour's reform strategy contains a mix of three of the four common forms of social organization. In particular it is suggested that fatalism is the organizational force that through the adoption of lottery-like principles binds together elements of hierarchy and network egalitarianism in New Labour's reform strategy. The third section of the chapter establishes the idea of a lottery strategy and its location in New Labour's fatalistic reading of its policy environment. The fourth examines the conditions that have made it possible for that strategy to emerge.

The contribution of grid-group theory

Grid-group theory is sometimes labelled and indeed promoted in social science as part of a wider cultural theory (Thompson *et al.*, 1990). Its intellectual origins lie in the work of Durkheim who in much of his work was trying to understand what enabled societies to hold together. Societies would not be able to sustain themselves if self-conscious calculation of costs and benefits by individuals – more broadly the world of rational choice – was all that was available to resource successful social functioning. Perri 6 (1999) offers the following explanation of Durkheim's key insight:

> [W]hatever institutional and social practices held societies together would not only take certain structural forms, but would show up in ideas, classification and cognition. In particular, he saw that whatever it was that explained basic success in functioning at all, and also explained particular types of social cohesion, would be given powerful moral authority and would be institutionalised as culturally mandated norms in law, religion and education, for it is by these cognitive means that the explaining phenomenon would be perpetuated.

Attaching the word cultural to grid-group theory is somewhat misleading in that it is about more than patterns of shared beliefs and values. It is about patterns of social relations and their institutionalization, so that they become part of the unconscious fabric of individual life. As Mary Douglas comments, Durkheim's key insight was to recognize the social origins of individual thought. Classifications, logical operations and guiding metaphors are given to the individual by society. Above all, the sense of *a priori* rightness of some ideas and the nonsensicality of others are handed out as part of the social environment (Douglas, 1982: 10). Institutions work because they help to determine how people think. They afford members with a way of understanding the world, they control their memory and they make sacred certain principles. Durkeim's insight has more in common with the approach of new institutionalists that see society as constructed, embedded and sustained in a range of institutional patterns of behaviour, norms and organizations (Lowndes, 2002).

Institutional grid-group theory postulates that certain forms of social organization keep recurring in human affairs. Its current dominant expression is associated with the work of Mary Douglas (1982, 1986) who adapted and developed insights from the work of Durkheim. She identified, through drawing on her work as a social anthropologist, various ways of functioning that tend to dominate in the processes and practices of societies. She identified certain biases in social organization that reflect patterns in people's assumptions about the way the world works and the nature of their relationship to others (see Figure 4.1). These forms of social organization can, in turn, be classified by reference to two dimensions: the grid dimension, which is characterized by the pervasiveness of societal rules that are envisaged, and the group dimension, which reflects the extent of group loyalty and solidarity that is involved. The grid dimension refers to the extent of autonomy that a social system allows or supports. Are the organizations and social structures constraining or do they allow individuals some considerable discretion and autonomy? A fatalist world is governed by a sense that fate will decide; the individual has little or no control. Similarly a hierarchical world is one where the rules dictate and constrain behaviour. The individualist world is one where there is considerable scope for choice and initiative. The egalitarian world again allows for choice but conducted through collective agreement and deliberation.

Different forms of social organization make different demands on us and so do different groups to which we belong. This is the concern of the group dimension represented in Figure 4.1. We may be very much part of a group, an integrated part of the collective. Alternatively we may be isolated from it and experience very view bonds of solidarity. The hierarchical and egalitarian functioning arrangements fall into the first group category. The individualist and fatalist fall into the second.

Figure 4.1   *Biases in social organization: an institutional classification*

Grid: Social relations are conceived as if they were principally involuntary		
Group: individual autonomy not always to be held to account	*Fatalism* *World view:* Sense of chaos and futilty leads to apathy for powerless, and a search for tools of temporary domination for the powerful *Insitutions:* suspicious of the efficacy of any institutional design *Co-ordination:* little prospect since all systems are capricious *Social networks: seen as* casual, shallow ties, occasion-bound. *Value stance:* personal withdrawal, weak trust, eclectic values	*Hierarchy* *World view:* social systems should be regulated and under central direction *Institutions:* seen as rational, rule-dominant, and capable of being steered *Co-ordination:* regulated systems are necessary; unregulated systems need management and deliberate action to give them stability and structure *Social networks:* centrally controlled and managed network *Value stance:* affirmation by rule-following and strong incorporation of individuals in social order	**Group: individual autonomy to be held to account always**
	Individualism *World view:* an effective social order emerges best spontaneously from individual action *Institutions:* self-restricting, transparent, facilitative, guaranteeing basic property rights and providing appropriate incentives and signals *Co-ordination:* by spontaneous exchange or hidden hand *Social networks:* open configurations characterized by weak ties *Value stance:* affirmation by personal entrepreneurial initiative	*Egalitarianism* *World view:* there is great value in partnership and group solidarity *Institutions:* laden with strong values and solidarity, governed by peer pressure and strong sense of ownership and attachment *Co-ordination:* through charismatic leadership or mutual and co-operative, networks *Social networks:* inward-looking, tight networks *Value stance:* affirmation by peer group, with scope for principled dissent	
Grid: Social relations are conceived as if they were principally voluntary		

Source: Adapted from Perri 6 (1999) Figure 1.

Grid-group theory is a heuristic device, a way of guiding investigation. It has been used in a variety of ways to explore a diverse range of topics (for reviews see Thompson *et al.*, 1990; and Perri 6, 1999). In this book it is used to stimulate propositions about the organizational understanding and strategic behaviour of New Labour and to comprehend how local authorities and other agencies of local governance have responded to challenges to change. In addition, the particular understanding institutional thinking offered in the work of Mary Douglas provides valuable insights.

As Perri 6 (1999) contends, 'the theory that underpins the heuristic is much richer and deeper than the banal truth that people with particular worldviews will, if they can, seek to institutionalize practices and norms and rules and solidarities that fit their worldviews'. He goes on to argue that it is important to stress that grid-group is not a classification of psychological types. No one individual person is an egalitarian or a hierarchist, and nothing else. People live in a variety of social contexts over the course of a week, let alone a lifetime. In many of those contexts, they operate within different and differently conflicting patterns of social organization. Some may try to integrate their perceptions and preferences about social organization across every activity; many neither can, nor feel the need to do so.

Moving to the level of institutional analysis in a similar way, no one form of social organization is ever likely to be wholly dominant. Again, as Perri 6 (1999) argues, each form of social organization produces particular biases in the capacity to recognize social phenomena, a range of institutionalized expectations, biases in understanding and attitudes to anomalies that give it certain blind spots as well as areas of focus. Moreover the organizational dynamics of each practice tends to undermine the world view of each bias. Egalitarians, for example, share a general belief in the equality of all but a particular organizational form that is favoured by that bias, the use of networks, can become an exclusive and closed form. The general orientation may be towards treating people equally but the practice of networks can over time undermine the achievement of that general principle. Some feminists identified, for example, how the loose informal network structures favoured by the women's movement had a tendency to degenerate into informal and unaccountable elite-driven organizational forms. Hierarchists think people should follow rules but set great store on leadership and the capacity for those leaders to 'think out of the box', that is beyond the rules. These attributes are in turn difficult to make wholly compatible with hierarchy. For these reasons institutional grid-group theory predicts that no one bias alone can constitute a viable pattern of social organization that can be 'rolled out' in an unproblematic and sustained manner. Indeed it expects in any one setting to see a compromise between a variety of organizational solidarities. Grid-group theory allows for the playing out of a dynamic between the four forms of social organization.

Grid-group theory, as has so far been argued, allows for the identification of four biases in social organization: hierarchy, individualism egalitarianism and fatalism. The organizational features of the first three tropes relate strongly to the familiar pattern of hierarchy, market and networks as three common forms of institution (see G. Thompson *et al.,* 1991). What is distinctive, although not unique, about the contribution of grid-group theory is its introduction of a fatalist orientation. Yet as Hood (2000:145) comments, 'although cultural theorists see fatalism as one of their most important "finds", only a few cultural theorists have given detailed attention to fatalism in practice'. The fatalistic world view sees all systems as capricious, an environment characterized by weak ties, low trust relations and modest prospects for effective co-ordination. The argument presented below is that to understand New Labour, at least as far as its approach to local governance is concerned, it is necessary to understand the extent to which it has been infected by a fatalistic outlook. The next section examines how a fatalist outlook has moulded the way that hierarchist and egalitarian organizational forms have been played out in New Labour's practice.

Control freaks, partners or bookies? Characterizing New Labour's approach to central–local relations

At the heart of New Labour, as David Marquand (1998) notes, there is a tension between command planning and pluralism, or, in the language of grid-group theory, between a hierarchist and a more egalitarian network approach to organizational solidarity. If asked to identify the strategy of New Labour towards governance beyond Westminster and Whitehall many of those in local and devolved government – and indeed many academic, journalistic and think-tank observers – would opt for a characterization that emphasized its top down, rule-bound, control orientation. In the language of cultural grid-group theory, New Labour's approach might be seen as a classic example of a hierarchist approach, or in more common parlance, control freakery gone mad. It is the trope of imposed structure that begins and ends with the centre setting down functions, means and relationships (Perri 6 *et al.*, 2002). It encourages a commitment to following rules, argues for group benefit to be subsumed in the wider achievement of societal goals and holds that transgressors that fail to become part of the project should be identified and punished.

There is no point denying that there are hierarchist facets to New Labour's approach to public service reform at the local level. Thus New Labour has laid out many of its programmes in great detail (such as Best Value or primary school literacy measures), demanded that they be adopted, and sent in the inspectors to make sure that its wishes are carried out. The Government has at times told local authorities and other bodies that their job is to help deliver national priorities:

> I want the message to local government to be loud and clear ... The people's needs require you to change again so that you can play your part in

helping to modernise Britain and, in partnership with others, deliver the policies on which this government was elected. (Blair, 1998a: 22)

Within many elements of New Labour there appeared to be a general view that although the task of governance had become more complex, and the range of institutions involved more diverse, there remained the need for a central core to provide direction and leadership (Pierre and Stoker, 2000). Yet the hierarchist frame does not appear to tell the whole story. New Labour has launched devolution programmes and initiatives galore aimed at building local partnerships. The rhetoric of New Labour is full of references to its commitment to an 'empowering' and 'enabling' state that works with people rather than does things to them. This approach draws on a trope of egalitarianism, mutuality and self-organizing networks in the language of grid-group cultural theory. This is New Labour in Third Way mode (Giddens, 1998, 2000), at ease with establishing a strong range of cross-checking institutions at different levels of governance and encouraging those institutions that are open and accountable and capable of working alongside private, voluntary and community interests. It was not just local government ministers who could be heard making these noises in the first term (see DETR, 1998; Armstrong, 2000). The Prime Minister himself has argued for a decentralized politics as part of a broader Third Way vision (Blair, 1998a,b; Blair, 2001). Even Gordon Brown, the 'Iron Chancellor', committed to localist approaches towards the end of the first term (Brown, 2001a).

Hierarchy and egalitarian themes can both be seen in New Labour's approach. The aim has been to use the strong arm of hierarchy to deliver a recognition of the need for change among those local governance institutions and yet also encourage a release of creativity and energy within those institutions reflected in a more egalitarian agenda. New Labour holds that neither hierarchy nor local autonomous partnerships can deliver on their own. The reasoning for this position is a product of the influence of another trope that has influenced New Labour: a trope of fatalism.

In many respects fatalism seems hard to reconcile with any description of a positive reform agenda. After all fatalism is a broad orientation to life which emphasizes the low likelihood of co-operation, the difficulties of overcoming the influences of fate and the improbability of developing effective trust. As such it would appear more suited to encourage apathy than action. Yet the fatalism of New Labour has led it to approach reform as if it were a lottery. A strategy of governance by lottery provides the glue to hold the two hierarchical and egalitarian parts of Labour's strategy together.

A fatalist reading in the hands of an agent with substantial formal powers can provide a focus for action. At a management level Hood (2000: 157–65) suggests that a strategy of contrived randomness could well be adopted in low-trust environments and describes it as a management recipe for 'positively designing institutions, using chance as the central part of the organizational architecture' (Hood, 2000: 157). A number of measures that deliberately introduce an element of uncertainty into the oversight functions undertaken by management would seem appropriate in such an environment. Moving staff around on a frequent and unpredictable basis might undermine the emergence of potential networks of collusion against the wishes of management or the interests of the organization. Audits arranged on an ad hoc basis, with considerable turnover amongst the designated auditors in order to avoid them 'going native', would also fit into the management strategy of contrived randomness.

It is worth dwelling briefly on the language that is used by Hood in order to grasp the wider implications of the analysis. The term contrived implies that the strategy is deliberate, a chosen course of action. The idea of the strategy being deliberate is crucial; otherwise the claim amounts to little more than that the perpetrator of the strategy is confused or unclear. There is also a hint in the term contrived that the strategy is manipulative. The word random could imply simply that the strategy does have a degree of haphazardness or chance built into it or that that each member of the targeted population has an equal chance of being selected by the strategy. The more exact second meaning – the statistical sense of the term random – should be laid to one side. What random captures for the purpose of this concept is that there is an element of uncertainty and chance present in both the processes and outcomes associated with the strategy.

A strategy of governance by lottery in a similar manner seeks to make a virtue out of conditions of low trust and an unpredictable environment by encouraging a change process driven by requiring or encouraging target organizations to participate in a complex and rolling game of chance. Fatalism for those with substantial formal power can provide a formula for action rather than apathy. Lotteries can and are controlled so the licenceholders achieve their purposes, usually to raise money. New Labour, like the high street 'bookies' or casino operators, has devised games to entice players but like them it aims to ensure it is always a winner, by getting the policy changes and performance improvements it wants from the players. The prizes on offer can be structured in various ways, providing a few major prizes or many smaller prizes, or some other combination.

The players themselves can increase their chance of winning through taking some action (by, for example, buying more tickets) and, if they are skilful, by working out the formula that drives the selection and sequencing of winners. Skill and luck combine in many lotteries to determine the selection of winners and the same would appear to apply in the case of the targets of New Labour's reform strategy.

The claim here is more than that New Labour's policies have been experienced as having the qualities of a lottery by the institutions and interests of devolved government. The argument is that the lottery principles reflect a chosen course of action by New Labour, a product of its world view, reform objectives and political contingencies that in turn reflect the context in which it has had to operate. These arguments are followed through in the next two sections.

The ingredients of New Labour's lottery reform strategy

New Labour's reform strategy exhibits the features of a lottery in at least four ways. First, the focus of policy attention and indeed priority is subject to complex shifts and much uncertainty. In the process many players in local governance are encouraged to believe that their number is about to come up. Governance, with its association with the introduction of a range of new challenging players to the game of local politics and service delivery, matches a lottery logic. Second, New Labour has encouraged a bidding culture so that to get prizes devolved units must form partnerships and a multitude of grants and initiatives have been aimed at institutions across spatial levels and sectors. Third, a new culture of audit and inspection has added to the environment of challenge. The Comprehensive Performance Assessment (see Chapter 5 for a fuller analysis) programme, that reached its initial high point in December 2002 with the categorization of all the primary local government units in England along a five-point scale from excellent to poor, can be seen as the ultimate expression of the lottery culture. In this case success in terms of a high rating is rewarded with special prizes of extra freedoms and decreased inspection. Finally, various rogue elements have been introduced into the reform process by the use of referendum and other mechanisms that take decisions out of the hands of local elites and give decision-making powers to the general public.

There can be little doubt about the mixed messages that local government receives from the Government about what its priorities are and where it wants policy to go. Early research assessments of Labour's programme revolved around the pressures caused by a reform programme driven by initiative after initiative. The large numbers of zones, pilots and initiatives led Perri 6 and colleagues (Perri 6 *et al.*, 1999: 24) to note the danger of 'initiativitis'. To quote the same group of researchers again, the early years of New Labour found ministers always on the look out for 'quick wins'. But there was something more than naïve enthusiasm at play on the part of the Government. New Labour appeared to have a deliberate strategy of letting a thousand flowers bloom, indeed this was given some legitimacy and substance by the commitment to evidence-based policy-making.

A further factor that explains the emergence of New Labour's strategy with its lottery pattern is the availability of a justifying smokescreen around the rhetoric of evidence-based policy. The commitment to developing policy through evidence gathering and learning is characteristic of New Labour's policy style (R. Walker, 2000) and a key feature of the pragmatism of New Labour's version of Third Way politics (Temple, 2000). The policy has much to commend it but in practice it has lent itself to a commitment to a plethora of initiatives, each justified as a pilot to provide evidence for a wider programme. However, much evaluation of the current string of New Labour initiatives amounts to no more than monitoring the operation of programmes (Stoker, 2000b). The lack of sophistication or depth in the approach to evidence-gathering means that a *de facto* strategy of lottery takes over from a more considered and reflective approach.

Modernization has been a core theme for New Labour as noted in Chapter 3. But the message to local government has been more muddied and mixed than in other areas or policy sectors. The ministers for local government, Hilary Armstrong (1997–2001) and Nick Raynsford (2001 onwards), have been strong advocates of both managerial and political change at the local level. The Deputy Prime Minister who had formal responsibility for the issue initially as head at the super-department of the DETR (1997–2001) and then at the much smaller Office of the Deputy Prime Minister (2002–) has not intervened to any great extent in the making of local government policy and has been content to guide from a distance. Yet it would be difficult to claim him as an enthusiastic supporter of all elements of the modernization agenda. Indeed he appears uninterested in local government and keen to promote regional government. The local government ministry was therefore populated by modernizers who had only limited faith in the ability of local government to reform and a Secretary of State who appeared to have given up on local government completely and focused instead on regional government.

Crucially, others have also wanted to play with local governance but they have appeared to favour different partners at different times. The Prime Minister's Office and its units have at different times wanted to work with local government, direct service providers such as schools, and local communities through neighbourhood renewal or private companies that might take over the running of failed services. The Treasury reached out to private companies through the private finance initiative but has also launched schemes aimed at the voluntary sectors, and offered the extension of public service agreements to local authorities. Many other departments threw new measures at local government. Ministers from other departments – in particular the Home Office, education and social services – have supported policy initiatives but appear to pay little heed to their overall impact. The emphasis for them is on education, health, crime prevention and job creation. Local government or other local agencies or organizations may well have a role to play in the delivery of these objectives, so a deliberate strategy of trial and error appears to have been adopted. Certainly there was no great trust in the ability of local government to deliver.

Second, New Labour has encouraged a partnership-based bidding culture. New Labour has showered devolved government agencies from local councils to schools with a variety of initiatives. There are now more than sixty centrally prescribed plans and strategies that a unitary local authority has to submit to central government. There are many prescribed statutory partnerships. There are many zones and initiatives, often not joined up. Within the first two years of the Labour Government's being in office at least ten different schemes were launched, with more than a hundred individual projects in various localities. Some authorities had four or five pilots or zones within their boundaries (LGA, 1999). New Labour encouraged a great range of initiatives and experiments in service delivery, the conduct of elections, the organization of public participation, and launched initiative after initiative aimed at particular target groups including the unemployed, single mothers and many others suffering social exclusion. The Neighbourhood Renewal Fund, Beacon status and local public service agreements are among the prizes that New Labour has offered councils and local communities in its third and fourth years in office. There is a plethora of separate incentive funding streams – especially in education – each of which has a modest motivational force and high transaction costs in both central and local government. The result 'is a Byzantine structure of plans, zones, and separate financial pots' (Filkin, 2001: 3).

Almost all of these initiatives have required the establishment of forms of partnership organization in order to bid for monies from the centre or present a local strategy to the centre. Without doubt a complex set of competing and cross-cutting networks has also been established in many localities, as Chapter 8 will explore further. The 2001 White Paper (DTLR, 2001) signalled a recognition that the range of initiatives and plans had placed too wide a range of demands on councils and suggested some modest streamlining but in turn went on to promote the idea of comprehensive performance assessment for local authorities: the ultimate lottery game as noted earlier.

If the Conservatives first gave support to a challenge culture in performance management, New Labour has certainly encouraged a continuation of that approach, as Chapter 5 will show. The separation of commissioner and producer, it is claimed, delivers not only a clearer focus on your particular task or function but a willingness to challenge others involved in a chain of relationships with you. There remains in Best Value – New Labour's flagship first-term reform aimed at local service provision – a strong commitment to separating the client from the producer function. Its fundamental rationale is that issues of the relevance, quality and cost of individual services will be brought into sharp relief by a rolling five-year process of review driven by those on the client side of local pubic authorities asking searching questions of the service and those responsible for producing it whether they are in-house or not.

The building-in of challenge can also be observed in the encouragement of peer review and arm's length inspection and regulation processes. The Improvement and Development Agency, IDeA, an institution established by the Local Government Association, under pressure from New Labour has launched an extensive programme of peer review, alongside more general training, management development and consultancy programmes. The world of inspection has seen an enormous boom in its work. Education and social services inspectorates have extended their activities, new Best Value and Housing Inspectorates have been launched, and police and emergency inspectorates have been encouraged to tighten their grip. New Labour has increased inspectorate spending by an additional 10 per cent at least from the Conservative era, which first saw an ethos of intensive inspection (Hood *et al.*, 1998). Under New Labour for the first time the whole of the local government functional and spending arena has been subject to not only audit but service-based inspection (Davis *et al.*, 2001).

As Goodin (1996: 3, 8–9) argues, there are good long-standing arguments for making what he calls disharmony a central organizing principle:

> In designing mechanisms for group decision-making, we are often well advised to designate someone to serve as 'devil's advocate', challenging

our shared presumptions and telling us things that we do not want to hear, as a way of improving the quality of the overall decision that we reach. We are often well advised to design institutions so as to encourage disharmony and hence dynamics, to force us to reconsider and perhaps change the way we are doing things from time to time.

New Labour believes in disharmony. That belief in turn reflects a sense that the world of service providers cannot be trusted to reform themselves. They have to be prodded into doing it.

New Labour has not just encouraged more challenge or disharmony, but has introduced a greater element of unpredictability in the process in part because of the sheer variety and range of those that are involved in the process. The aim is to check behaviour 'by making outcomes and operations unpredictable' (Hood *et al.*, 1998: 16). There are also new roles for the public in using performance material to challenge providers and in consultation processes around Best Value and budgets. In reforms of the political management system the public have the opportunity to initiate reform by organizing a petition that in turn could lead to a referendum on one of the mayoral options. The fundamental rationale behind much of New Labour's reforms is to make it much more difficult for local service providers and local political elites to rest on their laurels. The aim of many reforms, it appears, is to make life decidedly uncomfortable for those involved in local governance.

The making of the reform strategy

The adoption of a lottery strategy reflects New Labour's structural position, outlook and political contingencies. There are four main factors at work. New Labour's powerful position enabled it to act as the organizer of a lottery that local governance institutions felt obliged to play. New Labour's lack of trust in other actors and institutions meant that a strategy built of the principles of a lottery made sense. Divisions within New Labour helped to support a reform approach that encouraged a complex mix of reform strategies and targets. Finally, the culture of intensive media presentation of policy that surrounded New Labour supported the promotion of multiple cross-cutting initiatives.

First, such strategy would appear to be available only to those overseeing institutions that are able to exercise considerable power over the organizations that are targeted by the strategy. In the case of New Labour and the devolved governance of Britain there can be little doubt about the availability of sufficient power to undertake its reforms. Here we are in the familiar territory of the power dependence model of central–local relations; the centre may not be in a position to dictate to the institutions beyond Westminster and Whitehall but it can exercise a considerable influence (Rhodes, 1988). Control of legislation and statutory orders, government circulars, responsibility for raising all but 4 per cent of national public revenues (Travers, 2001: 135), not to mention a vast amount of media coverage and an ability to command attention, gets any organization much influence. Central government does not have the power to command change in the direction it desires but it does have a capacity to drive national programmes of reform. As with the Conservatives before them, New Labour has not been slow to use that power.

Second, the strategy is driven by New Labour's fatalistic outlook. There is a lack of trust between New Labour and the institutions of devolved governance, an argument that applies particularly strongly in the case of local government. The position is complex, as Vivien Lowndes (2000) has argued, with New Labour in some aspects showing more respect for local government through the establishment of formal summit meetings between LGA representatives and government ministers and officials, the signing of the Charter of European Local Self-Government and the provision of a new power of well-being, giving local councils greater legal freedoms than ever before in the Local Government Act 2000. But equally New Labour has not hesitated to intervene to encourage councils to carry through its national policy priorities, to name and shame devolved units and suggest that failure to improve various services will not be tolerated. From the Government's perspective it would appear that the return of trust is predicated on enhanced performance. As Lowndes (2000: 132) comments, in what might constitute an opening statement of a manifesto for the strategy of governance by lottery:

> Ministerial pronouncements clearly reflect the idea that local government must 'earn' a restoration of key powers, and that 'good' authorities will be able to earn faster than 'bad' ones.

In this light the strategy of governance by lottery provides a way of managing the lack of trust. The strategy is based in the context of the trope of fatalism and is a response to the problems posed by that trope's understanding of the inherently uncertain and problematic nature of co-operation.

The strategy might have a less random flavour to it if it were not for the influence of a third factor on New Labour's strategy, namely that of various perceived political and managerial pressures. New Labour would like many of the devolved institutions as partners in part because the drive to improve public services can only be achieved through the active co-operation of these organizations. Whether it is the elected institutions of the Celtic fringe or elected local government in England – where Labour was in 1997 in control or with a share of power in over half of all councils – it was not possible, for reasons of maintaining a support base of activists, for Labour to overlook the demands of its political colleagues. Indeed one of the guiding principles of New Labour is to avoid the perceived error of the previous Conservative administrations in allowing their activist base in local government to be undermined. As for head teachers or local authority chief executives – not to mention an array of other public sector but also non-public sector employees – New Labour is clear about the need to get their co-operation if successful change in public services is to be managed. At times, in response, New Labour has opted for a policy that in effect means prizes for all.

Divisions within New Labour also add to the sense of unpredictability, if not randomness, in its policy development. The Prime Minister favoured mayors. The Deputy Prime Minister supported regions and did not hesitate to express his dislike of the mayoral idea. Mandelson (2000) and some around No.10 expressed interest in the central role of cities and the idea of city regions as a better building block for further devolution. The Prime Minister's Social Exclusion Unit gave priority in its community renewal strategy to the neighbourhood level and argues for strategic partnerships that may involve local councils but do not give them a leadership role. Meanwhile the DETR was promoting the idea of community leadership and community strategies to be developed by local authorities. Lobby groups ranging from the Local Government Association, through the Campaign for English Regions, to the New Local Government Network provided sustenance and support for all of these positions.

The Treasury appears to have an explicit strategy of divide and rule: supporting neighbourhoods and voluntary organizations (Brown, 2001a), regional development through Regional Development Agencies (Brown, 2001b) and local councils through local public service agreements. Each is given the access to funds in return for placing themselves within the Chancellor's zone of influence. Each in turn has a sense that they are involved in a competition for approval.

An important factor that contributes to the tendency to randomness is what Peter Riddell, the political columnist of *The Times*, refers to as New Labour's commitment to 'the permanent campaign when calculations about how a policy will play with the public dominate decision-making' (Riddell,

2001: 36). The commitment to the permanent campaign in turn reflects a fatalistic reading of the fickleness of its support amongst public opinion and opinion formers. To claim that considerations of how a policy will play with the public now dominates decision-making compared to the past exaggerates the populism of New Labour and understates how governments always have a weather eye on public opinion. Yet as Riddell points out, the spindoctors or communication directors have more than before found themselves at the table where policies are discussed. More than ever the environment of policy-making demands ever stronger media management that in turn can impact on policy.

Civil servants work in a world where ministers and their advisers operate on a 24-hour news cycle, where rapid rebuttal and centrally determined 'lines to take'. Being on message is as important to careers as having a sound long-term policy. So the first question when a problem emerges is 'What is the line for the broadcasters and the press?' Reflection and deliberation are out, and a quick and catchy response is in. Media tactics come first, and a coherent strategy second (Riddell, 2001: 36).

Again some may argue that too glowing a picture of past practice is painted by Riddell but the commitment to campaigning and media management by New Labour has contributed to the rapid launch of multiple policies aimed at the institutions of devolved governance. Content as well as sheer volume may have been affected. Some policies may indeed have been launched primarily as media-oriented initiatives. Some opponents of the introduction of mayors have claimed that the policy was launched because Blair needed a big idea on local government. The reform of NHS administrative structures launched in 2001 was a product, according to some, of a need to produce a rapid Labour response to the Conservatives' plans to streamline NHS bureaucracy.

The sense of lottery that pervades New Labour's strategy towards devolved governance reflects four factors. First, the relative power of central government has given it the capacity to command the attention of devolved units with respect to the prizes on offer. Second, the centre's lack of trust in devolved government has encouraged it to adopt a strategy of conditional support backed in turn by a commitment to evidence-based learning. Third, divisions within New Labour and considerations of political alliances have added to the variety and complexity in the policy programmes of New Labour. Fourth, the commitment to media management has contributed to the tendency to launch a policy initiative first and think about the connections to other policies at a later stage.

Conclusions

Grid-group theory helps to illuminate the particular character of New Labour's reform strategy. It indicates that certain ways of social organization tend to dominate in human affairs and that these forms offer coherent collections of nostrums about what motivates people, the prospects of constructing collective action and generally the way that society works. These nostrums in turn provide guidance to actors in the construction of the actions and strategies to cope given the demands and contingencies they operate under. New Labour's reform strategy can be understood as a mix of three forms of social organization. Two are relatively familiar in the description of the intervention strategies of governments. New Labour, like the Conservatives before it, adopted a top-down, hierarchical approach to some of its reforms. However, it also placed an emphasis on a second reform rhythm that was largely neglected by the Conservatives. It looked to build support for reform through the encouragement of egalitarian networks that would facilitate mutual learning and partnership building and create the space for innovation. What is distinctive about New Labour's approach, it is suggested, is that it has also been influenced by nostrums associated within the fatalistic quadrant of grid-group theory. A sense that the world is unpredictable, that reforms cannot be assumed to work and that it is difficult to know which actors or institutions to trust pervades New Labour's thinking.

5 Improving Service Delivery under New Labour

Improving the performance of public services presents an enormous challenge to any government. For New Labour it provides a key political objective and test. As noted in Chapter 3, New Labour accepts much of the critique that first became prominent in the 1980s of the dangers of producer interests dominating in the provision of public services. Its solution to the problem posed by the potential for producer domination is complex and multi-faceted. Over time New Labour has attempted to move towards a comprehensive system of performance management. It has not sought to prescribe a particular institutional response such as the Conservatives' CCT scheme. Rather it has challenged local councils and other service providers to improve their performance through a locally managed system of review and restructuring. Yet centrally driven inspection and national performance indicators are seen as crucial to providing an information base on how service providers are responding to the challenge. A system of rewards and sanctions, again determined by national government, provides a further element in the performance management system. Training, organizational, developmental, and peer and other support activity for managing change processes complete the circle.

This chapter charts the progress of Labour's performance improvement regime for local service delivery. First, the nature of New Labour's initial strategy is reviewed. It emerges as a substantially top-down approach, but driven by an audited process not by prescription of methods. Next, the response of local councils to the Best Value regime is examined. Using grid-group theory potential positive and negative responses are identified. In a further section the extensive use of inspection by New Labour is detailed.

There follows an examination of how New Labour's strategy has responded to the limits of a simple top-down regulatory approach. The chapter examines some of the themes of the programme of comprehensive performance assessments that was launched at the start of Labour's second term. Inspection remains key to New Labour's strategy but the aim of the second phase of New Labour's performance management and service improvement plans is to avoid a one-size-fits-all approach and develop inspection, support

86

and intervention regimes to meet the particular circumstances of local councils. The final section asks whether New Labour will be able to develop an effective selective programme that targets sanctions and support on poor performers and grants lighter inspection and new freedoms to high performers. Can central government, to paraphrase the former world champion boxer Mohammed Ali, learn to 'float like a butterfly and sting like a bee'?

Best Value: a review of its style

The 1999 Local Government Act established the Best Value regime and rooted it in a commitment to an ongoing search for value-for-money (Martin, 2000). The general message of Best Value is in tune with much of the New Management rhetoric of the last two decades about reinventing public services to make them more efficient in the use of public finances and more effective in meeting user needs. It demands of local authorities a continuous improvement in the cost and quality of services in line with the needs and aspirations of local people. In that sense Best Value marks a continuation of the search for better management of public services first launched under the Conservatives (Stoker, 1999a). Yet its way of achieving change is different, less prescriptive and less reliant on the simple application of a market model and the introduction of competition mechanisms into public service delivery.

Martin (2000: 211–13; see also Geddes and Martin, 2000) outlines the main differences between Best Value and the Conservatives' regime of compulsory competitive tendering (CCT). First, Best Value applies to all local authority functions, whereas CCT applied to only a limited range of functions. Second, the key mechanism in Best Value is the requirement to undertake a rolling performance review of all services rather than market testing of some services. Third, market testing or eventual contracting out is not discouraged under Best Value but it is a matter of local choice and it is only one way in which a new relationship might be forged with private or voluntary sector partners. Indeed, if anything New Labour favours the creation of rather more long-term strategic partnerships with the private sector or other agencies (DETR, 2001). Further, whereas CCT made little allowance for consultation with users, such consultation is at the heart of Best Value. Finally Best Value is underwritten by a new inspection service and powers of intervention for central government in the case of service failure.

Best Value can be portrayed as a top-down approach. Local authorities are required to establish a performance review framework to challenge and clarify their service goals, to consult the public, to compare their performance with others and to embrace fair competition to test whether their services are securing Best Value for the public. The system is underpinned by a strong audit and inspection regime and driven by a new set of national and local performance indicators. Central government has powers to intervene if councils fail to improve service delivery. At first sight the Best Value regime falls into the 'classic' form of internal government regulation: the oversight model.

However, a closer examination of the Government's strategy shows an understanding that to put Best Value into effect demands a subtle mix of control and compliance techniques (McGarvey and Stoker, 1999: 8). Table 2.1, set out in Chapter 2, identified two ways of thinking about control in organizations, one of which emphasized hierarchical control and the other emphasized compliance delivered through peer review and control. There are echoes of both approaches in the Government's policy of Best Value. There are strong elements of classic oversight with the commitment to standard-setting, checking, inspection and sanctions. Equally there are elements of control through group processes and mutuality using shared learning and peer review and seeking to provide stronger incentives for self-policing.

Put another way, in developing the Best Value framework New Labour has made use of a wide range of mechanisms. A number of typologies exist which categorize the 'tools of government' (Hood, 1983). Government can communicate, and send messages to persuade others. It can bargain, offer financial and other incentives to change behaviour. It can provide services directly through its own staff and organizations. It can act with authority in a legal or official sense. A fifth broad tool might be added, namely the capacity of government to shape and influence cultures in order to make an impact (Perri 6, 1997). Governments also need tools for taking in information, for detecting what is going on. Best Value implementation has seen all of these tools in operation.

In respect of Best Value the Government communicated the virtue of the policy. Indeed Best Value has proved a very useful slogan; the term itself is difficult to argue against. How could anyone be opposed to Best Value? Indeed, as Martin (2000: 213–14) notes, the Government went out of its way to establish a broad consensus among local councils, trade unions and business about the virtues of the Best Value approach.

The Government has also been keen to provide incentives to encourage best practice. The Best Value scheme itself operates a star system on a scale 0 to 3. The Best Value Inspection Service 'sees itself as playing a major role in identifying and disseminating good practice' (Davis *et al.*, 2001). In addition to various other schemes run by the local government magazines the Government has given recognition to councils through its award of Beacon status for various service achievements since 1999 (DETR, 1999). There have been promises that successful local councils will be subject to lighter touch review in the future.

The Government has also lent its support to efforts to build capacity for effective change within local government. It established within the local government ministry a modernization team of practitioners able to advise and support councils. The Government has encouraged the establishment and work of the Improvement and Development Agency (IDeA) and other initiatives aimed at providing 'hands-on' help for councils in the Best Value process. In particular the Local Government Improvement Programme that offers week-long peer reviews of authorities by a team of experienced practitioners has been taken up by dozens of councils. The Government has also had strong support from both the Audit Commission (2001) and the IDeA (2001) in its campaign to change the culture of local authorities and their perception of the way local services should be delivered and how the public should be involved.

Yet, equally, a rigorous process of audit and inspection has been undertaken in order to detect failure. A systematic framework of regulation and information – gathering has been developed. The Government has taken legal powers to lay down a performance review framework and intervene in the case of failure both in relation to service delivery and also process, for example a failure to undertake any consultation with service users.

The power of intervention belongs clearly to the oversight model, as does the commitment to rigorous inspection. Yet also there are other control mechanisms at work that rely on group processes within the local government community, self-policing mechanisms and the spread of a sense of ownership for Best Value in local government.

The response of local authorities to the Best Value regime

Given that the construction of the Best Value regime makes space for, indeed encourages, local responses, it would be wise to expect local councils to respond to the demands of Best Value in a variety of ways. Drawing on the experience of those councils that were originally involved in piloting Best Value before the process went live for all councils in April 2000, Martin (2000: 215–23) develops an insightful model in which he identifies four broad approaches. He notes that each approach he describes relates to one of three generally available frameworks for achieving co-ordination for social purposes: hierarchical, market and collaborative. These various forms co-exist and interact. The first concentrates on improving and sustaining in-house services. The review looks at services as they are currently provided and seeks to assess what improvements at the margin might be possible. A second approach shows a stronger interest in outsourcing and Best Value becomes dominated by the search for new forms of contracted procurement. Deals may be cut with particular providers or there may be a strong emphasis on market-testing a range of services. A third approach is driven by the corporate centre and involves a focus on re-engineering services to tackle particular cross-cutting issues or meet the needs of particular client groups. For example, a review might be conducted into the way a whole range of service providers are meeting the needs of elderly people. Or a review process might take as its focus the needs of a particular community or neighbourhood.

This framework is helpful but it is limited in that it concentrates on positive rather than negative responses to the Best Value regime. Insights from grid-group theory can help overcome that weakness and produce a more developed understanding of the range of feasible responses to the Best Value regime. Table 5.1 presents a range of predictions about likely responses to the Best Value regime drawing on the different quadrants of the grid-group model that were outlined in Chapter 4. Table 5.1 is premised on the view that the presence of different combinations of social relations and cultural attitudes within institutions is likely to shape their response to Best Value.

Where fatalistic relations and attitudes have a grip on local government the attitude to change is likely to be that little effective can be done. This, in turn, can lead to the most negative response from the viewpoint of achieving the stated goal of Best Value, which is to drive a continuous and substantial improvement in the performance of local councils. From a fatalistic outlook Best Value is not an opportunity to think creatively about improving service delivery but an imposed external change process that is feared rather than embraced. Davis *et al.* (2001: 23) report the views of one Best Value officer:

> We don't really know what Best Value is. We're just waiting for the inspectors to fail someone then at least we will know what it isn't.

If such fatalistic attitudes predominate, at best some modest incremental improvements in services may be achieved; at worst nothing positive will be achieved. Indeed the sense of hopelessness and failure in the organization may simply be reinforced.

Table 5.1 *Responses to the Best Value regime: predictions from grid-group theory given different institutional cultures within local authorities*

	Institutional cultures in local authorities			
Issues	*Fatalistic*	*Hierarchical*	*Communit-arian*	*Individualistic*
General attitude to change	Lack of capacity makes directing change problematic, if not impossible	A willingness to comply combined with a recognition that someone must take control of the change process	Change viewed through the filter of its impact on the group, keen to protect and promote the group's values	Change seen as providing opportunity for individual advancement if the reward to risk ratio is favourable
Positive focus for innovation	The best that can be hoped for is incremental service improvement	Might encourage central political and managerial leadership to engage in substantial corporate dominated re-engineering of services	Could favour an approach that restructures service to meet the needs of a particular community or neighbour hood	Market-oriented procurement procedures, allowing scope for entrepreneurial reputation building and scope for bureau-shaping
Potential for negative approaches to change	Hapless going through the motions	Box-ticking compliance	In-house protectionism	Following the latest management fad
Predicted outcomes against stated goals of Best Value	*Worst case:* reinforcement of culture of hopelessness and failure *Best case:* survival, with minimum improvement to services although probably accompanied by further decline in morale of staff	*Worst case:* All that is achieved is muddling through. Processes are completed by no major service improvement *Best case:* potential step-change in services through strong local leadership	*Worst case:* A line-held, in-house providers survive without substantial service improvement *Best case:* opportunity is taken to achieve move towards community-focused services with staff ownership of change	*Worst case:* complacent compliance with regime, combined with tokenistic adoption of management fads *Best Case:* step change in service performance achieved through advanced procurement procedures and encouragement of a general culture of civic entrepreneurship

The presence of fatalistic modes of social organization would appear to be quite prevalent in local councils judging by early evidence from the implementation of Best Value. The Audit Commission's Best Value Inspectorate Service (Audit Commission, 2001: 7), for example, complains:

[F]ew authorities are ambitious or urgent enough in what they are seeking to achieve through best value. In many cases, BVRs (Best Value Reviews) are focused on delivering incremental change or gently confirming the need to keep the status quo.

Evidence collected by the IDeA (2001: 20) from a survey of 263 councils indicates where local government itself feels it has weaknesses in developing Best Value. Authorities asked to respond to a list of factors that might undermine the ability of councils to produce a fundamental challenge to existing services gave top billing to a lack of creativity in their organization (a factor cited by more than half of all respondents). More than a third indicated that their organization suffered from excessive inertia or caution. When asked to identify major barriers to innovation in their authority just over half cited a lack of staff time and more than a third focused attention on lack of skills and funding available to their organization.

Hierarchical patterns of relations and attitudes would appear to be also quite common in local councils. If hierarchical attitudes are dominant then the approach to change may reflect the decisions of the leadership of the organization. If that leadership is absent then the attitude may reflect a variation of the 'just tell me what to do' school of thought, a desire to know and follow the rules so that the organization is not caught out.

As Martin (2000: 219–21) records amongst the pilot authorities some local leaderships – usually a political and managerial combination – tried to take control of service delivery and push it in new directions. He cites several examples of where new joined-up forms of service delivery have been put into place focused on either client groups or cross-cutting issues. Yet there is a weakness inherent in the hierarchist mode of social organization that appears also to find reflection in the early experiences of Best Value. To quote from The Best Value Inspectorate (Audit Commission, 2001: 1) again, there is clear frustration on their part with what they describe as a 'compliance mentality' among councils. There is in many authorities too much emphasis on process and compliance rather than outcomes in terms of improved service performance:

Some authorities have concluded that best value is about process and proving to inspectors that they have been through best value processes ....

In some cases the real purpose of best value is forgotten and officers have focused almost solely on having a folder of evidence (showing that the review took place) for the inspector. (Audit Commission, 2001: 8)

As Martin (1999: 59) comments, the 'compliance culture' may itself be a product of past central government intervention against the local level. Local government politicians and officials after two decades of central prescription over funding and services were unaccustomed to having to take the initiative.

The commitment to group values and tight-knit social relations is an organizational feature that might be expected in all local organizations, including local government. Sometimes in respect of Best Value it has emerged in imaginative schemes to involve local communities in the future of service delivery in their area. Martin (2000: 222) identifies several examples of schemes where a strong emphasis on empowering local people has been given to Best Value initiatives. However, Martin (2000: 216–18) points out that rather more authorities have reacted to the demands of Best Value by seeking to defend the interests of in-house staff. Solidarity is the watchword: not solidarity with the community but rather it reflects commitment to staff. The IDeA survey provides some evidence to suggest that in-house protectionism is quite a common feature of local councils' relations and culture. In explaining why existing service provision could not be challenged, around a third identified the problem of legitimate interests such as staff jobs that could be threatened and about a quarter referred to the barriers created by vested interests (IDeA, 2001: 20).

Finally, it is the case that more individualistic orientations might be expected to exist among bureaucrats and politicians. After all rational choice theory and generally much of political science is premised on the prevalence of instrumental attitudes among human actors. The public choice critique of public service providers that, as we have seen, was first taken on board by the Conservatives and also to a degree later adopted by New Labour (see Chapters 3 and 4) rests on a view that providers will try to look after their own interests. The helpful twist to the argument in the context of public bureaucracies provided by Dunleavy (1986, 1991) is to emphasize how senior management in particular may seize opportunities to create for themselves a more desirable and pleasant working environment. They will bureau-shape rather than simply look to expand their budget.

What Table 5.2 suggests is that from the viewpoint of effective implementation of Best Value bureau-shaping may take a more positive as well as a more negative form. On the positive side it may lead to radical new approaches to procurement that may create new roles for key officials but in turn deliver step changes in the efficiency and effectiveness of service delivery. Martin (2000) and Filkin *et al.* (2001b) provide examples of some of the more radical schemes adopted by councils. Equally entrepreneurial bureau shaping can lead to the complacent and self-congratulatory adoption of the latest high-profile initiative in order to promote an image of being at the forefront of change. Long-term improvement in services is sacrificed on the altar of being up with the latest management fad (cf. Martin, 1999: 59).

One broad message of this section of the chapter is that it would be reasonable to expect a diverse range of responses to the Best Value regime. Just as the Conservatives found with their management reforms, local councils have a considerable capacity to take initiatives and develop in a variety of directions. As Lowndes (1999a: 28), reflecting on the Conservatives' reform period, comments: There is no one process of 'management change', as individual organizations and service sectors respond differently to system-wide triggers for change. Yet notwithstanding the message about diversity, the early signs are that Best Value is not delivering a transformation in ways of working in local government.

Fatalistic and hierarchical attitudes have been to the fore in local authorities creating an environment in which Best Value is seen as yet another central government initiative that local government has to survive. A survey conducted in 2001 (Enticott *et al.*, 2002) among a substantial range of local authority officers and councillors suggests that most local authorities are, indeed, learning to cope with Best Value. There is a widespread sense that the processes associated with Best Value have presented a major challenge but that they have largely been adopted, and led to small-scale incremental improvements in services in a wide range of cases. Best Value appears to have been absorbed by the established dominant organizational cultures of local government.

The rise and rise of inspection

Labour's commitment to regulation, like that of the Conservative governments before them, reflects a loss of confidence in professional self-regulation and a concern that the accountabilities of local politics were not sufficiently robust to guarantee that public services would improve their performance. External regulation provides another route to follow. One of the most common ways of keeping bureaucracy under control is through self-conscious oversight. A command-and-control style of regulation is given additional impact by the rigours of the inspection regime driven by central government appointees and backed up with the option of the removal of a service from local authority control through central government intervention. Control is exercised through an intensive process of target-setting, information-gathering about performance and the availability of sanctions.

The crucial change under New Labour has been the extension of a regulatory regime across the full range of local authority services, focused on service improvement. Auditors have checked the financial regularity of local budgets and made some efforts at encouraging efficiency. This work is supervised and overseen by the Audit Commission in England and Wales. But it was only with the arrival of the Best Value inspectorate that all local council services came into the orbit of inspectors of service quality. Long-standing inspectorates such as those for the police and fire services have been encouraged under New Labour to revise and develop the depth of their inspections. The Social Services inspectorate, that was set up in 1985, has been given an enhanced remit to undertake its work investigating the performance of social care. The Office for Standards in Education established in 1992 has continued its substantial role. A new Benefit Fraud Inspectorate has been established. But the major new kid on the block established in 1999 is the Best Value Inspection Service, which operates under the wing of the Audit Commission.

The direct costs for running these inspection systems for 2000/1 has been estimated to be £600 million (IPPR report cited in Davis *et al.*, 2001: 19). The compliance costs for local councils and other bodies in terms of staff time and effort in preparing for inspections is, in addition, considerable. So there is a debate to be had about whether the effort that goes into the inspection process from both sides of the fence is justified by the outcomes that are achieved. Does external inspection deliver the improvements in service performance that would justify the costs involved? The current state of both practice and research allows no definitive answer to that question.

For the present it can be noted that there is little call for the abandonment of inspection. Ministers clearly believe that it gives them a handle on service delivery that would not otherwise be available. A Local Government Association (LGA, 2001) of local councils in 2001 demonstrated widespread support for the principle of inspection, with service improvements seen as a likely if not inevitable outcome. The public seem keen on the idea of inspection, with nearly three-quarters approving of the Audit

Commission's role in checking local authority performance (quoted in Davis *et al.*, 2001). The value of some form of inspection is difficult to entirely gainsay. The real debate is about its style and substance. A survey in 2001 that covered 1800 local authority officers (Enticott *et al.*, 2002) reveals a great deal of scepticism about the conduct of inspection under Best Value measures. Two-thirds thought the costs of inspection were too high, with over half the respondents concluding that the costs of inspection outweighed the benefits. The main concerns were over the quality of the inspection teams sent out and the time and resources involved in responding to inspection processes.

One of the common themes of the literature on regulation is that different regulators tend to develop different ways of relating to their regulatees, with some developing a more punitive style and others developing a more supportive approach (Hood *et al.*, 1998; Day and Klein, 1990). In some respects Best Value inspection appears to have charted a course through the middle of those two options and ended up as not punitive enough to force change, except in a few cases, and yet burdensome enough in terms of regulation and oversight to make it difficult to welcome as a supportive process.

Labour's second-term agenda for service delivery

New Labour did not have much to show in respect of its drive to improve local authority services across the board at the end of its first term. Indeed the MORI Omnibus of satisfaction surveys found that public satisfaction with local government as a whole has declined slightly since the late 1990s (Martin *et al.*, 2001: 47–8). In 1997 56 per cent expressed overall satisfaction with their councils' service performance by 2000 this figure had dropped to 48 per cent. Of course a key explanation of these satisfaction ratings is that the expectations of the public have increased: a development due not least in turn to New Labour's ceaseless claims that it is going to improve public services. In terms of domestic policy issues New Labour has gone further than any other government in placing its record on improving public services as the key factor by which the electorate should judge it. The determination to manage the media has if anything led to a tendency to overclaim about performance and the prospects for improvement.

The broad theme of the second term reflects a shift from a control mentality tempered by a commitment to building local initiative and ownership of the change agenda for public services to an approach premised on a search for partnerships or initiatives that will deliver step-changes in service delivery at least in some localities or some aspects of service provision. Broadly New Labour no longer thinks it can name and shame its way to service improvements, although the occasional stern action against a failing service provider is to be expected.

The most obvious early expression of the new style for stimulating service improvement is the arrival of local (Public Service Agreement) PSAs. A group of twenty local PSAs were launched in the spring of 2001 and the Government is extending the scheme to all upper-tier or principal local authorities in the next few years. These agreements involve negotiation between individual councils and central government over areas where both would like to see substantial improvements in public services. These ambitions are then expressed in the form of stretching performance targets that if achieved will result in additional central funding being provided to the local authority. Certain flexibilities or freedoms from central government regulation can be built into these agreements. In a general way central government is buying the outcomes it desires, while local councils are to get the local ownership and freedom they need to deliver service improvement. Such an approach involves a shift from a strict oversight and top-down reform strategy to one that builds on more bottom-up processes (Balls, 2002). It is similar in many ways to the free local government experiments launched by the Nordic countries in the 1980s (see Stewart and Stoker, 1989).

There is also the prospect of a substantial initiative with respect to electronic access to services (Filkin *et al.*, 2001a). Here there is danger of letting each local authority go its own way in two senses: first, that much investment could simply duplicate services provided elsewhere and second, that the new technology provides the possibilities of a seamless service that should not be missed simply because of the historic split over functions between local councils and other service providers. A national network of locally managed call centres could provide a way forward, accessed by one number and offering one-call fulfilment for most contacts. More generally there is considerable scope for using the e-revolution to re-engineer local government functions and provide more information and more opportunity for interaction between local councils and their public.

Another focus of attention will be the building of opportunities to enable private and voluntary providers to add to the diversity of a market that is still dominated by in-house units (IPPR, 2001). The argument here is that the role of government is to procure services effectively but that in order to do so it needs a developed marketplace of potential providers in order that the forces of comparison and competition can deliver the benefits of innovation in service production and efficiency gains. Again the policy is unlikely to be developed by way of the imposition of national targets for facilitating diversity but more by incentive schemes to encourage new markets to grow.

One of the key innovations of the second term has been the development of a comprehensive performance management system. The heart of the 2001 White Paper, after the warm words about community leadership, is what is described as a 'national framework of standards and accountability' in service delivery (DTLR, 2001). Specifically it is proposed to:

- clearly define service priorities for local government that have been agreed through the Central Local Partnership (CLP);
- introduce a framework for the overall assessment of performance which addresses these priorities and includes the standards which councils will be expected to deliver;
- publish clear and concise information about councils' overall performance;
- in addition to freedoms for all councils, grant extra freedoms according to councils' ability to use them to make a real difference, including wide-ranging freedoms for high-performing councils;
- move quickly to a proportionate and co-ordinated inspection regime;
- intervene decisively where councils are failing (DTLR, 2001).

The comprehensive performance assessment of all authorities was to be based on analysis of data from a variety of sources about performance across a range of councils' services and an assessment by a team from the Audit Commission of the general corporate capacity of the authority. Councils were to be graded as performing at a level that would stretch from excellent, through good, fair and weak to poor. A package of performance support would be tailored to authorities in each of the categories. The proposals were to give more freedoms and demand less regulation for high-performing councils but to provide less freedoms and more targeted intervention for poorer performers.

The process of implementation started out with those 150 primary authorities in England responsible for most services: the London boroughs; the metropolitan districts; the county councils; and unitary councils (Audit Commission, 2002). In addition to their overall score, councils were scored from 1 to 4 in key service areas: education (based on Ofsted reports); adults' and children's social services (based on Social Services Inspectorate assessments); benefits (based on Benefit Fraud Inspectorate reports); and housing, resources, environment, leisure and libraries, based on Audit Commission and government data. A combination of these scores plus an assessment of corporate capacity at both officer and political level to lead change provided the base for the overall assessment. Results suggested that there are 22 excellent councils, 54 good, 39 fair, 22 weak and 13 poor. This means slightly more than half are in the good or excellent categories, and slightly less than half are ranked as fair or worse.

New Labour's reform agenda remains complex but at its centre is a belief that it can design a system for performance improvement with three clear elements (Office of Public Services Reform, 2002; ODPM, 2002a). The first is defined standards of service delivery that all authorities will be expected to achieve. The second is an inspection and review process in which not only performance in key services is measured but also an assessment is made of the corporate capacity of a council to manage change and undertake improvements. Finally, a system of rewards and incentives tailored to the circumstances of different authorities is proposed, with freedoms to high performers but with tough action planned against failing services and councils.

Following up Comprehensive Performance Assessment (CPA): lessons from enforceability analysis

There are grounds for thinking that in the CPA process the Government has found a system that will become fairly quickly institutionalized. The discussion below (pp. 99–106) develops arguments in McGarrey and Stoker (1999). As a method of judging performance and presenting a general assessment of local authorities the CPA process may not be perfect but it appears to meet the key tests that any system of enforcement is required to meet. It has a clear target, it has focused attention on corporate capacity as the key organizational ingredient of success and its method of judging performance appears to have been grudgingly accepted. What happens in individual authorities after the assessment is made is another matter. The collection of CPA scores is the start of a process not the end. The Government will have to deliver new freedoms and flexibilities to those authorities that are performing well according to the Government's own criteria. Even more critical though is the question of what to do with those councils that are rated poor, weak or even just fair. What kinds of intervention might be appropriate?

Some factors tend to make enforcement easier or more difficult (Hood, 1986a: ch. 3; McGarvey and Stoker, 1999: ch. 2). First, enforcement is likely to be easier if the 'population' to which the rule is directed is relatively stable and easy to identify. Here local authorities as the targets for comprehensive performance assessment would appear to be a straightforward and clear focus of attention. Moreover the focus of the corporate political and managerial responsibility of the local authority to put its house in order simplifies the task of investigation. The Government's position is that failure in a number of individual services reflects on a lack of capacity at the centre of the organization.

A second issue relates to how diffuse or varied the 'blameable' units are and whether oversight can be economically applied. There are concerns about the cost of the audit and inspection regimes applied to local government but despite the considerable number of local authorities the 'blameable' units do share many characteristics. While any explanation of failure is likely to have unique elements there is likely to be sufficient common ground for mutual learning and the development of general guidance in good practice. If the rule-of-thumb guide is that it is leadership that matters then comprehensive performance assessment has a heuristic that is manageable and sustainable.

A third factor is whether the standards that are required to be achieved can be measured relatively economically and 'objectively'. This factor is keenly felt to apply to the debate about the methodology of comprehensive performance assessment. The Audit Commission's (2002) approach involves an assessment of the existing service performance data on a local authority and the plugging of any gaps by way of a visit from a team of inspectors. Thereafter the second arm of the process involves an assessment of the proven corporate capacity of the leadership at official and political levels to drive forward improvements in services and over community leadership. The third element is a judgement about the context that the authority is operating, that would include some assessment of the scale of the challenge faced, reflecting social and economic deprivation in the area among other factors. Finally, an overall score is given to the authority on the back of a weighted and universally applied assessment framework. On the whole this methodology appears to be accepted by local government as valid, with some reservations.

A fourth general rule is whether there are sources other than those of main enforcer for cross-checking, then compliance is encouraged. Here there is evidence that comprehensive performance assessment is lacking since it has so far developed through an enclosed debate between central and local government. But the results of the assessments have been publicized and if the results of the exercise and the grading system enter the public consciousness – in the same way that school league tables based on examination results have – then there will be a strong external reinforcing of the internal assessment process.

So as a rating exercise CPA appears to have a good chance of becoming established. However, the key issue for central government is tackling poor performance (ODPM, 2002a). Excellent and good councils are to receive new freedoms and much lighter touch inspection and demands for plans. The fair and weak councils will receive packages of support co-ordinated by the Improvement and Development Agency (IdeA). Both excellent and poor authorities will have a 'relationship manager' appointed by central government to construct in the first instance an agreed package of freedoms and in the second case a recovery plan. The recovery plan for poor performing authorities will be overseen at the local level by a partnership or improvement board appointed jointly by the government and the authority. There would be a package of external support provided coming perhaps from the private sector, the voluntary sector or other practitioners in the public sector. There may also be an agreed set of changes in the management of the authority with the appointment of an interim management team. The political or governance arrangements of the council may be changed, with the option of an elected mayor possibly being put to local people.

The Government indicates (ODPM, 2002a) that its preference is for the package of changes to be agreed between its representatives and those of the council. But it indicates a willingness to use its statutory powers of intervention, in effect, to force any or all of the above measures onto a council that is designated as failing. The prospect of direct intervention against individual councils on such a scale takes central–local relations in Britain into relatively new territory. Again, enforceabilty analysis can provide some insights into the prospects for success (Hood, 1986a; McGarvey and Stoker, 1999: ch. 2).

Faced with failure to comply, the organization charged with enforcement can adopt a variety of strategies.

(1) Set aside the rule

This first response involves either setting aside the rule or modifying it in some way. It is a relatively common response often developed in the context of brinkmanship by, and bargaining with, the non-compliant agency. It may seem odd to recognize that one clear response to non-compliance is to let violators get away with it. However, it could be argued that in the context of an overall war it may be appropriate to concede a battle. There are a number of reasons why 'set aside' may be a viable option. The enforcer may consider it to be in a no-win situation and as a result back off. It may recognize that the non-compliant agency has a point and that alternative arrangements might deliver the spirit if not the letter of the rule. If the strategy was used all the time it would undermine the whole compliance process but it has a role to play. Even when it comes to enforcing the law it is widely recognized that strict enforcement is neither necessary nor always the most appropriate reaction. Jackson (1971) notes that strict enforcement of the law by the police would place excessive burdens on the service. For example, the enforcement of speed limits is usually selective and random. In the main, self-policing mechanisms such as road-design and signalling are used – direct intervention by the police force is infrequent and selective.

(2) Inform and guide

Rather than abandoning or modifying the rule a second response is to encourage compliance through publicity, education and guidance. The aim here is to enable the non-compliant to be supported and facilitated to achieve compliance through the provision of counselling, guidance and information. There may also be an element of warning in the guidance that is given. The rules may be explained, the best way to comply with them may be identified and in addition threats and warnings about the consequence of non-compliance may be outlined. As Stewart (1987: 22) argues:

> At the heart of most regulatory activity there is a choice that has to be made between enforcement and influence. The object of regulation is not to secure prosecution or to impose an enforcement notice but to achieve effective action. That can be achieved in different ways. Education and influence may be as, or more effective, than the imposition of sanctions.

These two enforcement strategies of set-aside and influence may be regarded as towards the 'softer' end of the spectrum. There are two 'harder' responses that a regulator can consider in response to non-compliance.

(3) Detect, pursue and punish

The most obvious response to non-compliance is to detect, pursue and then 'punish' non-compliers. The aim here is to take the decision out of the hands of the non-compliant agency and enforce the rule. As a response it is followed not only to take action against the non-compliant agency but also to make a wider point in the enforcement process. The approach has been labelled as a 'deterrence' strategy of enforcement. The logic is nicely captured in the following quotation:

> Chester Bowles, head of the US Office of Price Administration during World War II, once said that 20 per cent of the [US] population would automatically comply with the regulation, 5 per cent would attempt to evade it, and the remaining 75 per cent would comply so long as the 5 per cent were caught and punished. (Hood, 1986a: 56)

Whereas setting aside the rule may have negative 'knock-on' effects if others feel that an agency is getting away with it, a successful 'pursue and punish' strategy might be considered to have positive 'knock-on' effects. Bernstein (1955: 224), referring to the regulation of business, suggests that regulators face no choice but to be seen to be enforcing in a 'tough' manner at least in some cases:

> Unless it the [regulator] demonstrates a capacity to enforce its regulations, they will be honoured more in the breach than in the observance. Those who discover that violations go undetected and unpunished will have little respect for the regulator and will violate regulations with impunity if it is to their financial or commercial advantage.

(4) Remove from the frame: prevent non-compliance by restructuring

A fourth response is to avoid the problem of non-compliance by making it difficult or impossible to break the rules. In effect the potential non-compliant agency is removed from the frame by the enforcer. Its behaviour or actions cannot undermine rule enforcement because it is barred or removed from the situation.

In the context of comprehensive performance assessment it is clear that each of the four responses is available to central government. It could 'set aside' the framework if it felt that the circumstances merited such a response. In practice this option is going to be built into the process and driven by a judgement about whether councils designated as poor performers have 'some capacity to address their own problems' or whether 'their political and corporate leadership is so weak that they will require very significant external help and/or the use of statutory powers to direct them to take certain actions' (ODPM, 2002a: 11). In the first instance the option of set-aside and one more try seems likely to be taken. Probably for those councils seen as having a residual capacity for improvement it is more likely that the Government will choose a strategy of support, advice and guidance.

The Government has at its disposal a range of counselling techniques from general advice to provisions to require that the authority secure consultancy on the performance of a function or install an external management team to advise on the management of a function. Central government's third option to pursue and direct non-compliers is likely to be undertaken where the prospect of locally led improvement is judged close to zero. Councils in this position will be 'named and shamed' and forced to undertake a range of remedial measures. The final strategy of removing the non-compliers from the frame is present in the capacity to install both a new managerial and a political team to lead the authority.

The judgement about which strategy to adopt will in turn reflect a judgement about the motives of the non-compliers. Hood (1986a: 54–60) draws a broad distinction between unprincipled and principled types of non-compliance. In the first category can be found the 'incompetent' non-compliers that either do not understand or lack the capacity to apply the rules. From the perspective of the earlier discussion of local authority responses to Best Value it might be expected that it is those organizations with fatalistic orientations that such motives would be dominate. Another type of unprincipled non-compliance is seen as opportunistic: a calculated judgement made about the cost and benefits of compliance. Here it would be in those settings where individualistic values and social relations were to the fore that such motivations were likely to be found.

Principled non-compliance includes cases where there is a moral or ideological objection to the rule. More broadly the non-complier may see the rule as pointless, ill-conceived and quite inappropriate to its circumstances. This response could perhaps be seen as most likely to emerge in settings where there is a heavy emphasis on in-house group solidarity. Finally, non-compliance may reflect a broad rejection of the authority of the enforcer. There may be, in the case of central–local relations at least, within Britain few occasions where opposition is motivated in this manner; as was noted early in this chapter the overwhelming majority of councils have no difficulties with the general principle of inspection and so are unlikely to reject central oversight in general. Yet it is possible, with a growing sense of regional identity in England and perhaps a sharpening of political conflict between, for example, Labour and Conservatives, that such a principled objection might emerge.

The key point from the literature is that in judging what action is appropriate the organization charged with enforcement will have to consider what motivates the non-complier.

Table 5.2 examines the implications of various judgements about motivations for non-compliance for the strategy of the enforcer. Perhaps in the case of only the incompetent does removing the service from the council become

Table 5.2 *Non-compliance and appropriate responses for the enforcer*

Motivation of non-complier	Type of non-compliance	Appropriate responses
Incompetent	Non-compliance is explained by a failure fully to appreciate the need for compliance or a lack of ability to undertake the function or provide the service	Either guide towards competence or remove from the frame
Opportunist	Non-compliance which is deliberate and based on the fact that some advantage is gained by the non-complier	Detect and punish or remove from the frame. Name and shame if the evidence can be made to stick; giving one more chance is likely to stimulate non-compliance and guidance may also be likely to be ignored in the spirit even if followed to the letter
Principled rejection of particular rule	Non-compliance is explained by a rejection of the rule (or its implications) on moral or ideological grounds	Set-aside may reduce level of dissidence and encourage general compliance. But on the other hand, not to act may appear as political cowardice. Other strategies could be counter-productive. Naming and shaming could lead to martyrdom claims from the non-complier
Principled rejection of authority	Non-compliance is premised on a view that the authority of the enforcing agency is illegitimate or unacceptable on moral grounds	Removing from the frame would appear to be the only realistic response, all other responses would be unlikely to change behaviour. But the action would require considerable political will and confidence in the claim to legitimate authority in any dispute with the non-complier

Source: Adapted from Kagan and Scholtz (1984) and Table 3.1 in Hood (1986a: 55).

a mainstream choice and even here enforcing a recovery plan in detail would appear a more viable option. Opportunism might be met appropriately by removal of the service. Naming and shaming may work if the evidence can be found and made to stick. But such evidence is likely to be very hard to detect since a competent opportunist would have a number of defences and subterfuges in operation. Outright general or particular principled opposition, if expressed, will raise major problems for the enforcer. The Government may have to live with the possibility of creating martyrs and stirring up a wider campaign of rejection of the whole framework of comprehensive performance assessment. In both cases the Government will need to display political courage and be confident of its ability to win a battle over the legitimacy of its actions with the non-complier.

Conclusions

In the field of service delivery a government that prides itself on being evidence-based and looking at 'what works', has shown itself capable of adjusting and developing its policy approach. The Best Value policy was established in a relative rush after the Government's first-term election and has been judged to have been insufficient to achieve the change in service delivery desired by New Labour on two main grounds. First, its over-reliance on external inspection of the mechanics of multiple unfocused local reviews of services has consumed much management time and effort but not delivered the challenge to poor performance and the drive to creativity that the original designers of Best Value had hoped. Second, the Best Value scheme has not allowed a sufficiently differentiated response to the different circumstances of local councils, some of which are better performers in service delivery than others.

As a result of some rethinking the second term of the New Labour Government has seen a launch of a new scheme of comprehensive performance assessment. There are a number of dilemmas created by its approach and in particular around the intervention powers available to the Government as part of the comprehensive performance assessment framework. The dilemmas in practice will be even more acute because of the level of uncertainty about the judgement of the performance of an authority and the prospects for self-improvement. The task is a delicate one and it remains to be seen whether the Government can indeed 'float like a butterfly' – giving new powers or appropriate support to most councils – but 'sting like a bee' when it comes to poor performers that are reluctant or unable to change.

The Government's approach to the management of service improvement apes to an extent that of a head office of a big retailer in dealing with its branches. But there is a continuing recognition that local councils are more than local branches of a chain store. They are political institutions with their competences and capacities. New Labour's reforms aimed at local politics are the focus of the next two chapters.

6 Democratic Renewal: Getting People to Participate

The Labour Government stands in contrast to its Conservative predecessors very clearly in terms of its commitment to the renewal of politics at the local level. The overall aim has been to restore some political vitality to institutions that were judged to have lost touch with the public. The effort especially in the first term (1997–2001) devoted to the issue of democratic renewal was considerable. There have been three Acts of Parliament passed that have directly addressed issues of democratic renewal. One in 1999 promoted consultation in respect of Best Value processes in service delivery, another in 2000 encouraged experiments in voting for local elections and a third in 2000 established the base for the reforms in political management discussed in more detail in the next chapter. There has been also a considerable amount of associated guidance and advice from New Labour sources including a substantial part of a White Paper (DETR, 1998) and a pamphlet by the Prime Minister (Blair, 1998b), a number of good practice guidance documents (Lowndes *et al.*, 1998a; Copus *et al.*, 2000; Stoker *et al.*, 2002) and numerous speeches by government ministers. In the mixed range of partnership activities (examined in more detail in Chapter 8) that have been a feature of New Labour's programme there has also been considerable emphasis on consultation and participation. The scale and range of activities provide some evidence that the commitment to democratic renewal has been more than mere window-dressing.

The local government minister in Labour's first term, Hilary Armstrong, has argued that the democratic renewal strategy can be seen to encompass all of the Government's local government policy agenda (Armstrong, 2000). The broad philosophy behind New Labour's strategy stressed the need to seek active citizen endorsement rather than acquiescence. Prime Minister Blair (1998b:14) argued that:

> It may be asking too much to expect local government to get people shouting from the rooftops. But it is not too much to expect most people to care enough to vote or to know who to praise or blame for what is going in their locality.

There was a danger that local authorities would not be able to act as effective community leaders if they lacked a base of popular support. The challenge defined by New Labour was to find ways of engaging people on their own terms. Voting could be made easier and more meaningful. Consent beyond the ballot box can be obtained through various methods of public consultation and deliberation. New information and communication technologies offer a range of further opportunities to get people's participation in a way that is flexible, attractive to them and not too time-consuming.

The argument for finding new ways to engage with people is not just that government needs to listen and learn to design better policies and services, although that is important. Effective channels of communication are essential to achieving many social and economic outcomes. For example, to launch a waste recycling scheme or change driving habits requires an intensive dialogue and high levels of trust between the public and authorities. More generally there is a need to rebuild public confidence in political institutions and the most powerful way to do that is to seek active citizen endorsement of the policies and practices of public bodies.

Enhanced public participation lies at the heart of the Labour Government's modernization agenda for British local government. As the White Paper, *Modern Local Government: In Touch with the People*, states, 'the Government wishes to see consultation and participation embedded into the culture of all councils ... and undertaken across a wide range of each council's responsibilities' (DETR, 1998: para. 4.6). Yet the belief that local government should involve the public or 'get closer to the community' is hardly new. The history of British local government is littered with experiments in public participation and consultation over the last three decades (see, for instance, Gyford, 1991; Burns *et al.,* 1994; Stoker, 1997a; S. Young, 2000). What is notable about the commitment of New Labour is the national-level support for initiatives to drive forward participation levels.

This chapter looks at the impact of New Labour's policies. First, the experience of encouraging turnout in local elections is examined. Second, the debate about whether New Labour's reforms – premised largely on making voting more convenient – will resolve the problems of low turnout is examined. Third, the progress in developing more extensive systems of consultation within local authorities is reviewed. A story of increased use of a variety of consultation techniques is revealed. Fourth, a discussion is launched about whether participation and consultation schemes launched by local government can provide a basis for individuals or groups to re-engage with local politics. Contrary to the views of some, it is argued that it is possible to 'engineer' democracy. A strategy of public engagement led by public authorities is not without limitations or difficulties but there is evidence that it can stimulate more trust and a greater sense of involvement on the part of individuals or local groups.

Electoral reforms

The *Modern Local Government. In Touch with the People* White Paper (DETR, 1998: ch. 4) outlined a number of mechanisms to re-engage people with local elections. Two of the ideas that were floated in the White Paper were not followed through. There was a proposal to have more frequent elections and a note that while not on the immediate agenda the move to a different, proportional voting system for local government would be kept under review.

The talk of reconstructing the local electoral system in every authority (putting a third of seats up for grabs each year) so that there would be annual elections – a manifesto commitment of the Blair Government elected in 1997 – was dropped because on reflection it was argued it was likely to encourage a fatigue among voters. The 1998 and 1999 local elections saw turnout slump to an all-time low, hovering in both cases around 30 per cent. Ministers decided that annual elections were unlikely to improve the prospects for turnout and might if anything depress turnout still further.

Despite some considerable discussion about introducing proportional representation (PR) methods into local elections both in Scotland (McIntosh, 1999) and the rest of Britain (Dunleavy and Margetts, 1999; Rallings *et al.*, 2000) there was, in Labour's first term, only a flirtation with the idea and the practical introduction of a PR scheme in the elections for the Greater London Authority (GLA). There remains a strong possibility that PR might be introduced for local elections in Scotland in time for the next electoral round in 2007 but it would seem less likely that PR will form part of the agenda of reform for England and Wales in the next few years. The December 2001 White Paper (DTLR, 2001) makes no mention of PR but does promote the idea of further experiments in electronic voting and wider use of postal voting. Still, interest in introducing some form of PR into local government in England has not gone away in some quarters of New Labour.

There appears to be no 'in principle' objection to PR by New Labour given that they have introduced PR systems for Scotland's Parliament, the Assembly of Wales and the elections to the Greater London Authority. Moreover, the new regional assemblies are to be elected using a PR system (ODPM, 2002b). Thus far the judgement about whether to introduce PR appears to be a pragmatic one, coloured by personality, party political implications and the wider political context. It is widely held that the Deputy Prime Minister, John Prescott, is against PR as is the Chancellor of the Exchequer, Gordon Brown. The Prime Minister seems slightly keener and some of his advisers are supporters of PR but the costs to the party in terms of seats and the opposition of many activists within the party make any move to PR problematic.

The focus of attention during Labour's first two terms has been on experiments in increasing turnout by making it more convenient and easier for people to vote, facilitated by the Representation of the People's Act 2000. Around thirty-two councils committed to experiments during the 2000 May local elections, with some extending the times on which people could vote, others shifting the day of voting and some extending opportunities for postal voting. It would appear that the most successful schemes in terms of increasing turnout were those that allowed for full postal ballots in certain wards. In Bolton all postal ballots increased turnout by between 11 and 14 per cent compared to the 1999 elections. Doncaster saw a 20 per cent increase in a ward where an all-postal ballot was held. In Gateshead all postal ballots in two wards more than doubled turnout compared to the previous year's election: in one case turnout moved from 30 to 62 per cent (source www.homeoffice.gov.uk).

A further extension of the use of postal voting was undertaken in local elections in 2002, again there was a positive and substantial effect on turnout. A number of different initiatives were tried and by far the most successful in terms of increasing turnout was the introduction of all-postal ballots. In several areas where postal voting was piloted turnout was double compared to that previously achieved in local government elections. The Electoral Commission (2002a: 2) found that 'the average turnout for all-postal ballots was well above that for conventional ballots in the country'. There were differences between the pilots – those with a tradition of postal voting doing better than others. There also appeared to be an impact depending on the demands for a personal declaration on the postal ballot, with a requirement for a more austere and formal declaration putting people off. Opportunities to vote via mobile phones or over the internet appeared to have no great impact on turnout but, as the Commission argue, did increase choice for people. The security concerns that were raised about all these forms of remote voting were investigated by the Commission and judged to be manageable, although not entirely resolved. The Commission concludes:

Over time, remote voting may well become the norm for most electors, as it appears to be more convenient for many voters. In the medium term, remote voting may be achieved through postal voting; over the longer term, as internet access and digital TV ownership grows, through technology-based voting systems. (Electoral Commission, 2002a: 3)

A commitment to continued experimentation with postal and electronic forms of voting would appear to be part of New Labour's plans for democratic renewal, as the further round of experiments in the 2003 elections suggested.

What lies behind low turnout?

New Labour's measures to inject life into the local electoral process could perhaps be criticised for only scratching the surface of the problem. Making it easier to vote does not mean that you have addressed the problem of lack of motivation. There appears to be a wider malaise in the system given a turnout in the 2001 national General Election of just below 60 per cent, a historically low figure. Yet turnout in local elections has been a feature of the British system for at least fifty years and the gap between local and national turnout in Britain is the largest of any of the western democracies. It would appear that there may be problems with local elections that go beyond general difficulties with the political system. As Table 6.1 shows, turnout is especially low among younger people and black and minority ethnic groups. The issue of the voting behaviour of these two groups is

Table 6.1   *Turnout in 2002 local elections*

Actual turnout in 2002 local elections	32.8%
Estimated turnout among different age and social groups:	
18–24	11%
25–34	27%
35–54	33%
55+	47%
Black and minority ethnic groups	24%
Non-black and ethnic minority groups	34%

Source: Electoral Commission (2002b).

discussed in two reports commissioned by the Electoral Commission (Russell *et al.,* 2002; Purdam *et al.,* 2002).

As Rallings *et al.* (1996) point out, investigating turnout in local government elections can be done in a number of different ways. One broad approach uses attitude surveys to ask voters or non-voters why they do what they do. Another option is to examine aggregate data on turnout in local government elections over a number of years to see if any explanation for differences in turnout can be found. Each approach tends to lend itself to a certain direction in explanation.

Opinion survey-driven research leans to the argument that people may find local politics irrelevant or show how they are not important enough for a significant number of the electorate to engage with (Miller, 1980). Survey work conducted by NOP for the Electoral Commission in 2002 appears to confirm that broad line of reasoning (Electoral Commission, 2002b). Only 48 per cent of people feel that a local election makes a real difference in their community compared to 64 per cent who think a general election makes a difference. Seven out of ten respondents to the survey felt that they did not know enough about the candidates to make a choice. When prompted to explain why they did not vote nearly half the sample gave lack of time as a reason. But the key point emphasized by the Electoral Commission (2002b: 2) is that 'local elections are seen as being less important and less interesting than general elections and less likely to affect change'.

The work on aggregate data about local election turnout brings out other factors in explaining low turnout. Rallings and Thrasher (2000) conclude that it is the level of political competition that makes a difference to turnout. The more marginal a ward is (that is the smaller the majority held by the winning party) and the more contesting political parties there are in any one ward, then the higher the turnout. Political parties may be affecting voting behaviour by how effectively or otherwise they are contesting seats. It might also appear from this finding that a shift of PR system might increase turnout if it made parties compete for more votes and the electorate believe that their vote would make a difference. Rallings and Thrasher (2000) also found that smaller wards appeared to increase turnout and that multi-member wards tended to decrease turnout. This finding might indicate that concerns about knowing the candidates and what they are campaigning for, an issue also raised in survey evidence, makes a difference.

At the very least it can be concluded that making voting more convenient is likely to solve only part of the problem of turnout. Lack of time to vote is a factor for many but there are deeper factors at work. Turnout among young and black and ethnic minority voters is especially low and new, more convenient ways of voting are unlikely to be the complete answer to their disconnection from local politics. This is not to argue against the development of easier and more 'modern' ways for people to vote, using either postal ballots or electronic techniques. New Labour's reforms have taken some valuable steps forward by challenging a very traditional and unchanging voting practice. Yet Labour's strategy for increasing turnout appears not to tackle the entire problem. Making local elections more relevant and competitive are issues that remain to be addressed to a large extent.

More participation and innovative forms of consultation

The drive to encourage participation beyond the ballot box has also been a feature of Labour's policies towards local government. Guidance documents and a great deal of exhortation have been used to build on the growing practice of innovation by local authorities in this area. In addition steps have been taken to encourage participation as a key feature of other policy initiatives stretching from the service review processes of Best Value through to the commitment to neighbourhood renewal. In seeking to assess the progress that has been made the House of Commons Public Administration Select Committee (2001a: paras 75–8) comments:

> Our broadest conclusion from the very wide range of evidence sessions that we have held is that the period since the middle 1990s has seen an explosion of interest in involving the public more frequently, more extensively and in much more diverse ways in the conduct of decision-making within the public services ... Much of the progress in public participation methods has come and will continue to come at the local level.

There is a need, as the Committee recognizes, to ensure that best practice in this area is disseminated and extended. The Committee recommends a continuing period of experimentation at the local level extending to greater use of referendums, more electronic-based consultation and tests of different electoral systems.

Research confirms the view of the House of Commons Select Committee that over the last few years the number and range of participation initiatives in local government has expanded greatly, offering citizens wide opportunities to take part in local affairs. Two census surveys of local authorities, one in 1998 (Lowndes *et al.*, 1998b; also reported in Lowndes *et al.*, 2001a) and another in 2002 that followed the same line of questions (Birch, 2002) provide a comprehensive picture of what local authorities have been doing to engage their populations.

For the purposes of analysis (see Lowndes *et al.,* 2001a) the different forms of consultation techniques used by local authorities can be divided into five categories:

1. *Consumerist methods*: forms of participation, which are primarily customer-oriented in their purpose and are mainly concerned with aspects of service delivery. Key examples here would include complaints/suggestions schemes and service satisfaction surveys.
2. *Traditional methods*: methods, which have a long history of use in local government and are traditionally associated with public participation. Key examples here would include public meetings, inviting co-optees onto local authority committees, and consultation documents sent out for comment.
3. *Forums*: activities which bring together users of particular services, residents of an area, individuals concerned with specific issues (for example, community safety) or those with a shared background or interest (for example, minority ethnic groups), on a regular basis. Key examples here include the use of area or neighbourhood committees or forums that bring together young people or ethnic minorities.
4. *Consultative innovations*: new methods which seek mainly to consult citizens on particular issues rather than to engage them in sustained dialogue. The key examples here are interactive websites, focus groups, citizens' panels and referendums.
5. *Deliberative innovations*: new methods that encourage citizens to reflect upon issues affecting them and their communities through some form of deliberative process. Examples of this form of consultation include citizens' juries, visioning exercises, community planning schemes and issue forums.

Table 6.2 provides further details of the range of consultative and deliberative innovations that have been undertaken by local authorities that are, perhaps, less familiar to the reader. The categorization used in the research is inevitably crude and a case can easily be made for including some forms within a different category. For the purposes of analysis, however, it displays some important distinctions between different forms of participation.

Table 6.3 presents evidence on the consultation techniques used by local authorities in 1997 and 2001, based respectively on the 1998 and 2002

Table 6.2 *Consultative and deliberative innovations: participation techniques*

Technique	Description
Interactive website	The key here is a website that provides more than information but offers an opportunity for citizens to join in debates or send in messages about local issues or services
Citizens' panel	These are ongoing panels made up of a statistically representative sample of a local area. The panel is asked through regular survey-based consultation for its views about issues, services and local authority proposals
Referendums	These allow citizens to vote on a particular issue or decision such as which council tax option they prefer
Focus groups	Focus groups usually last between one and two hours and involve collecting together by invitation a relatively small group of people to express their views on an issue in a facilitated discussion. An effort might be made to gather together groups of relatively hard-to-reach social categories such as the vulnerable elderly
Citizens' juries	A group of citizens, usually chosen to represent as fairly as possible the local area, who are brought together to consider a particular issue. They have their discussions facilitated and receive evidence from expert witnesses before coming to a judgement. The process may last over several days and the citizens ultimately agree a report with recommendations on the issue
Visioning exercises	The purpose of this technique is to produce a vision among a group of residents about the kind of future they would like to create. A variety of techniques are usually combined in order to uncover people's preferences
Community planning exercises	Here citizens are tasked with giving priority to potential service developments in response to local authority suggestions
User management	A form of participation where the running of a service and direct control over resources is given to citizens. Examples include community-based housing organizations and community managed local centres

Source: Adapted from Lowndes *et al.* (1998b: 102–3).

Table 6.3   *Forms of consultation used by local authorities in 1997 and 2001*

Consultation technique	% of local authorities using in 1997	% of local authorities using in 2001
Traditional methods		
Public meetings	85	78
Question-and-answer sessions	47	51
Consultation documents	85	84
Co-option to committees	61	48
Consumerist methods		
Complaints/suggestions schemes	92	86
Service satisfaction surveys	88	92
Other opinion polls	46	56
Forums		
Service user	65	73
Area/neighbourhood	61	64
Issue	50	44
Shared interest	40	38
Consultative innovations		
Interactive websites	24	52
Citizens' panels	18	71
Referendums	4	10
Deliberative innovations		
Focus groups	47	81
Community planning	45	58
Visioning exercises	26	38
User management	23	18
Citizens' juries	5	6

Source: Drawn from data provided in Lowndes *et al.* (1998a: 16) and Birch (2002:12).

census surveys. Traditional and consumerist methods have a strong showing in both periods. Consulting the public through public meetings and consultation documents is close to universal local authority practice. Consumerist techniques such as service satisfaction surveys and complaints/suggestion schemes have also become commonplace. Indeed, when asked if their authority had ever used these techniques as opposed to whether they had used them in 2001, 98 per cent confirmed they had used service satisfaction surveys, 94 per cent had used complaints schemes, 93 per cent stated they had used public meetings and consultation documents (Birch, 2002: 17). The widespread use of these techniques reflects their relative low cost in organization and resources and the straightforward way in which they are understood and valued by both local authorities and many members of the public. According to further data collected and analysed in Birch (2002: 14–15) traditional techniques saw relatively steady growth in their use by local authorities from before 1990, with question-and-answer sessions rising from a very low base in the early years to become the practice of half of all councils by 1997. Consumerist techniques appear to have taken off in use from the early to mid-1990s onwards and have achieved saturation coverage in local government.

Various forums in which issues can be thrashed out and debated also appear to have been very widely used in 1997 and 2001. There is no strong pattern of growth or decline between the two periods. Where there is much more spectacular evidence of growth is in the use of some innovative and deliberative consultative techniques. In particular, as Table 6.3 shows, interactive websites, focus groups and citizens' panels, community planning and visioning exercises have seen sharp increases in use between 1997 and 2001. It is these forms of consultation that have seen the most substantial increases since New Labour came to power. Before 1997 the number of local authorities introducing these techniques was a mere handful but since the numbers have risen substantially (Birch, 2002: 16). In total by 2002 75 per cent of local authorities had used a citizen panel to consult the public, 91 per cent had used a focus group to consult, 55 per cent had undertaken a vision exercise and 73 per cent had gone through a community planning analysis (Birch, 2002: 17).

Two techniques despite the relatively high level of attention that they have attracted remain relatively unusual in the armoury of techniques used by local authorities. As Table 6.3 shows, referendums were used by more authorities in 2001 than in 1997 and so, marginally, were citizen juries. In total, looking back between 1997 and 2002, 21 per cent of local councils claim to have used referendums and 16 per cent have used a citizens' jury. The growth in referendums probably reflects to some degree the requirement to hold referendums over a move to a mayoral model of political management (see Chapter 7). Referendums have also been used to advise local authorities on the setting of their budgets in Milton Keynes, Bristol and

Croydon (see Stoker *et al.*, 2002, for an analysis of these experiments). There is a debate about what kinds of issues referendums are most suited for and the part they have to play. These are expensive to run and it would seem sensible that there had to be a significant issue at stake before they were chosen as the best consultative technique. Citizens' juries have probably not delivered on the promise held out for them by early advocates. There are doubts about how representative are the views that are unearthed by a jury, how open and free from manipulation the process is and whether the cost is justified (for a review of the evidence see Smith and Wales, 2000).

The growth in participation opportunities is more than simply a response to new Labour's democratic renewal agenda or, indeed, a party political programme. Rather, it demonstrates a sense of ownership within individual authorities of the democratic possibilities which such initiatives hold, and a willingness to develop them. There is, of course, evidence of considerable variation between localities. It would appear that Labour and Liberal Democratic authorities are marginally more likely to adopt a wide variety of consultative techniques but the differences are not great. What remains the case is that the smaller non-metropolitan district councils tend to trail behind other types of council in their capacity to use a range of techniques, although again the differences are not large (Lowndes *et al.*, 1998a: 33–7; Birch, 2002: 28–38).

The experience of local authorities has revealed difficulties as well as advantages in enhancing public participation (Lowndes *et al.*, 2001a). Top of most lists for local authorities is the crucial dichotomy between justifying expenditure on democratic activities when specific services are still in need of resources. Birch (2002: 41–2) also notes concerns about the resources spent on consultation and the time constraints that may dampen the enthusiasm of local authorities for participation.

Among many authorities there is a perception that there is little public enthusiasm for enhanced participation, particularly among those groups who are traditionally excluded from political participation. Birch (2002: 42–3) found a concern about consultation overload was held by two-thirds of local authorities. The key advantages of public participation as perceived by local authorities are: better decision-making, more fine-tuned services and improved citizenship.

From the perspective of the public a crucial issue is often whether the consultation had any impact on the decision. Birch (2002: 45–6) found that a quarter of all authorities claimed that public participation initiatives were often influential, slightly less than half argued they were fairly influential in final decision-making and about a quarter commented that they were occasionally influential. This mixed pattern of response does not suggest that consultation exercises, from the point of local authorities, are always key factors in making a decision but it does not indicate equally that all consultations simply disappear into some kind of decision 'black hole' and never have any impact.

However, even in the context of this modest conclusion the claim that the observed growth in participation initiatives represents democratic enhancement needs to be treated with some caution (cf. Lowndes, 2001a: 215). While many of the initiatives do provide new opportunities for individuals or groups to articulate their preferences, it is clear that, on their own, they often do not live up to the fundamental democratic tests of popular control and political equality (Beetham, 1999). Individual initiatives are often deliberately designed to discriminate in favour of particular groups or areas, especially where authorities are trying to reach socially excluded groups. If consultation methods are going to overcome these concerns there would appear to be a strong argument for a mix of methods that give access to a variety of groups. Indeed that is often a key recommendation of guidance documents on the issue (Lowndes *et al.*, 1998b).

Research suggests (cf. Lowndes *et al.*, 2001b) people do not participate for a number of reasons. If they feel alienated from and lack trust in the local authority they are likely to feel disinclined to participate. Lack of awareness of participation opportunities also appears to be a crucial factor. People do fear, it would appear not without foundation, that their views may be ignored. Equally some social groups assume that participation is not for the likes of them. Different groups appear to hold that the system is designed to exclude them. These arguments throw some light on common deterrents to participation in local government. On the other hand, it is important to challenge the idea that the public is universally apathetic. Survey and focus group findings indicate that people are more than willing to participate if the issue is important to them and if they were asked. The scale of potential involvement in any one year is substantial. Birch (2002: 23) calculates on the back of local authorities' estimates that in 2001 approximately 14 million people (about a quarter of England's population) were engaged in participation and consultation initiatives.

Moreover, local people have a clear idea about what they would like to see to ensure effective participation (Lowndes *et al.*, 2001b: 454). Succinctly stated in their own words, citizens' core criteria were: (a) 'Has anything happened?'; (b) 'Has it been worth the money?'; and (c) 'Have they carried on talking to the public? Consultation works then when it is sensitive to the environment in which it operates and is seen to have delivered some shift in the frame of decision-making. The key ingredients of successful consultation are:

- Address the stated priorities of local residents and involve all relevant agencies;
- Mobilize and work through local leaders (informal as well as formal);
- Invite or actively recruit participants, rather than wait for citizens to come forward;
- Employ a repertoire of methods to reach different citizen groups and address different issues;
- Recognize citizen learning as a valid outcome of participation;
- Show results – by linking participation initiatives to decision-making, and keeping citizens informed of outcomes (and the reasons behind final decisions).

The experience of New Labour is that consultation practice within local government has been expanded. Whether it has made a difference is the question that will be addressed more fully in the next section.

Can democracy be engineered? What difference does officially sponsored consultation make?

The use of participation schemes to 'engineer' improvements in democracy is regarded with scepticism by many. Cochrane (1996: 212) warns that democracy depends not on more flexible and extended forms of involvement alone but on the maintenance of active, locally based groups. 'Local democracy is not something that can be guaranteed, and it will only be achieved through the campaigning of local activists on a range of issues in the framework of a positive commitment from local government.' In short, there needs to be an active base from which participation can develop but which also stands outside official politics and challenges it. There are two types of argument that would appear to question the engineering approach to participation. Both rest on a bottom-up, community perspective. The first argues that a vibrant civil society and a civic culture provide the crucial underpinnings for democracy. The second warns that initiatives by political or bureaucratic government officials to engage the community in participation run the risk of disarming democracy rather than making it more vibrant.

The general argument that the key to effective democracy is a dynamic civil society is associated with much of social capital literature and in particular there is a view in that literature that a vibrant set of civic organizations provides the underlying foundations for an effective local politics (see Maloney *et al.,* 2000). In his study of Italy, Putnam (1993) argues that the relatively higher performance of local and regional government in Northern Italy can be directly correlated to the nature, vitality and density of associational life in the localities. These associations helped to create the social conditions to develop and maintain democracy by generating social capital, which can be defined as: 'features of social life – networks, norms, and trust – that enable participants to act together more effectively to pursue shared objectives. ... Social capital, in short, refers to social connections and the attendant norms and trust' (Putnam, 1995: 664–5). In the North of Italy there is a virtuous circle of social capital: 'Stocks of social capital, such as trust, norms, and networks, tend to be self-reinforcing and cumulative'; in the South there is a self-reinforcing destructive circle: 'Defection, distrust, shirking, exploitation, isolation, disorder, and stagnation intensify one another in a suffocating miasma of vicious circles' (Putnam, 1993: 177). Moreover Putnam argues that these two different sets of circumstances have historical and cultural roots and there is little that public authorities can do to reverse the situation in which they find themselves. The mechanisms whereby vibrant civic life and its associated social capital underpins better democracy are not fully exposed by Putnam but the assumption appears to be that a more active civil society keeps government on its guard and is better at offering solutions to those in government so that social and economic issues can be tackled (see Putnam, 2000).

On a rather different but still bottom-up tack there is a radical perspective that concludes that official attempts to seek participation rest on a flawed and limited conception of democracy. Blaug (2002: 102) suggests that participation schemes presuppose a representative core to democracy that participation is there to support. Participation is there to help elected politicians and bureaucratic officials – the key layers in incumbent democracy – do their job better. He advocates a more critical conception of democracy that would emphasize to a much greater degree the self-organizing capacity of individuals. Effective democracy from this viewpoint rests on people constructing their own decision-making systems and rules through face-to-face discussion. In this light the danger of attempts to institutionalize participation by incumbent democracy is that it will sap the energy of the grass roots. Applying for state funding, or working on agendas set by state officials leads community and grass-root organizations down the path to mainstream legal and bureaucratic ways of working that in turn take away the particular value of their contribution.

Democratic engineers, in viewing democracy in terms of institutions, encourage institutional solutions to problems, offer resources with colonizing strings attached and are, in the last instance, unable to relinquish the power they control. This kind of help closes down discussion, domesticates participation and gives rise to discussions and meetings which are, fundamentally, unengaging. It is little wonder, therefore, that no matter how democratic reforms seek to reduce the costs and widen the opportunities for participation, a recurrent problem for democratic engineering is the failure of the people to actually show up. (Blaug, 2002: 112–13)

Democratic engineering will fail because it rests on a flawed and limited conception of democracy and because its mechanisms offer bureaucratic and tame versions of democracy that people find uninviting and unattractive.

These bottom-up perspectives provide a useful corrective to any naïve assumption that official sponsorship of participation can work in all circumstances and captures the universe of politics. It can be conceded that the quality of the civic life will affect the way that official participation schemes are received and taken up. Equally for some of those engaged in direct action or DIY democracy official participation is irrelevant and to that extent a distraction. However, there is evidence to suggest that official attempts to sponsor participation provide in part the context of civic support needed for a healthy democracy and can indeed attract the interest and support of groups and individuals. More generally it is limiting to see government and civil society as separate from one another, as these bottom-up perspectives do. From a governance perspective it is the interpenetration of government and civil society that provides key insights into the operation of the polity.

Brady *et al.* (1995) have suggested that three factors explain the propensity of people to engage in public participation. A key factor is the impact of the socio-economic status (SES) of residents of an area. Resources essential to participation – such as time, money and civic skills – are distributed differentially among groups defined by socio-economic status and offer a convincing model of the causal relationship between SES and civic participation. This 'can do' model of participation explains a lot: having the necessary resources to engage makes a big difference. But, as Brady *et al.* (1995: 271) note, there are other factors to take into account when explaining participation. The first is people's engagement with politics. People have to feel part of something to have the motivation to take part in politics. Decisions about their community or group have to mean something. They have to feel involved, informed and to trust others in their community to a degree. The sense of engagement, it can be speculated, is connected to the social capital in an area. A further factor driving involvement in politics is whether people have been asked. People have to be mobilized into politics. The invitation to take part in politics reflects institutional arrangements within the local state (political and managerial) and within civil society (Lowndes *et al.*, 2002).

Local authorities through their strategies of engagement play a crucial role in moulding and maintaining a civic infrastructure of groups and organizations (Maloney *et al.*, 2000). The governance of an area is affected by social capital, but is itself an influence on social capital. Political institutions have a significant role, at least in helping to sustain civic vibrancy and probably also in stimulating its growth. Public authorities are deeply implicated in the shape and activities of voluntary associations through the institutions created to encourage engagement and participation or capacity-building programmes. Research (Stoker *et al.*, 2003) into local authority–community group relations in Birmingham, Glasgow, Stockport and Southampton suggests that a civic infrastructure can be actively generated and promoted by local public authorities through the use of mechanisms such as consultation forums, out-reach work, capacity-building and funding regimes. Positive and information-rich relationships can be established between local councils and a range of community organizations in their area.

Participation by individuals as well as groups appears capable of stimulation by official intervention. Research into levels of local participation show the impact that a long-term commitment to a more inclusive politics can have. Areas of similar socio-economic status show real differences in the levels of public participation they achieve and the difference is driven by how open the political system of the local authority is and how modernized is its management structure (Lowndes *et al.*, 2002). Whether the political party in control had a modernization impulse, and wanted to open out their council, was a factor in encouraging political participation. The absence of that factor appeared to hold back participation. Equally whether the council had moved from a traditional system of management to a more open consumer or community-oriented approach appeared to explain why some local authorities found a better response in their community to participation than others.

Active but sensitive intervention from local government can make a difference. It can provide a framework in which individual and group participation can be enhanced. People need to feel engaged and they need to be invited to participate and local authority interventions can help to support those conditions and thereby encourage political participation. That is not to say that the impact of socio-economic resources can be wholly overcome.

Participation rates in general do appear to be higher among higher status social-economic groups and within an individual authority higher-status residents may more easily mobilized. But social-economic status in not the only factor; the approach of the council makes a big difference. Half of all councils are worried that participation captures the views of dominant but unrepresentative groups according to a 2002 survey (Birch, 2002: 42–3). The argument of this chapter is that the solution to the perceived problem rests in part in their behaviour. Within limits, official attempts to stimulate participation can make a difference.

Conclusions

Democratic renewal was a key agenda item for New Labour. In terms of stimulating increased turnout in local elections despite the success of various pilots, especially those involving all-postal ballots, it would be difficult to conclude other than that local elections still remain second-order affairs. New Labour has addressed some of the elements of the electoral malaise but not all of them. As for official attempts to stimulate participation there is much evidence to suggest that local authorities have expanded on their previous commitment in this area to adopt a wider and innovative range of consultation techniques. There is also some evidence to suggest that these officially sponsored initiatives can, if sustained over a number of years, help to create a civic infrastructure supportive of community organizations and stimulate individual-level political participation. Official sponsored participation is not a panacea but it should not be dismissed either as doomed to failure because it cannot engage or as an attempt to buy off an activist politics. Indeed such participation schemes are effective precisely over the more humdrum, small-scale but important issues that make up the stuff of much local politics and their presence is unlikely to undermine the emergence of any radical direct action, protest politics or alternative political arrangements.

It is fair to conclude that whether it is possible to engineer democracy or not is a question where the answer depends in part on your conception of democracy. Yet for those who think that democracy relies on a complex mix of representative and participative forces then it would appear that officially sponsored participation has a positive part to play in engineering democracy.

7 Promoting Local Political Leadership

The Labour government in its first term introduced a major change in the way that local authorities constructed their decision-making, moving from a system without a formal political executive to a system that installed a form of 'separation of powers' between an executive composed of elected representatives and a wider assembly of councillors operating through a system of overview and scrutiny committees and general meetings of the whole council. Three models of a separate executive were offered in the 2000 Local Government Act. The first option was for a person directly elected by the people (called the mayor). Alongside the mayor a wider group of councillors would be elected (called the council). From that group, the mayor would ask a small number of councillors (called the cabinet) to join her or him to share in the leadership of the local authority but with executive authority for making day-to-day decisions, within a framework and budget set by the council, remaining ultimately in the hands of the mayor. The second option was for an executive headed by a councillor chosen by fellow councillors (usually called a council leader). All councillors would be elected by the public and together would form the council. The council leader or the council would, in turn, choose a small group of councillors (a cabinet) to share the leadership of the authority. Executive authority in this model rests with the cabinet. The third option was a person directly elected by the public (given the title mayor) and a salaried chief executive officer appointed by the whole body of separately elected councillors who together would form the council. The mayor and the officer (usually known as the council manager) would together provide leadership to the authority and share executive authority. The Act required all local authorities serving populations of more than 85,000, that is the overwhelming majority of English councils, to choose one of the three models: mayor–cabinet, leader–cabinet or major–chief executive.

The reform process was imposed against considerable opposition from within local government. That opposition had a long history. In their detailed study of local authority decision-making in the mid-1980s the researchers working for the Widdicombe Committee (1986) found 'little

126

evidence of lukewarm support, let alone enthusiasm, for any of the array of the 'separate executive' alternatives ... the overwhelming opinion among chief executives and particularly councillors was for a retention of the current arrangements' (Gyford *et al.*, 1989: 223). When the Labour Government decided to push ahead with the idea of a separate executive and a formal separation of powers there remained substantial doubts among most existing councillors and many officials; in particular, the more radical of the options trailed by the government in various white papers (DETR, 1998; DETR, 1999), which involved a move to a directly elected executive, were greeted with outright hostility. As Tony Travers (2001: 125), in his review of Blair's first-term policies towards local government, comments:

> [T]he topic of elected mayors stirred the most determined response from councillors of all parties. The idea that every council would be forced to choose between a cabinet, directly-elected mayor or mayor-plus-council manager ... proved hugely unpopular within local government.

A poll conducted in the mid-1990s found 82 per cent of councillors opposed to the idea of a directly elected executive mayor to lead a council (Miller *et al.*, 2000: 173). A later poll in 1999 found only 3 per cent of councillors in favour of the idea and general opposition to change but evidence to suggest that up to a third of councillors supported the idea of the leader and cabinet model (Rao, 2003). In contrast to the policies on electoral reform and public participation reviewed in Chapter 6, that received quite widespread support among councillors and officials; the reforms to political management did not, particularly among councillors.

The line of least resistance for many councillors, given that for most the 2000 Act forced a change, was to opt for the leader and cabinet model since it was closest to the informal practice of a group of leading councillors taking the prime responsibility for decision-making within local government under previous arrangements (Copus, 1999; Leach, 1999). The cabinet leader model was chosen by 83 per cent of all councils. Only 3 per cent of councils have adopted either of the mayoral options. Ten have gone for mayor–cabinet model and one (Stoke) for a mayor–manager model. In a concession granted late in the passage of the legislation the government allowed councils serving populations of 85,000 or below to choose whether to adopt a system without a separate executive and about two-thirds did choose to go down that route, adapting their existing committee system. As a result 14 per cent of councils have adopted alternative arrangements. The adoption of neither a leader–cabinet model nor alternative arrangements required the issue to be put to the public in a referendum. But if either of the mayoral options were proposed then a ballot of the local electorate would have to give its support. There was a right to demand a referendum on the issue given to the public, if a petition could be gathered, signed by 5 per cent of the electorate. A mayor–council system was also established in London for the strategic Greater London Authority in May 2000.

This chapter addresses the question why the reform of political management was opposed with such vehemence in the local government community and in particular why the mayoral models have failed to be taken up to any great degree. As noted above, councils were overwhelmingly negative about the mayoral options. The consultation exercises that were required by the 2000 Act over political management were in many instances exemplars of how to ensure that an official position on a decision was not seriously challenged. Indeed the government appeared to think that the local authorities would not be entirely even-handed over the issue and gave itself the power to review consultation exercises and, if necessary, impose a referendum of a mayoral option within an authority where there appeared to be evidence that substantial public interest in the idea had been overlooked.

Opinion polls conducted in the mid-1990s (Miller *et al.*, 2000: 112) and another conducted in the summer of 2001 (DTLR, 2001: 5) showed about three-quarters of the population in support of the idea of a directly elected leader or mayor. The public, as noted above, were also given the right to petition for a referendum on the issue. Yet it remained generally unengaged in a debate. For many, if they were aware of the issue at all, what appeared to be at stake was the obscure mechanisms of a local government system in which they had very little interest in any case. By the end of 2002 twenty-eight local referendums had been held on the issue of whether to adopt a mayor, with eleven leading to support for a mayor (see Table 7.1). Turnout in the referendums have been low on the whole and the mayoral elections that have taken place have not attracted larger-than-normal local election turnouts (Rallings *et al.*, 2002). Referendum campaigns were often conducted in a low key-manner with on many occasions most of the local political establishment lined up against a 'yes' vote. It is clear that the popularity of the elected mayor idea that was consistently expressed in opinion polls was not translated into enthusiastic support for the idea in referendums or polling booths. The mayoral elections were in most cases conducted in a low-publicity context, the great exception being the election for the London mayor that nevertheless saw only a third of the electorate turnout.

The mayoral model has a foothold in English local government but it has not been the driving force behind a wider programme of reform as hoped for

Table 7.1   *Mayoral referendums, 2001–02*

Council	Date	Result	For	%	Against	%	Turn out %	Type
Berwick upon Tweed	7 Jun 2001	No	3617	26	10212	74	64	Poll at time of General Election
Cheltenham	28 Jun 2001	No	8083	33	16602	67	31	All postal
Gloucester	28 Jun 2001	No	7731	31	16317	69	31	All postal
Watford	12 Jul 2001	Yes	7636	52	7140	48	24.5	All postal
Doncaster	20 Sep 2001	Yes	35453	65	19398	35	25	All postal
Kirklees	4 Oct 2001	No	10169	27	27977	73	13	Standard ballot
Sunderland	11 Oct 2001	No	9593	43	12209	57	10	Standard ballot
Hartlepool	18 Oct 2001	Yes	10667	51	10294	49	31	All postal
LB Lewisham	18 Oct 2001	Yes	16822	51	15914	49	18	All postal
North Tyneside	18 Oct 2001	Yes	30262	58	22296	42	36	All postal
Middlesbrough	18 Oct 2001	Yes	29067	84	5422	16	34	All postal
Sedgefield	18 Oct 2001	No	10628	47	11869	53	33.3	All postal
Brighton and Hove	18 Oct 2001	No	22724	38	37214	62	32	All postal

Table 7.1 *(Continued)*

Council	Date	Result	For	%	Against	%	Turn out %	Type
Redditch	8 Nov 2001	No	7250	44	9198	56	28.3	All postal
Durham	20 Nov 2001	No	8327	41	11974	59	28.5	All postal
Harrow	7 Dec 2001	No	17502	42	23554	58	26.06	All postal
Plymouth	24 Jan 2002	No	29553	41	42811	59	39.78	All postal
Harlow	24 Jan 2002	No	5296	25	15490	75	36.38	All postal
LB Newham	31 Jan 2002	Yes	27163	68.2	12687	31.8	25.9	All postal
Shepway	31 Jan 2002	No	11357	44	14438	56	36.3	All postal
LB Southwark	31 Jan 2002	No	6054	31.4	13217	68.6	11.2	Standard ballot
West Devon	31 Jan 2002	No	3555	22.6	12190	77.4	41.8	All postal
Bedford	21 Feb 2002	Yes	11316	67.2	5537	32.8	15.5	Standard ballot
LB Hackney	2 May 2002	Yes	24697	58.94	10547	41.06	31.85	All postal
Mansfield	2 May 2002	Yes	8973	54	7350	44	21.04	Standard ballot
Newcastle-under-Lyme	2 May 2002	No	12912	44	16468	56	31.5	Standard ballot

Table 7.1 *(Continued)*

Council	Date	Result	For	%	Against	%	Turn out %	Type
Oxford	2 May 2002	No	14692	44	18686	56	33.8	Standard ballot
Stoke-on-Trent	2 May 2002	Yes	28601	58	20578	42	27.8	Standard ballot
Corby	3 Oct 2002	No	5351	46	6239	53.64	30.91	All postal
LB Ealing	12 Dec 2002	No	9,454	44.8	11,655	55.2	9.8	Combination postal and standard ballot

Source: Taken from material corrected by New Local Government Network.

by some of its advocates. We begin the search for an explanation of this phenomenon by looking at the system established in local government prior to the reform process. What emerges from this discussion is a better understanding of the scale of reform that was envisaged since what is required is a move from a political system premised on party government to a model based on a much more explicit acceptance of the doctrine of separation of powers between a political executive and a wider group of elected councillors, leading to an ideal of strong leadership checked by effective scrutiny.

The next two sections review these broader arguments for the mayoral model as well as some of the doubts of the opponents of reform. It is concluded that while the opponents of the mayoral models make some worthwhile cautionary comments they were unable to undermine substantially the case for elected mayors. It is suggested, therefore, that the problems of implementation are not a reflection of an ill-thought-out, or wildly inappropriate idea, about how to construct the politics of local governance.

It is when we move to a deeper level of institutional analysis that an answer to what drives the resistance to reform begins to emerge. Drawing again from the neo-Durkheimian school of analysis an explanation is presented of why the mayoral agenda has met such substantial opposition in local government. The local political establishment never accepted the argument for a mayoral model and their resistance proved crucial to explaining the failure of implementation. The penultimate section returns to the issue of why in the light of local political establishment resistance central government was not more determined to push ahead with the mayoral project. The underlying cause of reluctance to force the issue at the national level is the same as that at the local: party politics controls the institutions of government and is unwilling to give up its grip.

A concluding section considers the future shape of political management reform in the light of the experience under the first six years of New Labour. The mayoral project is not dead and the level of focus on the London mayor suggests that the idea may not fade away.

The established system of political management and the reform proposals

It would be appropriate to describe the pre-reform model of local government as a committee-based system of internal decision-making overlaid by processes of party control and direction. Committees provided the formal structure through which decisions were processed but parties provided the decision-making drive and the focus of accountability. The essential legal features are that the council is a corporate body. Decisions are taken by, or on behalf of, the whole council – without any separate source of committee authority. Officers serve the council as a whole.

The Widdicombe Committee (1986) identified these legal features of the established system but recognized that councils can and do delegate their functions to committees who in turn can delegate functions to subcommittees and that councils, committees and subcommittees delegate functions to officers. Committees were the formally dominant player in the decision-making structure. As Gyford *et al.* (1989: 190) argue 'the committee' played 'a dominant role in the average councillor's life'. Councils had a variety of committee systems with usually some overarching committees dealing with finance and general policy and others focused on particular services and functions. These committees made recommendations about policy decisions that were usually formally ratified by the full council.

The formal system of committees was overlain with informal systems of political control. Gyford *et al.* (1989: ch. 6) identify differences between three main types of political control. They note that a few councils (about one-eighth of all councils in 1987) with a large number of independent councillors operated with low partisan arrangements. Most local councils were by the mid-1980s effectively politicized. Some two-thirds of councils in 1987 were under single-party control and one in five were in a position where no party was in overall control and where some combination of party support was necessary to enable decisions to be made. In most authorities decisions were not made in the council or committees but through party group machinery. The leadership of the group might in reality be the effective executive controlling the work of the council, although it was likely to operate through informal meetings rather than through the formal machinery of the council. Nevertheless it was party control that in theory delivered accountability to the system: if the political party in control on the council failed to deliver, the voters could kick them out.

The move to a system of party government occurred in a process that started in the late nineteenth century and went through a variety of stages of politicization according to Gyford *et al.* (1989: ch. 1). Even as late as the early 1970s barely half of all councils could be described as partisan but the advent of a further round of reorganization, combined with the continuing drive of political parties to stand candidates and, once they were elected, organize party groups on councils, led to a position that by the mid-1980s nearly 90 per cent of councils were fully party political.

There is little doubt about the extent of control exercised by parties over the machinery of decision-making under established arrangements. If a party was in the majority it took the leadership of all the committees of the council and majority of its members and party members were expected and generally did vote on block. According to the research conducted for the Widdicombe Committee (Gyford *et al.*, 1989: 37, Table 7) in Labour-controlled councils in 99 per cent of cases the party took control of all committee chairmanships and in 96 per of councils it took control of all subcommittee chairmanships. In 85 per cent of authorities the majority party had always voted as a party at committee meetings in 1985. With respect to Conservative-controlled councils 95 per cent of cases saw them in control of committee chairmanships and in 90 per cent of cases they took all subcommittee chairmanships. They too voted on block with 95 per cent of local authorities seeing the majority party always voting the same way in committee meetings. In both Labour- and Conservative-controlled councils there was more evidence of a breakdown of party discipline at full council meetings in part because the majorities were often sufficient to allow some sanctioned cross-voting and in part because of splits, so that discipline could never always be sustained. Nevertheless, overall these figures indicate a formidable degree of party control.

Parties saw their role in decision-making formalized (Gyford *et al.*, 1989: 17) with reference to party group and their rights in council's standing orders.

There was provision of rooms for party groups, officer support provided, arrangements for officers to brief groups and a range of mechanisms that recognized that in a majority-controlled council an effective informal executive was formed by the leading councillors in the group. In councils with no overall control various agreements and conventions were established to regulate relations between party groups in order to ensure that decision-making could proceed.

The Widdicombe Committee (1986: 78–82) saw the role of political parties in decision-making as legitimate but suggested that a split between decision-taking and deliberative committees should be created. The former should have proportionate representation from all parties according to the seats they held on the council and the latter could be composed of representatives from one party. Such a refinement would recognize that a controlling political group should have a private setting to develop its policy ideas, argued the Committee. In the end the Government rejected this recommendation and instead simply installed a requirement, in legislation passed in 1989, that representation on all committees should be proportionate to share of seats held by different political groups. This measure and some other minor changes introduced by the 1989 Act appeared to have little impact on the working of local government. A review of the position in the early 1990s concluded that the system had not substantially changed from the pre-Widdicombe period and that there was, in urban and majority-controlled councils, if anything, 'a tightening of party political organisation' (K. Young and Davies, 1990: 50).

The reform that was eventually introduced as part of the 2000 Act required radical changes in the internal political management structures of local authorities premised on a commitment to the doctrine of the separation of powers. This doctrine, as Gwyn (1965; 1986) notes, can trace its origins back to eighteenth-century political thought. At its heart is the idea that power needs to be checked and challenged if political liberty is to be maintained. Gywn identifies five distinct versions of the argument but two came to dominate discussions about the reform of local government in England. First, the doctrine argues that a separation between the legislative branch of government and the executive helps the former hold the latter to account by freeing the legislature from responsibility, thus enabling it to criticise, and by ensuring that the executive cannot dominant the legislature. Second, there is an argument, made on grounds of efficiency, that a smaller executive freed from the legislature will be able to take more effective action. Gywn goes on to argue that it is a mistake to assume that the application of the doctrine requires a complete separation between the two branches of government; rather what is required is that both executive and legislature have a certain independence of one another and certain powers at their disposal.

The main advocates of change had up to this point premised their arguments primarily on two issues. First, the committee system was seen as inefficient, consuming too much councillor and officer time for no great benefit. A second argument was premised on the value that strong leadership could bring to communities, hence the support offered for elected mayors by Heseltine and others. As noted in Chapter 2, there was a brief flirtation with the idea of elected mayors when Heseltine returned to the Conservative Government in the early 1990s but it was not pursued because of the strength of the opposition to the idea (Stoker and Wolman, 1992). At that time there was very little discussion of the accountability argument for change. The Commission for Local Democracy, an independent review of the state of local democracy in Britain, was instrumental in bringing this issue into focus in its final report published in 1995 (Commission for Local Democracy, 1995; Pratchett and Wilson, 1996). It argued that the accountability of local government was undermined by a decision-making system that obscured where decisions were made and where the leaders remained informal and impossible to hold to account.

The Commission for Local Democracy's report was largely ignored by the Conservative Government but some of its ideas did arouse interest in the then opposition Labour Party. Tony Blair, as leader of the opposition, expressed an interest in the mayoral idea, and Hilary Armstrong, as shadow local government minister, was interested in that idea and in the wider package of reforms proposed by the Commission. Robert Hill in 1996, who was subsequently to become Blair's local government adviser among other roles, wrote of the need for a radical reform of local government and emphasized the importance of effective leadership and the option of going for elected mayors (Hill, 1996). The possiblity of an elected mayor for Greater London was canvassed by Blair from 1996 onwards. On formation of the government in May 1997, the policy debate within New Labour developed in earnest and a pamphlet by Blair (1998b) and a White Paper (DETR, 1998) set out the general case for reform.

The general case for reform rested on a mix of the efficiency and accountability arguments. The established committee system was criticised as 'inefficient, opaque' and as 'weakening accountability' (DETR, 1999: 8). A lot of time was wasted. Decisions were not made in the right forums and there is a concentration of decision-making powers in small groups outside formal arenas:

In short, the traditional committee system, designed to provide an open and public framework for decision-making, has grown into an opaque system with the real action off-stage. People lose confidence in their council's decisions, individual councillors become disillusioned with their ability to influence local decisions, and local people are discouraged from standing for election ... unclear decision-making weakens the links between local people and their democratically elected representatives. (DETR, 1999: 8–9)

There was a great emphasis on the impact that visible leadership could make in providing both a more effective means of tackling community problems and a focus of accountability. The solution was to provide for a move to systems that allowed for 'a clearly identified executive to give strong leadership to communities and clarity to decision taking; and powerful roles for all councillors to ensure transparency and local accountability' (DETR, 1999: 19). All councils above 85,000 were required to adopt one of three systems that would deliver a separation between executive and non-executive actors in practice. The goal was strong leadership held to account by strong overview and scrutiny.

The doctrine of separation of powers is difficult to apply at the local government level in strict legal terms since local authorities do not have a significant function equivalent to legislation and the form is not strongly established in the British political system because of the dominance of the parliamentary tradition. Yet, as a broad set of ideas, the separation of powers has a substantial resonance. As Leigh (2000: 227) further comments:

Understood as a point about the lack of distinctive institutions responsible for policy formulation, implementation, and scrutiny, the point has some force. The existing fusion of these functions is said to be confusing, to obscure and distort public debate and lines of accountability, to be secretive and diverts councillors to time- and energy-consuming management rather than employing them in representation and scrutiny roles.

He concludes that 'the argument that the roles of backbench councillors and of the political elite should be strengthened by more clearly separating them appears compelling'. But he does warn that whether the new systems will work will depend on factors beyond the reach of the law and, especially, on whether the political parties genuinely work to change political culture and climate within which the new legal regime will operate (Leigh, 2000: 246).

The case for reform: leadership suited to the challenge of networked community governance

Much of the discussion in New Labour's ranks revolved not so much on the virtues of different constitutional forms and more on the need for effective leadership for local communities, which it was hoped that the move to executive forms of political management would deliver (Hill, 1996; Hodge *et al.*, 1997; Blair, 1998b; Jones and Williams, 2002). The challenge was to construct a form of politics that could find solutions to difficult social and economic challenges, and find ways in which people could be engaged and yet not forever active. The argument for reform was premised on the search for leadership to what was described in Chapter 1 as networked community governance.

Political leadership offers a unique contribution to governance in a number of ways. It provides a base for legitimate decision-making when technical arguments cannot resolve the issue. The nature of modern governance is characterized by conditions of considerable uncertainty about what is the appropriate policy response to complex, tangled social and economic problems; an increased awareness of the limits of expertise; and a recognition of a complex multi-layered system of decision-making in which local politics must place itself.

In a globalized world and complex environment leadership enables a community to express its shared voice. Elected leaders can with legitimacy articulate the demands and concerns of their town or city. In a world where networks and partnership are the key to effective action political leaders are often the key deal maker. They can demand from those both inside and outside government that people go the extra mile to find a solution or resolve a difficulty. Political leaders often play the role of deadlock breaker or the agent that can encourage the search for solutions when others may feel inclined to give up. Finally, political leaders provide a focus for accountability. They can be removed if their performance is judged to be inadequate by the public; at the very least they can be forced to render an account, to explain why something failed or why policy took a certain direction. In a complex governance system they provide a focus for public debate of the key issues.

So at the heart of the new arrangements was a desire to create a sharper and better-defined focus for leadership. The different executive options provide for different ways of putting together that leadership group. However, there is also a concern with establishing a role for other councillors in representing their communities and overseeing the work of the executive. Leadership in different forms could, as a result, be enhanced. The elected mayor could provide a steering capacity within and beyond the locality. The members of the wider representative body could become advocates for causes and interests and champions of the rights of individual citizens and neighbourhoods. The creative tension between the executive and representative body could bring a wider variety of issues and matters out into the open. The variety of access points for the citizen through both the executive and the deliberative body could in general enhance the openness of the system.

The mayor cabinet model would appear to have particular attractions when it came to political leadership (Stoker, 1996; Hodge *et al.*, 1997). The position of directly elected leader would, it was hoped, create a well-known and accountable figure. This higher profile in turn might help to make for a greater local dimension to policy-making. By playing up personality and leadership the role of nationally oriented party politics would be downgraded and local politics could be easily focused on local issues. Mayors, it was argued (Stoker, 2002b), would make a difference by turning their organizations outwards through providing visible, legitimate and accountable political leadership.

The mayoral model was not some wild untried experiment. It was and remains a commonplace feature of the local politics of many other democracies, not only in North America but also in Europe, Australia, Japan and New Zealand. What the direct election of mayors delivers, according to its advocates, is a leadership that is more likely to look outwards to the public and key stakeholders than the current system. It could also produce a leadership with a popular legitimacy and a capacity to speak for an area that cannot be matched under the established system.

Mayors could deliver a facilitative leadership capacity better suited to the new tasks and challenges that face local governance and service delivery. The environment of local politics has changed and along with those changes has come a new understanding of the challenges faced by local politicians. From the 1930s onwards until the early 1980s local politics defined itself and organized its politics around the challenge of delivering the welfare state at the local level. This was a politics of distribution. The challenge was to gain control over the local machinery of government and make sure it served the interests of working people by delivering the basic infrastructure of a good environment, followed by better houses, education and later quality leisure services and community arts and culture. The system of council committees, tight party group discipline and party control of elections (and to some extent appointments) delivered the machine and the appropriate style of politics to the task that had been set. From the 1980s onwards it was clear that the previously dominant style of local politics was no longer sustainable or desirable. Indeed, Labour councils were among the first to begin to experiment with schemes of decentralization to reach out to the public in a different way and with a shift in focus away from a narrow concern with service delivery towards an interest in economic development. Not all the initiatives were successful or clearly thought through but they did indicate that times were changing (Burns *et al.*, 1994).

Looked at from the perspective we have at the start of the twenty-first century, local councils have not only to widen their role but change their approach to service delivery. National programmes in turn driven by public opinion mean that in some areas such as education a national agenda dominates, although local councils have a crucial role in ensuring its delivery and in providing additional dimensions to the national strategy. Solutions offered by new communication and information technology mean some services no longer require a local spatial base. People should expect to receive services based on their needs and life-cycle circumstances rather than the artificial divisions between different institutions of public service delivery. Interest in linking housing, crime prevention strategies or anti-drug initiatives to a felt level of community brings into play provision at the neighbourhood level. These factors combined mean that the arguments for a local council machine to deliver the welfare state at the local level are no longer as valid. In practice service delivery has become a complex task of co-ordination between different spatial levels and institutions.

For networked community governance to work requires local politicians who can act to facilitate the expression of voice in diverse communities and reconcile differences, develop shared visions and build partnerships to ensure their achievement. Leadership in these new circumstances is not about seizing control of the state machine; it is about building coalitions, developing networks, accountability and steering in a complex environment. Leaders are there to deliver a sense of direction or vision to communities, to support people as they struggle to find their own solutions and to bring the parts together in order to create the capacity for things to happen. They are also there to take responsibility for making positive change happen – for achieving public value in the public service sector – and to be held to account for their performance and those that they have commissioned to undertake work. In the previously dominant committee system effective leaders could emerge; however, leadership operated in a context where the millstone of the council machine and group politics were a major constraint. The mayoral model and to some extent the leader–cabinet model was seen as more suited to the tasks demanded by the adoption of networked community governance.

The case against reform

Various arguments have been levelled against the mayoral options (for a fuller discussion of these see Stoker, 1996; Jones and Williams, 2002).

In this section some of the main arguments are reviewed and they are found to make some telling points. But equally they were not arguments that undermined the case for mayoral reform. They rather presented design challenges for the mayoral model to meet.

(a)   *The separation of the executive and deliberative institutions will lead to a system that will be less effective or responsive, or both*

One common argument was that the reform would concentrate too much power in the hands of the elected mayor and would deny a worthwhile role to the councillors in the council or wider deliberative body. Related to the argument were two subsidiary points: that the system would be more prone to corruption because of that concentration of power, and that decision-making would be more secretive and closed as the elected leader wielded his/her influence to strike deals and progress policy and other matters, in private.

A second argument, which to some extent contradicts the first, is that the split between the executive and the deliberative body would create a stale-mate. Rather than being too powerful the elected leader could become a prisoner of the wider range of elected representatives in the council. Alternatively, if the executive leader cannot guarantee a working majority in the council a stand-off between the two institutions would result, made worse by the fact that both could claim the legitimacy of election to justify their stance.

Although there is a surface contradiction between these arguments they share a common scepticism about the creative nature of the tension between the executive and assembly. Either one side or another will win, or a stale-mate will result in which no one wins. Is this a reasonable objection?

The answer to the above question is that if the checks and balances in the system are inappropriately drawn then the mayor could end up as too pow-erful, without power, or the system could be stuck in perpetual stalemate. However, if effective checks and balances were built into the system it would appear perverse to insist that the tension between executive and assembly cannot be resolved successfully and to the benefit of local democ-racy. The broad principles are clear. First, powers should be divided between the executive and wider body of representatives, thereby giving each side something to bargain with and exercise influence through. Thereafter it is assumed that politics kicks in, that compromises are reached, deals are struck and that common objectives are found.

Getting an effective mix of checks and balances is a considerable institutional design challenge. It is certainly not clear that the regulations that followed the Local Government Act 2000 met that challenge. The mayor has the responsibility for selecting his or her cabinet and the authority to take day-to-day executive decisions. On all major matters relating to policy and budget the agreement of other elected representatives will be required in order to make decisions and spend taxpayers' money. All the options contain features designed to ensure that the rights of the public are protected. Under all arrangements planning, licensing and other 'semi-judicial' matters are dealt with in a way that ensures that all points of view can be heard and the interested individuals have the right to present their case. Meetings of the leading group of politicians make key decisions in open, public session as far as possible and with notice of the decisions being provided in a forward plan. Information about all decisions is made available. All the options have standards committees and procedures to ensure that politicians behave in a manner that is appropriate and ethical. All of the options require an overview and scrutiny function to be run by councillors who are not part of the executive.

The opponents of reform make some telling points about whether the checks and balances in the system would work. It is too early to judge but it would appear that, if anything, there is a danger that the mayors will not be sufficiently powerful in circumstances where they face unified political forces in the council. One factor here is that mayoral models have been put in place against the teeth of significant local political opposition in some cases. Thus, for example, in North Tyneside a small Conservative group not only undertook the campaign to get a mayor but then fought a successful mayoral campaign to get a Conservative mayor elected in 2002, although the rest of the council remained firmly in the hands of the Labour Party, as it had done for many years before. The tensions between the Conservative mayor and the Labour council have been considerable and various legal arguments have developed over their respective powers. A fairly poisonous atmosphere provided the backcloth to events that led to the resignation of mayor in April 2003, although in the mayoral election that followed, a Conservative candidate was successful again.

*(b)   The reform has the effect of over-personalizing local
politics and encourages the trivialization of issues*

The elected mayor, it is argued, will attract inappropriate media attention. He or she will become a 'personality' to be built up and then knocked down.

Issues of public policy will become reduced to supporting or opposing a person. George Jones (G. Jones and Williams, 2002: 79) comments:

> The directly-elected mayor will tend to encourage the politics of celebrity as against the politics of policies, programmes and principles as embodied in political parties seeking to promote the public interest ... Business people, the rich, popular media performers, actors, wrestlers and clowns who attract media attention because they challenge parties and distract voters, are likely to rise to the top, and thus diminish the quality of political argument.

Of the eleven mayoral candidates so far elected in mainstream local government, five style themselves as independents. Ken Livingstone was elected to be the Mayor of London as an independent. But the only one that might be described as having trivialized politics is the Mayor of Hartlepool, who in the early stages of his campaign wore a monkey suit, the costume of the mascot of the local football team. Even he had to offer some serious local campaigning issues. All the other independent candidates have had serious manifesto commitments to change their local community. Indeed there is some evidence that mayoral elections have made people more aware of local issues and what the choices are in respect of the various candidates. As we saw in Chapter 6, lack of knowledge about candidates and what they propose to do is one of the most common reasons for disengaging from local politics.

Opponents of a mayor are right to argue that it does allow greater scope for personality politics. Yet within limits, the enhancement of personality and greater scope for charismatic figures might be seen as a positive gain for local politics, a way of gaining prestige and attention for local government and local issues. It is certainly not automatically a bad feature of the reform. Nor is the mayoral model inherently anti-party politics – since half the successful mayoral candidates have a party allegiance – but it does require parties to work in a different way.

(c)   The committee system has advantages that the
reformed systems are in danger of losing

The committee system, it is argued, has a number of key advantages. It allows each councillor a formal role in decision-making. It enables councillors to develop specialist interests and knowledge. The proposal to separate executive and assembly loses these advantages of the committee system. Yet committees, so the counter-argument goes, broadly defined as groups of people deliberating in public, have not disappeared. Meetings are still where most decisions are made. The advantages of collective, reflective decision-making can still be obtained under the new arrangements. Still, it could be argued, that if councillors do not have hands-on control over policy and operational matters they will lose the incentive to stand for office. The counter-argument put by reformers is that in part the formal role in decision-making was to an extent illusory, since the real power was elsewhere within the decision-making of party groups.

Another argument is that the formal participation in the detail of executive decisions was under the old system bought at too high a price in terms of the time commitment and involvement of councillors. The result is that those willing and able to stand for election are drawn from a narrow band. When it comes to recruitment many do not so much volunteer to become council candidates but are rather pushed into standing by party colleagues and friends. The role of councillor is not an attractive option for many and in private all parties admit to difficulties in recruiting candidates. If the system was designed in a different way, with a range of opportunities and a diversity of representational roles, then a wider variety of people might well be attracted to stand.

In short, many of the activities undertaken within the existing committee system could continue under the proposed reform. What would be lost is the committee's formal executive role both in the authorization of decisions and the detailed supervision of the operational matters in relation to service delivery. What impact this will have on local government is an open question but it cannot be assumed that it will be entirely negative.

*(d)   The creation of a strong executive is incompatible with the
       development of a decentralized politics and wider
       public participation*

The argument here is that the strong executive tends to centralize power while much of the governance agenda is about the need to develop a more decentralized and involving form of politics. Is there a contradiction here? George Jones, again, expresses this viewpoint effectively:

> A single person cannot represent the complex economic, social, ethnic and cultural diversity of Britain's localities ... or provide such close contact

and access to government for individual citizens as can a cabinet and large council. The more representatives there are, and the more collegial the government, the more representative will be the system. (G. Jones and Williams, 2002: 82)

The reply of the reformers is to aim to balance opportunities for leadership with a commitment to a variety and openness in terms of participation. Given the diversity and particular experiences of different groups and individuals in society, wide decentralization and participation are necessary to provide effective voice and commitment. Equally, however, there should be opportunities for expressing shared concerns, for bringing the fragments together. A directly elected executive could provide such a focus. In a practical sense a mayor can be made compatible with a broader politics of decentralization as mayoral towns and cities in many places outside Britain have shown (Stoker and Travers, 1998; 1999).

(e)   The reformers have missed the point: the key to revitalizing local democracy is to restore powers to local government, not changing its institutional structures

Lack of interest in local politics reflects the lack of power in local government. If local government had substantial control over its finances including its own revenue-raising it would attract public interest. Moreover, if local government was given greater freedom from central control then the vitality of the system would be enhanced. The kind of institutional tinkering proposed by the mayoral advocates will prove to be irrelevant and will fail to have any impact unless these more fundamental issues are tackled.

The main reply to these comments falls into two parts. First, it can be suggested that the problem of local democracy is multidimensional rather having a single cause. Lack of local autonomy is an issue and one that needs to be addressed. However, a lack of dynamism in the institutions of local representative democracy is also part of the problem. Local government needs both more scope for local decision-making and more effected institutions of representative democracy. The two are complementary and supportive. In particular it would be difficult to justify the former without the latter.

This section of the chapter has reviewed the arguments for and against change. The argument for the mayoral model may not entirely convince but the model emerges, if not unscathed, at least as a coherent and plausible option. Given that mayors operate in many other western democracies, it would be implausible to suggest that the model has potential as an ideal but always fails in practice. The mayoral option met the criteria to enable it to reach the policy agenda. It appeared to be addressing a problem recognized and regarded as salient by powerful political actors, namely the need for stronger leadership in local government. It offered a solution that appeared to be feasible in terms of the time, political capacity and technical knowledge it demanded in the crafting of the legislation to make it happen. The explanation for the sturdy and steady resistance of much of the local government community to the reform plans lies less in some of the inadequacies of the reform proposals but rather is attributable to the nature of the institutional attachments that the reform plans threaten.

The interest and institutional bases of resistance to the mayoral model

Reforms often meet resistance. That resistance may reflect a calculation of interest. Hall and Leach (2000: 157–60) argue, for example, that the diverse response of different elements of the local government community to the re-organization plans of the 1990s was the product of calculations by leading councillors as to whether it would advance their careers or not. It would, using a similar logic, be possible to suggest that councillors opposed mayoral reforms because crudely the mayor was unlikely to be them. The vast body of councillors opposed the mayoral option because they saw it as a threat to their power and influence. The difficulty with the argument is that, as we have seen, there remain many roles for all types of politician under the mayoral models. Overview and scrutiny roles, membership of the cabinet and involvement in planning and licensing are available options. Many of the existing incumbents were likely to have an opportunity to have some role and some influence under new arrangements and objectively it would be difficult to insist with certainty that for many of them their opportunity to exercise power would be reduced. Nevertheless, the perceived loss of power appears likely to have been a key factor in the position of many councillors. A survey, conducted in 1999, found that nine in ten councillors agreed that a consequence of the mayoral model would be an excessive concentration of power and a substantial loss of influence for ordinary councillors (Rao, 2003).

The seeds of resistance, however, may reflect forces deeper than simple calculation or even miscalculation of interest. The key is to recognize how the mayoral models threaten the fundamentals of the dominant institutional practice and culture of local government. Best Value and other service delivery reforms also present a challenge especially if they involve using private or voluntary sectors in the organization of provision. But the political management reforms pinch even further in challenging ways of organizing and thinking that have come to be regarded as 'sacred'. The neo-Durkheimians (see Perri 6, 1999) would predict a strong reaction to reforms that go to the heart of institutional beliefs. People are seeking to make sense of their world and institutions provide them with explanations, reasoning and argumentation that enables them to comprehend their environment and justify its form. A challenge to institutional form represents a challenge to a whole way of thinking. According to Mary Douglas institutions do the thinking for individuals:

> Any institution that is going to keep its shape needs to gain legitimacy by distinctive grounding in nature and reason: then it affords to its members a set of analogies with which to explore the world and with which to justify the naturalness and reasonableness of the instituted rules, and it can keep its identifiable and continuing form. (Douglas, 1986: 112)

As argued earlier in the chapter, the role of party politics and group control in local government is a relatively recent but powerful institutional form. The positive features of party politics are summarized by Wilson and Game (2002: 296–7), although they go on to identify how each of these might be turned on its head. For present purposes it is sufficient to identify some of the commonly cited benefits of party politics in local government. Party domination is justified as a way of ensuring that disciplined and clear political direction is given to the local authority. In a complex world that discipline is needed. Without it there would be too much policy and management uncertainty, and also instability as independents voted on various issues in an unpredictable manner. Worse still the officials would dominate as it would be all to easy for them to divide and rule the elected representatives. So parties deliver the democratic process. Parties offer manifestos or, at the least, known policy stances from which the electorate can choose in a practical way that is not too demanding of its time and effort. The competition between parties, as in other walks of life, promotes efficiency and effectiveness. The mayoral model, as we have seen, threatens these justifications of the current political system.

Institutions do not simply have to provide justifications for their rightness; these justifications have to be ingrained. Again, as Douglas (1986: 112) argues, an institution starts to:

> control the memory of its members; it causes them to forget experiences incompatible with its righteous image, and it brings to their minds events

which sustain the view of nature that is complimentary to itself. It provides categories of thought, sets the terms for self-knowledge, and fixes identities.

It is clear that party groups are not just about providing the immediate mechanism for driving decisions in local government. They provide the mechanism for recruiting candidates, they instil in new members a way of thinking and working, they provide a framework of discipline and organizing the decision-making processes of the local authority in group meetings and in caucuses held prior to decisions (for descriptions of these processes at work see Dearlove, 1973; G. Jones, 1969; Game and Leach, 1996). The problematic features of these arrangements tend to be overlooked, such as the taking of key decisions in private and without appropriate professional advice and the trivialization of the formal decision-taking meetings as an elaborate array of committee meetings are endured in which all the main decisions have been taken elsewhere. The claim of parties to provide a conduit for local democracy is also hotly disputed by many observers, yet in parties it is taken for granted that they are elected and therefore legitimate. The mayoral models threaten the selective promotion of the virtues of party politics and its dominance over the political process.

The mayoral model is treated as if it is an attack on sacred features of local democracy. Again as Douglas (1986: 112) argues, institutions secure their social foundations by 'sacralizing the principles of justice' and any attack on those principles is viewed as dangerous:

> If the sacred is profaned, terrible things will happen; the world will break up and the profaner will be crushed. ... Any attack on the sacred rouses emotions to its defense. (Douglas, 1986: 113)

Elected mayors challenge central tenets of the existing system such as the formal equality of all councillors in the decision-making process, the ceremonial role of the existing non-executive mayor and the key role of party loyalty in decision-making (cf. Leach, 1999: 79). Reaction to the mayoral proposals, because of the challenges they pose to these sacred features, has often been very strong with emotive overtones. The DETR guidance on consultation over the new models of political management provides several examples of council publicity literature that exhibits a tendency to emphasize how the mayoral models go against the grain of British decision-making. It is described as a North American or European model in contrast to the home-grown cabinet leader model; the 'implication is that it is your patriotic duty to choose the latter' (Copus et al., 2000: 25). The mayoral model is charged with undermining the role of the traditional First Citizen, the ceremonial mayor. It is viewed as creating the prospect of 'tin-pot' dictators up and down the land. 'The mayor and the queen seem to be on a par in terms of security of tenure' according to one councillor (quoted by Simon Parker in Guardian Unlimited, website, 2001). These jibes at the mayoral model are all capable of being replied to and dealt with in a reasoned debate, as the previous section has shown. But their regular use, within the local government community in attacks on the mayoral project, give some idea of the scale and nature of the response that the mayoral issue has evoked.

It would be wrong to suggest that local government has shown no interest in the mayoral model or that neo-Durkheimians hold the view that it is impossible to achieve institutional change. Neither proposition would be accurate and the nature of institutional change will be explored in a different context in Chapter 8. There have been forces for change within local government even with respect to the mayoral agenda, as the activities of some authorities such as Newham, Watford, Lewisham, among others, testify. Indeed it is in part because neo-Durkheimians see institutions as not permanent and always in a potential state of flux that they have developed such strong arguments about how institutions achieve stability through influencing the way their members think. As Douglas (1986: 111) comments:

> We have insisted ... that it is highly improbable that institutions could emerge smoothly from a gathering momentum of converging interests and an unspecified mixture of coercion and convention. We have too much experience of how easily they come apart and collapse. The thing to be explained is how institutions ever start to stabilize.

So change is a constant feature of institutions. Surprise and shocks can drive change. As can the constant clash between the institution's explanation of its activities and those provided to individuals from other groups and sources. The constant drip, drip of such challenges can tip a set of people in an organization from one social bias to another, in turn stimulating radical change (M. Thompson et al., 1990). The resistance of the local political establishment, although deeply ingrained, might have been overcome if New Labour had managed the politics of implementation better. This proposition will be explored in the next section of the chapter.

New Labour's compromised implementation strategy

The political context for the reform of political management and in particular the mayoral project was far from favourable but the politics of implementation was probably made more difficult by four factors that were within the orbit of the national Labour Government to control but which were addressed in an unsuccessful way.

First, there was little or no effective political management of the reform agenda. The opposition of the local government establishment was clear but not even Labour leaders were directly approached to discuss the merits or otherwise of the policy. There was no charm offensive coming from the Prime Minister's Office on the issue. The message from the Department responsible for local government was, at best, confused and, at worst, undermining of the whole implementation process. While the local government ministers Hilary Armstrong and, after her, Nick Raynsford were articulate advocates for the reforms, the Deputy Prime Minister, John Prescott (1997–2001; 2002), and even his short-term replacement Stephen Byers (2001–2), at Secretary of State level, were lukewarm. Putting John Prescott in charge of the mayoral policy was like asking a non-swimmer to enter a competition to swim across the English Channel. In private, and later in public, John Prescott made no secret of the fact that he was not a supporter of mayors and was backed in his opposition by Jeremy Beecham, Chair of the Local Government Association throughout the period. Together they, in effect, advised everyone to avoid swimming if at all possible. Mayors received no encouragement from these quarters.

Second, there was no clear enforcement strategy. A series of mini-scuffles took place between the Prime Minister's Office and the Deputy Prime Minister that tended to undercut the prospect of developing any implementation strategy. There was a proposal, at one stage, for a certain group of councils, unitary urban authorities above a certain population size, to be required to hold a referendum on the mayoral issue on the same day. This measure would have put the decision out to the public and would have enabled a co-ordinated campaign, attracting large levels of publicity, to take place. This option was rejected by the Deputy Prime Minister and instead the calling, timing and organization of referendums were left in the hands of local government. The Prime Minister's Office promoted the idea of the public being able to call for a referendum if 5 per cent of the electorate signed up for it. There had been a proposal for a higher threshold but the Prime Minister's Office won on that issue. In public there could be agreement that this policy allowed for local people to make choice, a policy on which all could agree. In private all recognized that the local political establishment – known opponents of the policy in most places – was left to run the consultation exercises and largely determine what would happen, with the long-stop option that if the public were really dissatisfied it could push for a referendum. Given the level of the public's disengagement from local politics that in part inspired support for the mayoral idea, it appeared optimistic to imagine that the public that had been inactive were going to be mobilized over the issue. It was a bit like expecting the dead to rise from its grave. Indeed, that there was some recognition of that point is indicated by the power given to the Secretary of State to force a referendum if, in his or her judgement, the consultation exercise required to be undertaken by a local authority had been mishandled or led to a failure to recognize that there was some considerable support for the mayoral idea that should be tested in a formal referendum. Even here compromise kicked in. The power to force a referendum was only used once; in the case of the London Borough of Southwark. Otherwise, despite considering using the option in respect of Birmingham, Bradford and other places, where consultation exercises appeared to show high support for the mayoral idea, no referendums were forced. The decision not to force referendums was taken on pragmatic political grounds and because in none of the locations could a credible enough Labour candidate be found. To put it bluntly, a mayoral election was only valued if it was likely to result in a Labour victory.

Third, party politics and tribal loyalties among its elite appear to have played a more general part in tripping up the mayoral agenda. Ken Livingstone's campaign for the Labour nomination to stand as Mayor of London was blocked by the New Labour hierarchy in an inept manner. His subsequent victory in the first London mayoral election probably helped set the first alarm bells ringing in New Labour about whether mayoral elections were going to be a source of triumph or failure for the party. The victory by independents in some of the early local government mayoral elections confirmed the grim logic of those who take a look at elections through tribal eyes. 'If we can't win we are not sure that we want to play', would appear to have been the attitude of some high-ranking members of the New Labour administration. What is also surprising is how slow the Conservatives were to take advantage of opportunities afforded by the new system. The stunning success of the Conservatives' campaign and candidate in the Labour stronghold of North Tyneside has not been followed by other interventions, which is somewhat puzzling for a party struggling to achieve local representation in urban areas. Parties, in general, have been slow to adjust to the new politics of mayoral contests and their slowness to change made the agenda of change in local government more difficult.

The final factor in making implementation more difficult is the design of the new constitutions that local authorities have been required to adopt. The Commission for Local Democracy's proposal and that of others

(Hodge *et al.*, 1997) was that the mayoral authorities would have their matching assemblies elected by some form of proportional representation (PR). With the exception of the London model, this option was not followed through. The aims of these plans for a PR-elected assembly were to encourage the prospects of a broader political representation in the assembly and allow more freedom for manoeuvre for the mayor in negotiating with the assembly. The explanation for the Government's confused position on the issue again lies in the outcome of tussles between the Prime Minister's Office and the Deputy Prime Minister. In London the PR battle was won by the former and elsewhere it was won by the latter. The issue of PR in local elections, as noted in Chapter 6, was too challenging an issue to open up. As a result several mayors face majority-controlled assemblies not of their own perspective, one as a Conservative in North Tyneside and the others as independents in places such as Middlesbrough. The delicate balance between the mayor and the assembly may be difficult to sustain in such circumstances. More generally the implementation of political management arrangements was left to individual authorities to construct under guidance from central government official regulations. Unfortunately the regulations have proved to be very cumbersome and complex and there remain in mayoral, but also other, councils some uncertainties about the division of powers between the executive and the council.

Conclusions

It might be argued that the campaign to reform the political management structures of English local government is a formal success, in that in all authorities with a population above 85,000 a separate executive has been established. What is equally clear is that the wider ambitions of the reformers have not yet been met. The mayoral models have been adopted in only a handful of councils. There is not much sign that either a dynamic new political leadership cadre has emerged or that a new relationship has been forged between governors and governed. The leader–cabinet system dominates in local government but it is far too early to draw strong conclusions about how different it will be in practice from the system under pre-2000 Act arrangements. The leader-cabinet model is that closest to past informal practice but there are signs to indicate that behaviour with local authorities is beginning to change as a result of the structural changes (see John *et al.*, 2003 for a development of this argument and for a contrasting and poorly researched alternative view see House of Commons, 2002a). A census survey of all local authorities revealed a view that the efficiency and accountability of decision-making had been improved in many cases but that party attitudes and loyalties were continuing to play a big part in shaping local decision-making (see the research evidence from the University of Manchester team led by the author on the website www.elgnce.org.uk.).

The London model offers some hope for the advocates of mayoral reform. Early assessments of the London model (Pimlott and Rao, 2002: ch. 10) suggest some strengths, as well as weaknesses in the new system. The weaknesses relate to the gap between the strategic responsibilities of the mayor and the legislative and financial powers that he has at his disposal. Yet Mayor Ken Livingstone had picked up on issues that are central matters of concern to Londoners, his style of politics has been relatively inclusive and yet he has been willing to show strong leadership over, for example, the introduction of congestion charging in central London and budget-setting in general. Neither his temperament nor his powers have allowed Livingstone to offer a 'city boss' or commanding role but he has taken on other mayoral roles commonly displayed around the world (Pimlott and Rao, 2002: 175–6). He has been entrepreneurial over promoting London's Olympic bid, he has been an honest broker in piecing together various small-scale deals for London and he has been a crusader not least over the deal to reconstruct London's Underground. He has certainly attracted much media attention. There appears to be no shortage of high-profile candidates who are prepared to challenge him for the job when he comes up for re-election in 2004. There is nothing to suggest that the radical mayoral changes either in London or elsewhere will be swept away in a tide of public or political opposition. The mayoral model has something to build on.

8   Partnership and Joining Up in an Era of Multi-Level Governance

This chapter focuses on local partnerships and intergovernmental relations. Together these two concerns capture the essence of the idea of multi-level governance. As argued in Chapter 1, to understand the challenge of governing today requires a recognition that decision-making has multiple locations – spatial and sectoral – and is driven by a complex interplay of forces across these multiple locations. The pursuit of partnership and joining up by New Labour reflects its clear embrace of governance. Multi-level governance is both the present and the future; the issue is how to manage it, as far as New Labour is concerned.

Commitment to partnership is a key feature of New Labour's rhetoric (Sullivan and Skelcher, 2002). Although 'partnership' is a word that is 'sprinkled liberally in academic and policy discussions' it does carry a clear commitment to the long-term building of joint decision-making and implementation in order to achieve shared purposes for New Labour (Sullivan and Skelcher, 2002: 5–7) More generally the term 'joined-up government' has been developed to capture New Labour's commitment to working across organizational and sectoral boundaries. The challenge is on the one hand to achieve co-ordination and on the other to achieve integration. The underlying task of joining up is to align commitments and capacities in various organizations in order that critical tasks can be addressed (Perri 6 *et al.*, 2002; National Audit Office, 2001).

There are two basic arguments for joining up (see Perri 6 *et al.*, 2002: ch. 2). The first is that more complex challenges, such as tackling crime, require input from a variety of sources if they are to be met. The second is that people have joined-up problems, the difficulties they confront do not necessarily, indeed rarely, follow the bureaucratic demarcations of government. Joined-up government and the even more ambitious commitment to holistic government stand in contrast to government by muddling through, that is collaborative without being consistent about objectives. Joining up also stands in contradiction to baronial government, where each part of the machinery does its own thing and in opposition to fragmented government, that sees constant battles over who is responsible for an issue. Specialization is not the enemy of joining up since expertise is to be prized in any governance structure; rather the opposite of joining up is fragmentation.

The chapter begins by presenting an analysis of the changes in the institutional map at the local and more generally subnational level encouraged by New Labour. There has been no great bonfire of local quangos but a staggering growth of a whole series of partnerships at the local level, leading Sullivan and Skelcher (2002: 224) to comment: 'the state is joining up with a vengeance and in the process is constructing a configuration that is significantly different from that found prior to the 1990s'. The second section looks at how New Labour's progress towards joined-up governance was undermined in the early years of the first term by what has been described as 'an excessively hierarchical bias in the design of the programme' (Perri 6 *et al.*, 2002: 95). Indeed some go further and argue that joining up has an inherent centralizing bias. Does joining up open the way for a subtle form of steering from the centre or does it, as some argue, give local councils a chance to shine as the community leaders for their areas? The third section explores how both arguments are reflected in New Labour's thinking.

The concluding section notes that joining up is not fully institutionalized in the British governance scene. Whether it survives and in which form it is likely to survive is subject to analysis using an understanding of the processes of institutionalization derived from neo-Durkheimian insights.

Mapping New Labour's institutional framework for local and regional governance

New Labour has not disappointed governance anoraks in its willingness both to add new institutions to British local governance and contribute to the overall complexity of the system of multi-level governance. Beyond the formal institutions of the core executive in Westminster and Whitehall and the operation of elected local authorities there is a vast world of regional and national agencies, local quangos and local partnerships that are all players in modern local governance. In discussion below we look at New Labour's contributions to the institutions of governance under three headings: its devolution programme, its maintenance of a local quango system and its promotion of myriad forms of new local partnership.

The devolution programme

The five parts of the devolution package are outlined in Box 8.1. It is possible to see some shared connections between Labour's programmes of

---

Box 8.1   *New Labour's devolution programme*

The Northern Ireland Assembly: The Belfast or 'Good Friday' agreement in April 1998 proposed a 108-member Assembly with full legislative and executive authority in respect of most domestic social and economic affairs. The Assembly was elected in July 1998, using an STV proportional system, and legislation to establish its powers has been rushed through the UK Parliament. The political executive of the Assembly consists of a First Minister and Deputy First Minister chosen by and from among Assembly members on a cross-community basis. The procedures and operation of the Assembly are designed to require cross-community support on major or crucial issues.

The Scottish Parliament: Elections for the Parliament were first held in May 1999. The Parliament has substantial legislative and executive authority over domestic policy except in areas reserved to the Westminster or UK Parliament such as Social Security. The Parliament has 129 representatives elected on an additional member proportional system (76 first past the post, 56 from regional lists). The Parliament in its first term had a coalition government formed by Labour and Liberal Democrats. This looks set to continue in its second term.

The National Assembly for Wales: The Assembly was elected in May 1999 for the first time and sets policies for Wales in the context of primary legislation enacted by the UK Parliament. It has a wide discretion over a large range of domestic, social and economic policies and has the authority to promulgate its own secondary legislation. The Assembly of 60 members was elected on an additional member proportional system. The Assembly was governed through a minority Labour administration for its first term. A further Labour administration will dominate the second term.

The Greater London Authority: The Greater London Authority (GLA) elected in May 2000 consists of a directly elected mayor and a 25-member Assembly. It covers the same area as the Greater London Council abolished by the Conservatives in 1986. The first Mayor, Ken Livingstone, was elected using a supplementary vote system, with the Assembly elected using the additional member system. The GLA's main functions are its strategic responsibility for transport, economic development, environment, planning, police, fire, culture and public health.

Regions in England outside London: In the remainder of England, 8 Regional Development Agencies (RDAs) were established in April 1999. They are non-departmental public bodies and responsible directly to ministers and onwards to the UK Parliament. The RDA boards are appointed by central government. Alongside RDAs, regional chambers have been established composed of local councillors and other local stakeholders to monitor the work of RDAs and develop regional strategies. A White Paper published in May 2002 set out the procedures to move elected regional government in England. The proposals are to allow the English regions outside London to establish regional assemblies if there is public demand for the development. The first referendums on the issue are likely to be held in 2004.

---

constitutional reform. There is an underlying commitment to embrace some devolution of power from Westminster to the 'nations', the regions and localities. There is recognition that developing leadership capacity at sub-Westminster levels of decision-making is an appropriate response to the complexities of the emerging world of multi-level governance. Yet beyond these general factors it is important to recognize that there have been and remain particular driving factors behind each element of Labour's reform package.

The case of Northern Ireland makes the strongest argument for uniqueness. The move to a new political settlement was one of the great events of the Blair Government's first year in office. The proposed Assembly is part of a broader agreement designed to bring peace and political progress to the province. The basic structure of the settlement is what might be described as a consociational agreement. It includes: cross-community executive power sharing; proportionality rules applied throughout the relevant governmental and public sectors; community self-government (or autonomy) and equality in cultural life; and veto rights for minorities. These and other complex features of the Belfast Agreement are designed to regulate ethnic and national conflict.

The demands for a Scottish Parliament, too, reflect a complex set of pressures and influences. The rise of Scottish nationalism and its political expression, from the late 1960s, in the ability of the Scottish National Party (SNP) to win a sizeable proportion of votes is a key driving factor. The reaction of the mainstream UK political parties was mixed. An attempt at reform failed in the late 1970s. Crucially under John Smith's leadership in the early 1990s Labour committed itself to a parliament, a promise that the Blair Government has been able to deliver. A body called the Scottish Constitutional Convention, which was set up in March 1989, played a major role in Scotland. The Labour Party and Liberal Democrats participated in the Convention along with representatives from local authorities, trade unions, churches and other organizations. The Convention delivered a blueprint for the future Scottish Parliament, demonstrated a capacity for cross-party and beyond party joint-working and led the growing elite and non-elite consensus that some form of political devolution for Scotland was essential.

The case of Wales is different again. There was, and is undoubtedly, greater ambiguity compared to Scotland about the nationalist dimension and the case for devolved government, a feature which explains the extremely close referendum vote in favour of reform in 1997 and the less-developed nature of the proposed Welsh Assembly.

In London the argument for a new strategic authority began almost as soon as the Greater London Council was abolished in 1986. With the exception of the Conservatives there was cross-party support for such an initiative and a largely favourable reaction among the public, although the issue hardly reached the top of the list in terms of political salience. However, the particular form of the new Greater London Authority (GLA) reflects the thinking of the Blair Government rather than the product of a cross-party or political/civil elite consensus.

A White Paper, *Your Region, Your Choice* (ODPM, 2002b), published in May 2002 on regional government reflects the demands of regional enthusiasts, not least the Deputy Prime Minister, but the relative weakness of the model it offers reflects some considerable doubts within New Labour (in particular the Prime Minister) about the suitability of a regionalist agenda for all parts of England. The Regional Development Agencies (RDAs) established in Labour's first term are not the product of a groundswell of regionalist sentiment but rather a pragmatic policy tool designed to deliver more effective economic regeneration. In the 2002 White Paper the Government is concerned to present any new regional tier that might emerge as a matter for local choice and as a streamlined and focused form of government. A relatively small assembly for regions that vote for change of around twenty-five to thirty-five representatives is proposed. The key function for the Assembly will be to draw up strategies around economic development. The RDAs that are currently responsible to central government will come under regional direction and will lead the drive to economic renewal in each area. The assemblies will also have a key say over spatial development plans. In addition it will be the task of the regional assembly to establish some key policy objectives for a number of other policy fields including transport, housing, skills and culture. The White Paper makes a powerful argument for regions to develop their own approaches to sustainable economic regeneration and to provide a more general tool for joining up a range of strategies in order to maximize the benefit of public spending and intervention in their area. Taken as a package the functions associated with the proposed new regional assemblies can be seen as central to any attempt to drive economic performance in an area. The measures constitute a form of decentralization in that many of the decisions taken by the new assemblies are currently taken by the government's own Offices of the Regions.

The White Paper suggested that the core budget of the regional assembly for the North East would be in the region of £300 million; in addition it suggested that it would be able to influence the budgets of other agencies worth £500 million. These two figures combined, however, are only slightly greater than the gross budget of Newcastle City Council for 2002/3 that stands at £677 million. Newcastle, just one of the local authorities in the North East, will spend almost as much as the proposed regional assembly. The assemblies will have a block grant to fund their core activities that will be subject to a few central objectives and a modest power to raise additional income through a precept on council tax. The proposed new regional tier for England has to be characterized as a financial mouse rather than a roaring lion. It remains to be seen if enough people will vote for one in their region. The powers of a regional assembly appear to rest rather more in drawing up strategies and influencing rather than through direct control. It will be able to steer the activities of its RDA and have responsibility for allocating other funding. Otherwise it will have to rely on the power of oversight with respect to the activities of other agencies, and the 'obligation', as the White Paper puts it, of other bodies to take notice of it. It will also, as the White Paper notes, have to rely on influencing other bodies, including central government and the EU as best as it can.

In the modern world of multi-level governance where the construction of intervention relies on the promotion of partnership and joint working it may be appropriate that a new regional assembly will have to rely on techniques of building networks, constructing strategies that people can buy into, spreading good practice and learning, using finance to cajole policy shifts, checking performance and holding organizations to public account. In many respects the new regional system of government that is proposed offers an archetypal form of governance institution that has to rely on influence rather than direct control.

No bonfire of local quangos

Despite the demands of some, reported in Chapter 2, New Labour has largely resisted calls for the abolition of local quangos. As a careful investigation by the House of Commons (2001b) Public Administration select committee found, the number of local quangos in 2001 is similar to that identified in studies undertaken in the mid-1990s. There are a number of definitional difficulties, and some uncertainty about what to include and what to exclude, but the figure of 5338 local bodies is offered by the Select Committee as assessment of local public bodies in the UK. This figure is, in fact, slightly higher than that produced by audits in the mid-1990s, although direct comparison is difficult because of the issues outlined above. New Labour did abolish some quangos such as grant-maintained schools but replaced them with foundation schools. It replaced Training and Enterprise Councils with Learning and Skills Councils, although not by the time of the census reported in Table 8.1. As noted earlier it established the new RDAs to take forward regional economic development.

Broadly speaking New Labour has left the world of local quangos unchanged, in large part because the agencies are focused on delivering a

Table 8.1   *New Labour's local quangos in England and Wales, 2000*

Name	Number
Further education institutions	511
Foundation schools	877
City technology colleges	15
Training and enterprise councils	47
Registered social landlords	2166
Housing action trusts	4
Police authorities	41
Health authorities	99
NHS trusts	373
Primary care groups	434
Primary care trusts	40
Dartmoor steering group	1

Source: Adapted from House of Commons (2001b, Table 6).

service that is valued by New Labour. What New Labour has done is generally encourage all appointed bodies operating at the local level to consult with the relevant local authorities about their plans and intentions. In the case of RDAs, the new Learning and Skills Councils and in the health sector the commitment to ensure that connections are made with local government has been given statutory backing. The Public Administration Select Committee welcomes this trend to improve the links between local authorities and local quangos and suggests that it should be extended further. It remains convinced, however, that significant accountability issues remain for local quangos (House of Commons, 2001b: paras 40, 41).

The burgeoning world of partnership

If, in the world of local quangos, New Labour has adapted rather than transformed the Conservatives' legacy, with respect to the use of partnership it is fair to argue that New Labour surpassed their predecessors' legacy. Sullivan and Skelcher (2002: 5) identify four aspects of local partnership working that mark out the New Labour era as distinctive from that of the Conservatives (see Sullivan and Skelcher, 2002: 21–5).

First, there has been less emphasis on partnership as a particular tool for urban regeneration and a stronger emphasis on the role of partnership in service delivery. There is a concern with using partnerships to ensure the delivery of outcomes in terms of improving the well-being of communities rather than 'bricks and mortar' property-based renewal. Second, there has been an inflation in the time horizon of partnerships, with many set up to run over relatively long periods (ten years or more). Third, there has been a great use of neighbourhood or more generally area-based initiatives. Finally, there has been the creation since 2001 of a new form of overarching partnership – a Local Strategic Partnership (LSP) – usually covering the whole of a local authority area.

Not surprisingly the interest in partnerships has resulted in the establishment of partnership bodies. Sullivan and Skelcher (2002: 26–7) suggest that there are some 5500 individual partnership bodies at local and regional level created by government in the UK, with a direct spend of £4.3 billion. Table 8.2 provides some of the details of those bodies that are responsible for the larger elements of that spend, created by New Labour between 1997 and 2001. There have been over a dozen different schemes backed, each carrying a major spending commitment in excess of £50 million in 2001/2. Many of the partnership initiatives focus on issues of deprivation and seek to target resources either at deprived neighbourhoods or at services directed towards the deprived. As Table 8.2 shows, New Labour has in addition continued the large commitment to property-based regeneration through the Single Regeneration Scheme (SRB) started under the Conservatives.

New Labour's centralizing implementation strategy for joining up: first-term mistakes

New Labour has not only sustained the use of local and regional appointed bodies and added new institutions of devolved government, it has further contributed to complexity through its sustained drive to encourage partnership. Yet for much of the first term its approach to implementation was chaotic and over-centralized. When New Labour came to power in 1997 it was enthusiastic, committed to developing new approaches and new practices. A great variety of initiatives were launched promoting joined-up ways of working and new forms of partnership. It also showed a great faith in the virtues of plans and strategies. Another approach used, and loudly proclaimed, was a highly prescriptive form of top-down policy implementation, such as the literacy hour scheme introduced into primary schools and the policy to reduce the number of rough sleepers.

Perri 6 and colleagues (2002: 96–101) accuse the Government of several faults in the development of its strategy. First, there was a problem of

Table 8.2 *New Labour's major local multi-agency partnerships*

Partnership name	Start date	Number	Identifiable funding 01/02 (m)	Purpose
Children's Fund	2001	40	£150	Tackle child poverty
Coalfields Programme	1998	–	£135	Regeneration of coalfields
Crime and Disorder	1998	376	£160	Tackle community safety and fear of crime
Early Years Development and Childcare	1998	150	£435 approx	Develop nursery provision and childcare
Education Action Zones	1998	73(plus 100 small zones)	£72	Raising educational standards in groups of schools
Employments Zone	2000	15	£56	Help long-term unemployed
Excellence in Cities	1999	58	£75	Raise education standards in major cities
Health Act Partnerships	1999	64	£637	Joined-up working between health and social services
Health Action Zones	1998	26	£160	Targeting health care and treatment
Healthy Living Cities	1999	–	£60	Promoting health
Neighbourhood Renewal Fund	2001	88	£200	Improve services in most deprived areas
New Deal for Communities	1998	39	£112	Tackle deprivation most deprived neighbourhoods
Social inclusion	1999	48	£50	Tackle social exclusion
Sports Action Zones	1999	30	£75	Promote sport in deprived communities

Table 8.2   *(Continued)*

Partnership name	Start date	Number	Identifiable funding 01/02 (m)	Purpose
Sure Start	1999	500 by 2004	£284	Promote development of children from deprived families
Single regeneration budget	1994	900	£700	Regeneration in deprived communities
Local Strategic partnerships	2001	400 approx	–	Develop and oversee long-term vision for an area

Source: Adapted from Sullivan and Skelcher (2002) Appendix 2, 228–37. Includes all local partnerships launched in New Labour period in office up to Autumn 2001, spending more than £50 m in 2001/02. In addition includes continuing commitment to Single Regeneration Budget and support for strategically overarching local strategic partnerships.

impatience as ministers in some instances made unrealistic demands for partnership to work overnight. Second, there were just too many joined initiatives so that in any one area there was a multiplicity of schemes and programmes. Many of the individual initiatives, calls for new plans and prescriptive interventions had much to commend them. But taken as a piece it is probably true to say that initial interventions were often experienced by those in local government and in other local units of service provision as a 'chaotic centralism' where it was never entirely clear what demand was going to hit your desk next (cf. Corry and Stoker, 2002). Problems arose in part due to the scale and speed at which New Labour tried to move. Sullivan and Skelcher (2002: 20) refer to a 'congested state' in which considerable amounts of time and resources are just chewed up in getting new organizations off the ground and in constructing partnership relations so that something can get done.

All of this frenetic activity relating to zones, pilots and initiatives posed a real danger of overload for local government. Indeed researchers warned of the dangers of 'initiativitis': 'This is the syndrome in which public managers end up swamped by the volume of special projects, discretionary funds and demands to produce plans' (Perri 6 *et al.*, 2002: 96). An excessive demand for plans and strategies can create demands that divert managerial time and resources from the actual business of improving services, a point now conceded by the Government in the 2001 Local Government White Paper (DTLR, 2001).

Partnerships were also launched against the backcloth of badly designed bidding competitions and inadequate evaluation schemes. What partnership can do in these circumstances is hone up people's bidding skills but not make much real progress in tackling problems. Getting money was about displaying skills that might or might not be appropriate to the delivery of your objectives. The culture of measurement of performance was too often not flexible and adaptable enough and as a result could take value out of programmes rather than put it back in. 'Hastily set measuring systems can either quickly become irrelevant in practice as the project acquires its natural focus (causing problems with later accountability), or can from the outset skew and distort the initiative' (Perri 6 *et al.*, 2002: 98).

The Government's programme also suffered because in many ways despite the rhetoric they were not committed to learning. Evidence-based policy development is often seen to be part of the rationale for joined innovations or new partnership arrangements. But if there is a great deal of political capital set by the success of these schemes then their value as experiments can be lost. The Government's strategy allowed little tolerance for failure. Moreover it was not geared up to share lessons about what worked as well as it might have been. The distribution of best practice advice was often highly centralized and hasty. There are several difficulties here. First, given the official central flavour of lesson-learning some managers might have been 'more concerned to cover up failures than to discuss the lessons learned frankly with colleagues' (Perri 6, 2002: 98). Moreover, lessons are often very specific to local circumstances and conditions. Finally, deciding what works often takes more time than the production of good practice guides six months or one year down the line can allow for.

The Government has, at times, employed a highly prescriptive model of top-down intervention. The Performance and Innovation Unit report (PIU, 2001) on models of policy design regards the literacy hour as a classic example of this kind of approach:

> There was clear evidence on how to deliver improvements in reading ability. Government implemented a highly prescriptive model, pushed through the policy despite initial opposition, invested high level political support, provided substantial resources to those implementing the policy and in time achieved widespread support from key stakeholders. (PIU, 2001: 17)

A similar approach might be observed in a co-ordinated blitz on street crime in 2002. Crucially, as the PIU report went on to make clear, the potential for such strong-arm top-down tactics being effective on a large-scale is limited. Such models can only work when the solution to a problem is clear and universally applicable. It is only when clear objectives can be set and communicated that the level of sustained political capital necessary to back the scheme from the centre can be mobilized. The Government has largely taken to heart the criticisms of its early period of chaotic centralism (Corry and Stoker, 2002). It has promised to cut back on the number of initiatives and encouraged local authorities to set up local strategic partnerships to help to bring together and make sense of a mixed range of schemes in their area. It has committed to significantly reducing the number of plans and strategies it demands of local authorities. But was the period of chaotic centralism a blip or a standard feature of any drive to join up government?

New Labour's competing visions of effective multi-level governance

Some argue that joined-up government is inherently centralizing and as such bad news for the devolved units of government. The bad news argument is driven by the view that for New Labour joining up builds on an old Fabian commitment to state engineering in which an all-seeing centre seeks to impose a new integrating order on the various other agencies of government. In the words of Rod Rhodes (2000) it is about establishing 'a new central command operating code'. Joined-up government in this interpretation assumes that the centre can devise and impose tools that will foster integration and facilitate the achievement of the centre's objectives. From this perspective joining up would appear to be a centralizing plot and plainly bad news for local and subnational government.

Others argue that effective territorial organization is prioritized by the demands of joining up, as the functional or silo mode of organizing is downgraded; as such it is good news for local and regional government. Joining up gives a special place to organizations with a multifunctional structure rather than a single goal. Out goes the argument for organizations that focus like a laser on a single task and in come the arguments for organizations that can operate across several fields and knit together the different elements of a solution. Local government and other forms of devolved territorial government would appear in this light to be the big gainers from joining up.

Supporters of the bad news interpretation can point to some considerable evidence of centralizing tendencies in the way joining up has developed in Britain. Much of the formal practice of joining up is the product of a myriad range of centrally inspired, funded and monitored schemes, as we have suggested earlier in the chapter. Many of these schemes are devised to achieve centrally defined outcomes, although it has to be noted that many leave considerable discretion in the hands of local and regional players as to how the work is done and the precise focus of activities. Each of the joined-up partnerships has its own funding and accountability mechanisms that orient it towards the centre distorting, so it could be argued, the priorities of local and regional agencies as they go in search of the central money, much of which requires match funding to be provided by the local and regional bodies. In any case the management time and effort put into such schemes at the behest of the centrally inspired initiatives constitutes a significant opportunity cost for local and regional agencies.

The good news case does not deny some of the failings and foibles of the rolling out of joined-up government in the last few years. In a way the advocates of the good news case would see the limitations of centralized version of joining up as proof that their way, the path of decentralization, is likely to be more effective and will ultimately be seen to be so. The advocates of this line of argument make particular play of the capacity of local government to join things up at the local level and the capacity to do more if the centre would encourage or allow it. Nor do they see the issue as one of creeping centralization since many of the priorities of the centre that lead to calls for more joining up, such as child development, crime prevention, getting people back into employment, are indeed shared by local officials and politicians. Further there is evidence that, in contrast to central departments, local agencies and local authorities in particular are rather good at doing joining up. They have the commitment, skills and capacity to make joining up work and the main block on progress is the heavy hand of the centre.

Labour has offered a number of models aimed at identifying the role of local government as part of a wider system of multi-level governance. The visions are not without points of contact and there are elements of overlap. However, one model sees local government as a community leader, with a wide role in determining priorities and expresses the concerns of communities in partnership with other stakeholders. The second sees it as an institution with significant discretion but one where the key partnership is with central government, enabling it to deliver on its agenda. One model sees networked community governance as locally led. The other sees it as a subordinate partner to central leadership.

The networked community governance model

Local government's job is to facilitate the achievement of community objectives. Its role is to lead the debate, develop shared visions and help to ensure that appropriate resources – both public and private – are found and blended together to achieve common objectives. As a result the political processes necessary to local governance involve a subtle mixture of leadership capacity and opportunities for wider participation and involvement. Because they are elected then, councils are uniquely well placed to undertake a leadership role. In the words of the 2001 White Paper:

> Thriving communities and strong democratic leadership go hand in hand. Such leadership helps enhance the quality of life of individuals and communities, boost the local economy, improve the environment, and contribute to the achievement of wider regional and national policy goals. Councils are uniquely paced to provide that leadership. (DTLR, 2001: para. 2.1)

This vision of local governance sees that services can be commissioned or co-produced rather than directly provided by the state. It also gives prominence to a wider role of community leadership and citizenship. Local government is there to influence the major social and economic dimensions of its locality even if it is not directly responsible for a particular service provision or policy issue. It is there to be a community leader. It is there to steer the governance of a locality. As the 2001 White Paper comments, successful councils ' enable individuals, families and communities to find solutions to their own problems, provide resources and opportunities to help them to do so, and work with others to contribute to those solutions' (DTLR, 2001: para 2.7). The community leadership role requires local government's commitment to achieving outcomes, desired by local people, in co-operation with local stakeholders. Community leadership also involves recognizing that communities are interdependent. Local government has a key role in representing areas in wider regional and national matters. 'Someone needs to champion their communities' interest at these wider levels ... councils are best placed to do this' (DTLR, 2001: para. 2.9).

The constrained discretion model

Under the second scenario the future lies in the centre managing multi-level governance (cf. Pierre and Stoker, 2000). The view here is that although the task of governance has become more complex and the range of institutions involved more diverse there remains the need for a central core to provide direction and leadership. In this scenario the core is seen to reside around Westminster and Whitehall – among the political and managerial elites. Through regulation, manipulation and sheer organizational skill the aim is to ensure that the fragments both inside and outside government are brought together to achieve collective purposes. It is a matter of ensuring that all the institutions of multi-level governance are guided to perform in a manner commensurate with the ambitions and objectives of the central Westminster/ Whitehall elite. Central steering is the key and what is required at the local level is sufficient discretion for local service providers, including local authorities, to have the flexibility to shape central steering to local circumstances.

A Treasury adviser to Gordon Brown, Ed Balls, has described the approach as the 'constrained discretion model of policymaking'. It is not a matter of straightforward central control; rather it is a system with local discretion guided by central steering. For New Labour it is viewed as an innovation in management style. As Balls (2002) explains, just as with running parts of the economy through institutions such as the independent Bank of England New Labour has learnt that running public services through a command-and-control model does not work. The 'old approach to policy where goals were not specified, lines of responsibility unclear, power guarded jealously at the centre and proper performance information concealed from the public' is not appropriate 'for running a modern health service or delivering the best local public services' (Balls, 2002).

The Balls argument is not only against ad hoc, non-strategic government. It is also against a government that believes that a simple top-down model of command and control can work. It goes to the heart of a debate within New Labour and against a line of argument associated with Michael Barber. 'Barberism' holds that if you specify what you want, provide the tools to achieve it and measure performance, you will get the results you want. The literacy hour within schools is seen as an example of this approach. Yet the argument of Balls and others is that in the long run the approach will not work (PIU, 2001).

A changed world demands a changed management approach. As Ed Balls explains:

> As with macroeconomic policy, so effective public service delivery requires discretion for public service managers with the maximum devolution of power to encourage flexibility and creativity and meet consumer demands; but this discretion must be constrained by clear long-term goals and proper accountability. Today it is simply not possible either to run economic policy or deliver strong public services that meet public expectations using top-down one-size-fits all solutions of the past. Because new information technologies, greater competition, a premium on skills and innovation, a wide-ranging media, increasingly demanding consumers, and varying local needs all work to expose the contradictions of

old-style centralization and a command and control approach to delivering public services. (Balls, 2002)

Underlying the model of constrained discretion is a set of new principles to guide policy-makers. They are, in the words of Ed Balls:

- Clear long-term goals set by the elected government;
- A clear division of responsibility and accountability for achieving those goals with proper co-ordination at the centre;
- Maximum local flexibility and discretion to innovate, respond to local conditions and meet differing consumer demands;
- And, alongside this devolution of power, maximum transparency about both goals and progress in achieving them with proper scrutiny and accountability.

The model offers a decentralized image of management but a centralized image of politics. The key accountability is seen to rest at the centre with ministers. An overhead view of democracy remains in place. This can create difficulties as Ed Balls notes:

> there is sometimes a tension between the desire to devolve flexibility and encourage local innovation with the fact that, often, it is ministers at the centre who remain accountable to parliament and the public for fiscal stability, tax, value for money and performance.

This model of joining up ultimately sees legitimacy resting with national government. Democracy is a tool for offering national accountability but not in the search for solutions itself. Local government's challenge is to use the flexibilities granted to it to deliver to the government's agenda. As the 2001 White Paper (DTLR, 2001: para 3.6) puts it:

> [C]entral government has not been clear enough about what it expects from councils. In future priorities will be more clearly identified ... Councils will make their most effective contribution if, alongside central government, they take responsibility for key national priorities and instigate corrective action when standards are not met.

Local government is a partner in the delivery of national programmes of service provision and societal change.

Multi-level governance: which way for New Labour?

New Labour, in a manner consistent with the argument presented in Chapter 4, appears to operate different codes in its approach to joining up with devolved governance. In the early years it was a rather simple-minded top-down, impatient demand that devolved units in local and regional governance join up in partnerships of a great variety and number. There has followed a commitment to a more enhanced community leadership role for local government and eventually in England for regional government as well. Running alongside this is the concept of earned autonomy or what a leading Treasury adviser has called constrained discretion; this suggests a different rhythm to multi-level governance of hands-off steering by the centre.

The crude model of top-down direction appears to have been dismissed at least in theory. A Performance and Innovation Unit report in 2001 comments that:

> The delivery of public services always depends on the actions of people and institutions that cannot be directly controlled by central government, departments and agencies. Although short-term results can be achieved through direction, in the long run it is more efficient to motivate and empower than to issue detailed commands. (PIU, 2001: 4)

The report goes on to note that the government is seeking to define a new balance in its operating code for multi-level governance.

But which model is most likely to become institutionalized of the two outlined in the previous section? Is it the community leadership model that implies a commitment to a plurality of local decision centres, where elected representatives, public officials and stakeholders from other sectors and the community combine to identify and pursue a local common purpose? Or is the future going to be dominated by the constrained discretion model, where the centre is the sole or prime focus of public accountability but in which local government, along with others, is given freedom to deliver on an agenda agreed with the centre? To put the issue more abstractly: is joining up about a new form of horizontal or vertical integration?

Both codes are new, neither is established. To address the question as to which is likely to become institutionalized it is helpful to use a framework derived from neo-Durkheimian scholars and presented in work in which the author was involved (Perri 6 *et al.*, 2002: ch. 10). To become institutionalized any paradigm in governance or management has to meet a stiff set of challenges. It has to have a certain legitimacy, to be seen to be appropriate in some way. It has to have a capacity to guide the career paths of those involved in affected organizations. It needs to have some 'name recognition', to become part of the commonplace of the world it is seeking to influence. It needs to be able to survive challenge and demonstrate a level of robustness. The post-war welfare state role for local authorities had the quality of being institutionalized. It was seen as a legitimate part of the post-war settlement. It developed and sustained a variety of administrative and professional careers. The welfare state, and the role of the town or county halls, in providing it became part of everyday language and understanding. It was able to survive and demonstrate a certain robustness. As noted earlier in Chapter 2, the destabilizing of this model in part explains the rise of governance.

There are six factors to consider in understanding the process of institutionalization of a governance or management paradigm (Perri 6 *et al.*, 2002: 219–33). The first is whether it is seen to be able to address a perceived challenge in the socio-economic environment. Does it present a viable solution to a set of problems perceived by policy-makers?

Second, it has to establish its own narrative of what needs to be done and what kinds of things can be achieved. 'Indeed, for many writers one of the tests of whether something is institutionalised is whether, on being asked a question, the representatives or advocates of an institution typically answer with general claims about the nature of the world, human life and motivation, fundamental values and where history is expected to take us (Perri 6 *et al.*, 2002: 220). The institutional form has to come to be seen as normal and natural. Institutionalization is present when there is evidence that the institution shapes the way people think through formal training and through informal understandings that guide what is perceived as important, how to make decisions and what is an acceptable risk.

Third, institutionalization requires not just the shaping of ideas but also the shaping of interests. To launch itself an institution needs to gain a group of users and supporters who identify with the institution. To sustain itself it needs to create sets of incentives, rewards and sanctions for those that engage with it. It needs to be able ultimately to shape roles and career paths. The appeal, when it comes to public service and governance, has to be more than about simple self-interest; there is a need for an ethical dimension. Institutions need to be able to convince their participants that there is a broader goal they are serving. People value themselves as other-regarding and want to work in an environment where a public service ethos is promoted (House of Commons, 2002c; Aldridge and Stoker, 2002). Institutions need an ethic.

Fourth, institutions need to create the standard trappings of organizational life. There need to be rules of decision-making and mechanisms for holding individuals to account. However, it is not the case that institutionalization requires all rules and roles to be set in concrete. '[I]nstitutionalised paradigms of public management need not micro-manage, but they must at least implicitly allocate specific powers to groups, roles, professions, political structures. Sometimes these powers may be explicit and written in legislation or judicial decisions, but more often the important institutional powers are implicit until such time as they are challenged' (Perri 6 *et al.*, 2002: 225). Indeed a certain ambiguity can help to sustain institutional life: uncertainty and scope for interpretation allow a variety of coalitions and interests to co-exist under the same umbrella. Alongside flexible rules for followers there need to be rules for leaders. A governance paradigm needs to be clear about the kind of leadership that it expects and where it expects to find it. In the post-war welfare state it was professional leadership that was most lionized. With the arrival of new public management in 1980s it was the top managers in the organization that were seen as key. The community leadership and constrained discretion models make other, indeed rather complex, leadership demands. Ultimately, of course, any paradigm of governance needs a formula to guide interorganizational relations.

Institutions need also to be able to shape emotions as they 'are intensely emotional things' (Perri 6 *et al.*, 2002: 229). Fear, loyalty, commitment and a sense of allies and enemies are all central to organizational life. Institutions shape experience and shape emotions. In terms of grid-group theory a more hierarchical organization fosters respect for superiors and fear of failure. And a more egalitarian organization encourages a team spirit and a sense of an exclusive bond between members. Institutions need to be able to select their friends and identify their enemies. They need to be able to identify rivals, to present threats and make claims of survival, resilience and robustness. Above everything else all institutional arrangements, as Hirschman (1970: ch. 7) recognized, require loyalty. Loyalty is often a key to effective management of organizational life alongside the capacity to threaten exit and express dissatisfaction. Loyalty reflected in 'a special attachment to an organisation' (Hirschman, 1970: 77) gives time and space for voice to work and helps to prevent a too easy and destructive use of exit. People need to become attached to an organization and institutional forms; that formulation of commitment 'comprises a whole cluster – indeed, a highly organised cluster – of emotional processes' (Perri 6 *et al.*, 2002: 231).

Finally, institutions need rituals. '[I]nstitutionalisation cannot be achieved without some form of visible, tangible and bodily performance, which conveys the meanings and commitments of the institutions, both of those who are already in return committed to it, and to others more sceptical or hostile'

representatives constitute a ritual that expresses both a commitment to hierarchy and formal democratic accountability. 'Underlying different protocols and practices may be different sets of values' as Sullivan and Skelcher (2002: 110) note. These in turn may create tensions in developing partnerships, as for example those from a voluntary sector tradition or business world struggle to come to terms with those from a state bureaucratic or party political decision-making framework.

Table 8.3 illustrates an application of the framework for analyzing the processes of institutionalization applied to the two models of multi-level governance community leadership and constrained discretion outlined earlier in the chapter. Not surprisingly neither model is close to meeting all of the conditions given their relative newness. Both score highly in terms of their perceived capacity to address an identifiable problem and both offer coherent, if not entirely comprehensive or consistent, narratives of how the world should work. Both have some key interests and supporters aligned behind them. The prospects for the future are going to rest on progress that the two models make on the last three of the institutionalization attributes. The community leadership model in terms of core organizational trappings has made some progress as best practice has been built on, the constrained autonomy model has much less experience on which to draw. In terms of emotional attachment and ritual expression both paradigms are underdeveloped.

Conclusions

The challenges presented by governance are complex and what this chapter shows is that New Labour was initially willing to embrace governance but unwilling to embrace its complexity. Yet a substantial innovation in institutions and agencies has occurred with the creation of a whole new tier of devolved government stretching from the Parliament in Scotland to advanced proposals for regional government in England. Some adjustments to the world of local and regional quangos have been made and a whole raft of new partnerships arrangements have been established. What was initially absent was any new thinking about how to manage the world of multi-level governance and instead New Labour relied on an over-centralized set of mechanisms for stimulating joined-up governance. The result has been that a considerable amount of resources are consumed in constructing relationships without a clear sense of direction and purpose to guide those involved in the system.

However, this chapter argues that a joined-up agenda is not necessarily a centralizing one and that, moreover, there are signs that New Labour is rethinking its approach and searching for a new operating code to manage multi-level governance. Two possible models are seen to be in play: a model that gives prominence to community leadership through elected local and regional government working alongside various stakeholders and a model where the key accountability rests with the centre but in which considerable discretion is given to other agencies and organizations to deliver to an agenda agreed with the centre. Neither model is fully institutionalized. Yet the key point is that New Labour has started the search for an effective system of multi-level governance.

9 Local Finance: Coming to Terms with Governance?

As noted in Chapter 3 New Labour's approach to local finance for much of its first and second terms has been cautious and pragmatic. In part this approach reflects the sheer scale of the damage done to the system of local government finance by the Conservatives, as described in Chapter 2, but it also reflects the fact that the debate about what to do over local finance has got stuck, so that the same arguments are raked over again and again. In its first two terms New Labour has attempted to ameliorate rather than directly confront the legacy of the Conservatives. It has given local authorities more money to spend but, whereas the commitment to governance has led to rethinking and reforms on the ground with respect to partnership, service delivery and politics, when it came to the issue of finance, radical options have not been on the agenda for New Labour. However, with the launch of the Balance of Funding Review in April 2003 and a range of measures proposed by the Government as part of the post-2001 White Paper policy development there will be an opportunity to provide some significant moves forward. The argument of this chapter explores how to develop a local finance system that takes into account the arrival of a system of local governance and a changed political world. Its tone is rather different from Chapters 5–8, in that the focus is much more on what might be done by New Labour.

The chapter develops arguments in Stoker and Travers (2001) and Stoker (2001) and begins by outlining how the circumstances of governance, public and elite opinion and past policy will need to be taken into account in any long-term reconstruction of local finance. A second section argues that we need to move beyond the parameters of the established debate and sets out some of the core qualities that might be expected from a local finance system. A third section outlines two broad directions in which local finance policy might go. One emphasizes the commitment to universal service provision in key public policy areas and moves to a more transparent recognition of responsibilities of central government and a limited scope for local choice. A second localist approach tries to build on the idea of networked community governance more fully. It aims to limit but recognize national responsibilities and expand the scope for local choice. A fourth section examines the strengths and weaknesses of the two ways forward against the criteria for a system of local finance outlined earlier. A concluding section explores the prospects for a universalist or localist solution winning through in New Labour's policy choices over local finance.

Governance and local finance

As noted earlier we have moved from an era of traditional local government to the wider sphere of 'governance'. The challenge imposed by this role is one that suggests the need to rethink the requirements of an effective local finance system. Local authorities in this new world operate in the context of a mixed economy of providers with a key role in commissioning services and regulating their quality. The issue is no longer simply whether a local council can generate the resources to deliver a service from council tax, charges or centrally allocated funding, although all these issues remain important. The local authority as the commissioner may seek investment from the service provider in the service, in return for a long-term contract. It may have land or property assets that can be thrown into the equation in order to construct a relationship with a provider that can yield resources and investment for the area and a service. Getting things done is not a task that is always best done by a local authority on its own.

The world of governance is one where the capacity to join up the activities of different agencies is often the key. What is required is some element in the system of public finance that enables these agencies jointly to plan their budgets and to find ways of co-funding shared endeavours to meet the challenges faced by individuals and communities. Typically, the local council will be responsible for one quarter of public expenditure within its area: the remaining three-quarters will be under the control of other institutions. The debate about local finance needs to take into account these realities.

A further area in which a significant change of context can be observed is the growth in strength of a view among opinion leaders, and probably more generally the public, that certain services should be a matter of national standards and not local variation. Education is perhaps the most clear-cut example of where there has been a shift in thinking both among elites and the general public as compared with the 1960s and 70s. Education is now clearly defined as a national service delivering outcomes central to the nation's economic future. A 1999 British Social Attitudes Survey (Rao and Young, 1999: 51–3) found more than two-thirds of the public supported central government's right to decide school standards. Social services is another area where elite opinion has moved against what is referred to as the 'postcode lottery' of differential access to services depending on where you live. Public opinion is perhaps less clearly in support in this instance, although the judgement probably depends on the sort of decisions or services that are being questioned. The same 1999 survey found, for example, the public were split half-and-half in their judgement about whether the allocation of home helps should be a matter of local or central decision.

There is no great base of support in Britain for an exclusive local citizenship tied to people having paid local taxes. An ESRC survey in 1995 (Miller, Dickson and Stoker, 2000: 66–7) asked if people should be excluded from local voting on services if they had not been in tax paying residence for over two years and found very little support for the idea. People may have a sense of local identity, to some extent, but do not appear to have a strong sense of local citizenship. On the contrary, social citizenship – in terms of rights to universal education, health and other core services – is clearly seen as part of national citizenship and as such national responsibilities (see also Miller *et al.*, 1995: 154–5). The national tax system is seen as the instrument to fund those services that are to all citizens essential to their well-being and access to equality of opportunity. In designing a system of local finance the realities of people's perceptions of their citizenship need to be taken into account.

Any debate about local finance needs to take account of how the responsibility for what spending takes place, and how it is distributed has a multi-governance dimension. The European Union is a relatively modest contributor to local projects but its funding in those areas where it is available is eagerly sought after. National government (including the Scottish Parliament and Welsh Assembly) has the key role in ensuring that different areas of the country have the resources to provide the same level of services given their different needs and their different capacities to raise revenue. The Conservative governments from 1979, despite all their market-liberalism rhetoric, significantly increased the sophistication of local authority equalization grants. New Labour, under pressure from most stakeholders in the system, has also remained wedded to an extensive system of equalization. It has changed the details of the way that a grant is calculated and given the redistributive grant a new name – formula grant – but there can be no doubt that the finance system for local government in England still goes to great lengths to equalize fully taking into account the tax resources available to local authorities and the needs and levels of service demand they face. It may well be that the amount of centrally provided funding is greater than that necessary to achieve equalization to a reasonable degree but the commitment to some concept of fairness in the distribution of resources is deeply embedded in elite and public opinion debates about local finance. A final contextual issue, that was identified in Chapter 1, can be highlighted. There is a broad loss of trust in government and as a result there may be an enhanced need to persuade people that any increase in the tax burden is justified. It should not be assumed that any proposal to increase taxes will be met with an automatic refusal but the assumption might be that any increase will have to be negotiated and perhaps tied to a specific package of benefits (cf. Fabian Society, 2000). It was, perhaps, never given to government to tax in a popular manner but in the context of new governing conditions the demand to justify spending and achieve value for money appears to be increased.

Moving beyond the established debate: four criteria for a local finance system

Finance, like so many policy areas, is all about choice. The problem is that the choices on offer are often false, in part because they reflect outdated thinking at their heart. The Layfield Committee (1976) that reported a quarter of a century ago in 1976 has largely framed the debate over the finance of local government. Layfield argued then that central government had a vital choice to make. It expressed concern about the growth in central funding provided to local authorities; a level of funding where two-thirds of resources came from the centre undermined local accountability. National government had to choose between a continuing drift towards further centralization or a reaffirmation of local responsibility by providing local government with a more extensive and robust tax base. If the centre funds local government spending it will ultimately have to take responsibility for that spending and therefore extend centralization. The only other option is to create the conditions for local choice and local democracy by ensuring that local politicians have to raise the money to pay for their decisions about policy choices and service levels.

The debate, articulated by Layfield, about the proportion of local government revenue raised from local taxation has continued to dominate all discussion about the future of local government finance. In fact, in the years after Layfield reported in 1976, the proportion of local authority revenue expenditure financed from local taxation rose from about 34 per cent to

55 per cent by 1989/90. The grim convulsions that accompanied the introduction and removal of the poll tax cut this locally funded proportion back to 20 per cent. It had subsequently risen to around 25 per cent by 2001/2. It is impossible to discern any particular link between local autonomy and the changes in these percentages. It would certainly be bizarre to insist that local government was more autonomous in the late 1980s than in the mid-1970s simply because it raised more of its own income in the late 1980s.

The issue of whether or not it is necessary to increase the proportion of council income raised locally has become virtually theological. On the one hand, local government traditionalists assert that only an increase in this proportion will ensure real local accountability. On the other, governments of both parties have behaved as if they believe there is no such link between local taxation and political freedom. In truth, governments make decisions about the proportion of local authority income to be funded from local taxation on a number of grounds, including the constitutional needs of local government in Britain, national economic circumstances, the personal concerns of particular ministers, general taxation policy and electoral advantage. Those who believe that the constitutional position of local government is the key, overriding concern delude themselves.

Moreover, there are overseas examples of countries that have more settled and visibly autonomous systems of local government – almost all of which enjoy higher local election turnouts – with (in some cases) higher and (in others) lower proportions of revenue income raised from local taxation. Thus, for example, all the Nordic countries have local income taxes and considerable degrees of local government autonomy. But the Netherlands and Italy have very low proportions of locally raised income as the basis for their healthy local democracies. International evidence suggests that national political expectations and traditions are the key to an acceptable balance between central and local government funding.

For New Labour the options for a radical policy over local finance were limited. The political climate could hardly have been less favourable. Local government – with its sustained low profile and poor electoral turnouts – seems a highly unlikely prime candidate for a major new tax-raising power such as the local income tax favoured by Layfield. The debacle following the introduction of the poll tax in 1989/90 (which, it is worth noting, did create a high-profile but deeply unpopular new form of local tax) suggests that it would be a major political decision for any government to consider a substantial increase in the burden of local tax (or, for that matter, a significant shift in local tax burdens). Moreover, the claim to have the business rate returned to local government following its removal in 1990 (as part of the poll tax changes) is not consistent with Layfield since the burden of the tax falls on businesses not residents, so local accountability to voters is not enhanced. In short, New Labour, like previous national governments, has not been prepared to choose the option favoured by Layfield and local accountability supporters have not come up with any way of enhancing local revenue-raising capacity that is politically feasible.

One of the most frustrating things about much of the post-Layfield debate is the way it has focused attention on only one aspect of a local finance issue: that of accountability. In designing a local government finance system there are at least four dimensions that need to be considered.

A key aspect of any finance system is the one Layfield focused on, namely the need for transparency in connecting spending decisions, tax-raising and voters' choices. But the issue is more complex than some of the post-Layfield debate has allowed. Layfield's (1976) basic argument was that accountability requires that those responsible for spending money should also be responsible for raising it. The argument followed that if local authorities were to exercise discretion over the way they carried out their functions and were to determine the level and pattern of expenditure on them, they should also be responsible for finding any money through local taxes for which they are accountable (LGA, 2003). This form of accountability has been called average accountability and it requires that those who pay should control what is done with it, and vice versa (Watt and Fender, 1999). A popular form of the argument is 'that he who pays the piper calls the tune'. So the Layfield line of argument leans towards the conclusion that if local councils rely on their services to be funded from the centre those services will ultimately be under the control of central government.

However, there are other ways in which transparency issues can be addressed. A key alternative requires a focus on local discretion over marginal shifts in spending (Stoker, 2001). From this perspective receiving funding for services, especially if there are relatively few strings attached, does not undermine accountability as long as there is some scope for discretion in the system. Marginal accountability requires that those who pay for *increases* in expenditure control what is done with it (Watt and Fender, 1999). Financial discretion at the margins is the key. Accountability requires clarity over any provision of central grants or monies and freedom to vary spending and taxes at the margins. Local councils need to be more than managers of others' monies in order to strike political deals with their own communities. Local authorities need to be in a position to top up spending and intervene in the realm of education and social services. To be an effective partner often requires the bringing of funds to the table. To be a community leader means at times being able to underwrite the activities of community and voluntary organizations. Public perception of the transparency and accountability of tax-and-spend decisions is important but in terms of budget-making it is at the margins where the real public interest exists and potential for engagement rests. Marginal accountability can deliver transparency without the sharp division in funding responsibilities demanded by average accountability.

Given the scale and complexity of modern financial arrangements and associated packages of service delivery the conditions for average accountability are not easy to achieve in a pure sense. There are good reasons why local and central government share responsibility for many functions. Is transport a local or a national function? When is a road local or national, or does it depend on who is driving on it at any time? Is there an unchallengeable case for primary education, so vital to achieving equal opportunity in life, to be a local function and for higher education – a key element in local and regional economic development – to be designated as a national function alone? Moreover, the world of public spending has a certain 'messy' quality. If local authorities raised the taxes for all education costs in their areas then the formal requirements for average accountability would be met. But then if the costs of employing teachers went up because of national insurance payments set by central government, for example, there would still be a row between local and central government as to who was responsible for the hike in local taxes that might follow. The full requirements of average accountability would seem hard to secure and as a result those that follow this line of reasoning tend to pluck arbitrary figures out of the air and argue, for example, that local authorities would be accountable if they raised half the money they were responsible for spending. But why half, why is that a magic tip-over point?

Advocates of marginal accountability also have problems in constructing conditions for that form of accountability to work in practice. The key difficulty is in holding all other things steady so that marginal shifts in tax can be related to marginal shifts in spending. If grant levels go up or down, or if some cost base is reduced or increased in some arbitrary way then it is difficult to be sure that voters will be in a position to see with complete clarity what they are getting for any marginal increase or decrease in local taxes.

The lionization of transparency by the post-Layfield debate does seem to belie some of the complexities surrounding the local finance debate. Finally, just to muddy the transparency case further, there is much survey evidence that indicates that the majority of people have very little idea about the way that local government is financed or for that matter exactly what government level is responsible for which service. As a review of the evidence concludes:

> There is little evidence one way or the other on the relationship between the balance of funding in support of local government and democratic engagement. While public knowledge of the reality of local government finance (including the balance of funding and the balance of control) remains poor and patchy it is difficult to establish clear causal links with political behaviour. (Kleinman *et al.*, 2002: 69)

In the light of the current state of public understanding of the local finance system it would appear that full transparency may be a laudable but somewhat utopian goal. This is not to argue that understanding could not be improved (Spencer *et al.*, 2000) or that consultation over budgets is undesirable (Stoker *et al.*, 2003).

Crucially, in judging a local finance system there are issues other than transparency to consider. A second issue rests around a concern with justice in the distribution of resources. The question of equalization, as it has become known, is about recognizing that a system of local government finance needs a capacity to give additional resources to areas of high need or with a low taxable base. Layfield's commitment to local accountability surely implies a willingness to accept a considerable unevenness in both service provision and local tax burden in different areas. If you advocate local accountability you are to a degree also advocating greater territorial inequality in distribution of public services and taxes. There can be little doubt that the Layfield Report recognized this choice but all too often in subsequent years people have made ritual calls for more local accountability, followed by a demand for the nth degree of fairness in the distribution of national funds. It may well be that to achieve an acceptable degree of equalization of resources available in relation to need does not require the full-scale complexities or levels of the current grant system but any finance system is likely to have built into it some mechanism for distributing funds in a manner that is seen as fair and in a way that compensates poorer areas.

A third feature that designers often look for in a local finance system is a certain flexibility and buoyancy in the capacity to raise revenue. The art of government, so the argument goes, requires a mix of revenue-raising powers in part to cope with contingencies and in particular shortfalls in some revenue streams. Another factor is that a mix of different taxes enables pubic perceptions of the tax burden to be manipulated in order to achieve what Adam Smith referred to as 'easy taxes', which do not hurt the payer too much because the burden is in some way disguised or is felt indirectly. Expressed in this manner the case for flexibility is an argument that dare not be heard for fear of accusations of supporting 'stealth' taxes. Yet the argument can be expressed more positively, namely, that a degree of buoyancy and flexibility in respect of taxation gives government the capacity to deliver in the context of a modern democracy. In this sense, greater freedom in local taxation might better deliver what voters really want. In helping to ensure service delivery a flexible tax system supports the development of a level of trust in government and enables government to act with greater effectiveness in meeting people's concerns. Local government is not well served against this criterion at the moment. Council tax, although a relatively easy-to-collect and stable yielding tax, is not very buoyant because the number of households expands only relatively slowly. More generally, local government is hamstrung by its heavy reliance on that one tax.

A fourth desirable aspect of a modern system of public finance is that it facilitates a holistic approach to funding to ensure consistency in the activities of the diverse sets of agencies that in a complex world form part of the governance system. At present, it proves incredibly difficult to get public bodies to work jointly in the provision of, say, the criminal justice system or services for old people. Until and unless local authorities and other institutions are given incentives to fund services jointly, there is virtually no chance of achieving consistent and seamless provision.

Transparent accountability, an equitable distribution of resources, sufficient flexibility and some capacity for consistent budgeting to enable government to act effectively are all desirable features of a system of local government finance. There are, of course, tensions between the various valued features. The balance between them will be very different in Britain to what is desirable in another country (for example, equity appears to be particularly prized in this country). Not all are entirely consistent with one another. There are trade-offs, as has already been argued, between local accountability and a concern with territorial equity. In a similar manner there is a potential trade-off between absolute transparency and the flexibility needed by government decision-makers. To insist that every tax is so painfully obvious that it hurts to even think about it let alone pay it is not a recipe for effective governance.

Designing a local finance system involves judgements about how to balance out the various desirable design elements. Political realism needs to combine with principle. Layfield so emphasized one virtue – transparency – that it undermined the potential for a settlement that could give due recognition to other desirable design features – much demanded in modern

Britain – such as equity or flexibility. If we add in the requirement that the system delivers the framework for joined-up government or effective partnership it becomes clearer still that a complex challenge confronts us.

Choices over local finance facing New Labour

As Chapter 3 makes clear, a decisive choice of a new direction in respect of local finance has not been made by New Labour, but rather it has muddled through on the back of largely pre-existing systems and arrangements. The name of the grant distribution system may have been changed but the fundamentals of central funding have largely remained in place. Some new revenue sources for local authorities have been identified but there is no overarching new system established to derail council tax as the main and dominant source of local finance. Some moves to 'passport' education spending direct to schools and other services has been made but the centre has not moved finally to take over funding of at least primary and secondary education. However, a decision point may soon be reached and a decisive jump in one direction or the other may need to be made. But the choice facing New Labour cannot best be understood as a contest between centralization and local accountability. Rather it is possible to identify what might be called new universalist and new localist perspectives.

Moving to new universalism

Local authorities in the new universalist scenario become franchisees, authorized to produce a service subject to the achievement of certain standards. The concern would not be about detailed control over the local organizations but rather how best the centre can create the incentives and controls to ensure that the outcomes it wants are delivered. The new universalism is therefore not demanding direct control over spending but rather the delivery of outcomes that achieve social and economic opportunity for all. The concern is at least as much with social opportunity or justice as with spending or fiscal constraint. The rationale for the system is provided by a commitment to achieving equal access to key services at a guaranteed quality throughout the country.

As a model it could be designed to fit in with the constrained discretion approach to multi-level governance outlined in Chapter 8. This perspective would recognize the reality that both elite commentators and the public have come to expect many local government services to be universally provided, though with no substantial concern about which particular institution provides them. Demands for territorial equity (i.e., similar treatment for people living in different places) and universality are immensely strong within Britain. A system which fully reflected the reality of public and elite expectations would probably require central government to guarantee levels of public expenditure and the outputs achieved by such spending, at least in a number of so-called core 'welfare' services. Such provision would definitely include education and personal social services. On the basis of modern political expectations, the police – not a welfare service in the normal use of the term – could also be included in this list. It would be up to the government to decide if any other services were of such overriding universal importance that they, too, should be included among those to be provided in this way. Accountability at the political level to citizens would rest with central government largely on its own.

The finance system underpinning such a system would, to be consistent, have to make Whitehall explicitly responsible for the amount spent on every individual institution. In a system of this kind, the government would probably have to contract with each local authority about the amount of money that would be paid for the delivery of a specified level of service. There would be no need for an equalization formula to allocate resources since each department of state would negotiate with individual local authorities about the sum that would be paid, per annum, for a particular service. There would be 100 per cent central funding for the services concerned, though it would be necessary to adjust grant and council tax levels accordingly. If an authority failed to deliver, the service would be taken away from it and provided by another agency or company.

It would no longer be possible for central and local government to pass the buck between each other as to who is responsible for a particular level of spending or service failure. If education provision did not operate effectively within a particular area, the relevant central government department would be held fully responsible. Any school which did not deliver would be seen as the Secretary of State's personal (or, at least, departmental) failure. A centrally determined system of this kind would put immense pressure on central departments responsible for education, personal social services and the police. To run a system of this kind, civil servants would have to advise ministers about the detail of these services in every city, town and village in England. This need to provide detailed, legally robust, advice would be an immense new burden on central government. Because there was a contract between the government and a local provider (who might or might not be a local authority), there would inevitably be a risk of litigation if contracts were believed to have been broken. But, crucially, the public would be absolutely certain where the responsibility for the universal service standards lay. Those services not tied up in universalist arrangements would be designated unambiguously local services. In many authorities they would be funded entirely out of local sources, with some form of central grant to support those councils that cannot raise sufficient funds to underpin funding for these functions. They might include, for example, waste collection, environmental protection, street scene and load roads, leisure facilities and a range of other functions. It would appear likely that in all councils these services could relatively easily be funded by keeping local council taxes at or indeed below the levels they are now, as long as some modest central funding was available for those unable to raise enough funds themselves. There would certainly be no need for additional tax-raising powers for local authorities.

A new localist solution?

There is another route open which is more compatible with allowing extended local choice in the delivery of networked local governance. The new localist solution would separate out local 'welfare' state services such as education and social services (as discussed above) and fund them using a grant system similar to that currently in operation, that is there would be a near full equalization of the resources available to local providers based on their tax-raising capacity and their level of need. However, in this localist option, authorities would then be free to top up central funding for such provision or to reduce it below the government norm. It would be entirely clear how much expenditure the national government felt was needed, and how much each authority was then prepared either to add or take away from that figure. A similar approach would be adopted for social services, police and any other 'universal' services.

In a pure version of the new localist solution, for all other services there would be no grant support at all. Authorities would finance them out of local council tax and also other sources with no equalization of any kind. This would mean that the fire brigade, environmental provision, local roads, planning, street lighting, arts and leisure and all other services would be financed from a local tax or a range of other taxes (and, in some cases, fees and charges). There might also be scope for local authorities to earn income to underwrite service provision from trading activities. Top-up spending for education, social services and the police would also be funded in this way. Authorities with larger local tax bases, charging options and earning capacity would be able to fund their services more easily than those with smaller ones. In this model, local government could be given access to new local taxes and charges as part of the localist deal. Indeed there are already a number of moves in the direction of providing additional sources of funding. The Transport Act 2000 gave local authorities the power to introduce road user (congestion) charges and workplace parking levies. A Government amendment to the 2002/3 Local Government Bill proposes to give local authorities a right to benefit from any increase in local business rate that is a result of their planning and regeneration activities under the name of the 'growth incentives' scheme. The Bill already allows local councils to raise additional council tax from second homes in their area, introduces a series of additional charges for dog fouling and other matters and allows higher performing councils to develop trading activities. The yield of these taxes would then be available to fund local services and also to add extra amounts to the Government's funding of education and other 'social' services.

The addition of new income sources could give local government – overall – greater flexibility to determine local service provision (including additional provision, potentially, for 'welfare' services). It would be essential for new taxes to be transparent and widely understood. The public would then be able to decide whether additional (or reduced) local tax were a price worth paying (or not) for services. It is important to note that this pure localist solution would produce very significant differences in the taxable capacity per head from authority to authority. Some councils (notably central London boroughs) would be able to support relatively high levels of expenditure with relatively low local tax rates. Others (particularly older towns and cities in the North of England) would find themselves in the reverse position (lower spending and/or high tax rates).

The need to create incentives for joint activity, possibly led by local authorities, is another goal for an improved system of local government finance – indeed it could be a key element of a new localist approach to funding local services. Local government could be given a lead role in proposing spending programmes within their area, which brought together the budgets of the council with one or more other agencies. For example, a council could publish proposals for a joint spending initiative that involved improved services for the management of juvenile delinquency. Such a local spending partnership could, subject to light oversight by national or regional civil servants, be made binding on the public bodies concerned.

This kind of public expenditure co-ordination would represent an enormous step forward in the achievement of consistent and effective government.

Strengths and weaknesses of the options

Unlike the choices laid down by Layfield, the new universalism and localist perspectives are not mutually exclusive, as our discussion so far suggests. Both are more attuned to the complexities demanded of any local finance system in Britain/England and give appropriate respect not only to accountability but also to the virtues of equity and effectiveness. It may be that different mixes of the two options might be suitable for different services or even different local authorities. In short, the two perspectives may provide the starting point for a new consensus on finance that breaks through the current stalemate.

However, there would be strengths and weaknesses in both the new centralist and new localist approaches. Table 9.1 summarizes these strengths and weaknesses as compared to the four criteria for a system of finance set out at the start of this chapter. Thus, for example, the new universalist approach scores highly in terms of 'transparency'. It would be clear how far central government was prepared to control and/or fund a number of universal or national services, while local government would be held to account for all the rest. It would be easier to show how far central and, separately, local government were respectively responsible for the funding and regulation of two sets of services. The new localist option would not be quite as sharp in its designation of national and local services but as long as top-ups/downs were clearly designated and explained to voters, and if new taxes were introduced with clarity, then transparency would be enhanced in comparison with the current system.

'Equity' would be more likely to be achieved by the new universalist model, as it rests on providing 100 per cent national funding for welfare-type services, with the option of some top-up central funding for local services in

Table 9.1 *A comparison of the strengths of new approaches to local finance*

	Transparency	Equity	Flexibility	Holistic
New universalist	High	High	Low	Low
New localist	Medium	Low	High	High

areas with a very low local tax base. The new localist option, by contrast, would reduce equity, as it is currently understood: the quality of services provided in different areas would vary more.

'Flexibility' would be no worse than at present under the new universalist model. Arguably, an arrangement where council tax funded a large proportion of remaining wholly local services would give councils greater freedom than at present (the 'gearing' ratio between spending changes and tax changes would be made far more favourable for local authorities). Under the new localist model, flexibility would almost certainly be greatly enhanced by the introduction of new local taxes. Local authorities would be put in a position analogous to that found in many countries overseas (e.g., France, the United States) where councils have access to more than a single, highly visible, tax.

Finally, how would the two options fare in terms of 'holistic' or consistent public service provision? Arguably the new centralist model would score badly in its propensity to deliver holistic local services. Because central departments would contract directly with local authorities or other local providers for the supply of services, the notorious functional-orientation of Whitehall would be entrenched for ever in services such as education, social services and the police. Local government would, of course, still be free to ensure consistency in the remaining locally controlled services. The new localist model would be rather more effective in terms of holistic governance, because authorities would still be free to determine local spending levels on all services. There would also be an incentive for joint service provision, involving not just local government but also other public providers.

Both the proposed options would be likely to require changes to the capital finance system. For example, any system which transferred the responsibility for funding services such as education and social services to Whitehall would also, for consistency's sake, need central determination of capital spending in each authority, or institution. Indeed, it might also be necessary to finance all such capital using grants, rather than relying on authorities to fund debt. For locally provided and funded services, it would be consistent to move to a far more liberal control regime, possibly relating control to a prudential ratio of outstanding debt to taxable capacity or annual expenditure.

Conclusions

There is at the heart of local finance a debate between those who argue that what is crucial is the overall proportion of expenditure financed locally and those who argue that the crucial issue is how any extra local spending is financed locally under democratic control (average versus marginal accountability). One of the main arguments of this chapter is that the autonomy or otherwise of local government is not something that can be simply read off from knowledge about the level of revenues that it raises itself. One issue is the extent of local control over the way in which money is spent. The Scottish Parliament for its first four years has raised no income itself but it is not an institution without autonomy because it has almost complete discretion over how its allocation of monies is spent.

New Labour faces a difficult choice over local finance. This chapter identifies universalist or localist options. What is the most likely way forward? The commitment in both elite and public opinion to equal access to core services (education, social services, police) demands a level of equalization that requires substantial non-local funding of services. But a total universalism in which the same services are provided everywhere at the same cost is neither achievable nor desirable, so some marginal discretion will be part of any future system. If these arguments are right the only politically acceptable option is likely to be one that focuses on marginal accountability. But how much local discretion remains the key issue. Should education and other services be reserved for universalist treatment and national funding? Or should, as the localist model argues, local choice be exercised across the board with the centre using national funding simply to guarantee the core funding of key welfare services?

New Labour would reject the option of total universalism but it might still be tempted by the option of funding all education spending directly itself. The choice goes to the heart of wider competing hierarchical and communitarian perspectives buried with New Labour's thinking, as suggested in Chapter 4. The new localist option could have considerable attractions and could be developed over time, creating a wider degree of local discretion and thereby expanding the scope for marginal accountability over time.

To signal a shift to a greater degree of local discretion and accountability there is an argument for giving local councils one large and substantial new tax. The Fabian Report *Paying for Progress* (2000) argues that the nub of the problem of local finance is not the percentage of total revenue raised locally but rather the ability of local councils to vary their budgets at the margins. The Fabians argue for a mechanism to allow for local variation of income tax. There may be merit in the Fabian proposal but it would take time to establish, and by their own calculations, would have considerable set-up costs. One big new tax for local government is one way forward to consider. Another option is not one new major tax but a variety of small-scale taxes, charging and fund-collecting opportunities to support a modified and fairer council tax system. The fairness of that system could be enhanced, for example, by allowing greater differentiation between council bands and the amounts levied in each band. The British system of local finance suffers from an over-reliance on just one main source of own source income and a rather ad hoc and incoherent set of charging options. As we have seen in this chapter and in Chapter 3, there are a variety of relatively small-scale measures that together could enable local discretion to be considerably expanded.

For either a top-up local tax option or the mixed bag of marginal taxes to work effectively it will be essential to ensure as much predictability as possible over resources allocated to local authorities from the centre. Local decisions should reflect local choices rather than an attempt to cope with the vagaries of year-on-year central resource allocation. Some degree of predictability over central resource allocation (including an effective system of floors and ceilings) is essential to the working of all of the marginal tax/spend discretions outlined in this paper. Yet no public body should demand or expect total predictability in its budget-setting. The new politics of marginal accountability will require a willingness to take responsibility and initiative by local councils and greater trust from the centre in the capacity of local councils to be a focus for accountability. In short, for a new system of finance to work will require not only new arrangements but a willingness on the part of local and national actors to make them work.

10   The Challenge of Governance

This chapter reflects on both the challenge of developing governance arrangements at the local level and the dilemmas of the emerging networked community governance model as a mode of governing. The chapter is divided into three sections. The first looks at various environmental constraints on modern governance: the realities of multi-level decision-making, a decline in public trust of political institutions and dysfunctional institutional legacies. The second examines several difficulties associated with the process of transition in modern governance, difficulties connected to the learning of new skills, roles and orientations by public service managers and politicians and more broadly by systems of government. It raises the issue that governments need to learn to cope with failure in their governance strategies and develop a capacity to mix approaches. The third set of challenges revolves around structural contradictions inherent to governance: the dilemmas of state-sponsored network steering and network accountability and the issue of equality of access to decision-making in governance. Whether the focus is on the state-steering or the self-organizing capacity of networks, the processes of governance raise some difficult constitutional issues and challenges in relation to the nature of the democracy it can provide.

Making history in challenging circumstances

The rise of governance, as was argued in Chapter 1, is a reflection of wider changes in society. Environmental factors not only provide a stimulus to governance but help to define the challenges involved in its practice. Three are given particular attention below: the interpenetration of institutions that characterizes an era of multi-level governance, the decline in public trust that seems to have accompanied the emergence of a changing governance environment and the continuing presence of flawed institutional legacies which limited and constrained the capacity of the governing system to respond to new demands.

The interpenetration of multi-level governance

For Rhodes (1997a) governance is predominantly the product of the hollowing-out of the state from above by emerging international interdependencies and from below through administrative and political decentralization. We have as a result entered an era of multi-level governance. A base-line definition of multi-level governance is that it refers to negotiated exchanges between systems of governance at different institutional levels (see Pierre and Stoker, 2000). Multi-level governance emerges as a co-ordinating instrument in institutional systems where hierarchical command and control mechanisms have been relaxed or abolished. It draws on bargaining rather than submission and can, for example in the provision of services, draw on public–private mobilization rather than public sector specificity. As Peters and Pierre (2001: 3) comment, 'multi-level governance is assumed to differ from traditional intergovernmental relationships in three respects: it is focused on systems of governance involving transnational, national and subnational institutions and actors; it highlights negotiations and networks, not constitutions and other legal frameworks, as the defining feature of institutional relationships; and it makes no prejudgements about a logical order between different institutional tiers'.

It is worth emphasizing here that the claim of this book is that we are seeing an increased influence for the forces of multi-level governance but it is not that the capacity of the nation state has been entirely hollowed out, that central–local relationships are unimportant or that legal or constitutional frameworks do not have an effect. Indeed, part of the complexity of governance in the last two decades or more rests on a mixing of governing styles reflected the half-finished and by no means inevitable nature of the transition to different governing rhythms. Crudely put, those who argue we are not in an era of governance without government are correct (for a review and development of this argument see J. Davies, 2001: ch. 8).

The challenge of multi-level governance is not simply that politics operates at different spatial levels: the neighbourhood, local, regional, national and international, although that in itself is a significant task. The key difficulty arises from the interpenetration of all the levels. To achieve many goals, certainly the more demanding ones, it is necessary to act at a number of levels. To tackle an environmental issue such as traffic pollution in cities may require national legislation, local powers to enforce congestion management schemes, neighbourhood-based commuter car-sharing schemes and European action on the control of emissions from cars. Multi-level governance is a world of institutional interdependencies.

Modern governing faces an extremely demanding set of power dependencies (Rhodes, 1997a). Power dependence implies that: (a) organizations committed to collective action are dependent on other organizations; (b) in order to achieve goals organizations have to exchange resources and negotiate common purposes; and (c) the outcome of exchange is determined not only by the resources of the participants but also by the rules of the game and the context of the exchange.

The nation state needs to be able to operate at an international level and at the same time encourage action it favours at the regional, local or neighbourhood level. In all of these settings it cannot command although, especially within its boundaries, it may be able to dominate the exchange. However, even in these settings the costs of seeking to impose control may be felt in considerable unintended consequences, or by a failure to achieve control except in a narrow range of issues (Rhodes, 1997a). Looking at the issue from another perspective it is increasingly meaningless to argue for independent local government. To tackle the social and economic challenges confronting its area a local authority needs not only to reach down to neighbourhoods and communities and across the voluntary and private sector partners but to place itself in the context of a complex of regional, national and international connections. Local government can offer itself as a valuable partner, even community leader, but it cannot command independence.

Power dependencies, and the opportunistic behaviour they allow, add to complexity and encourage uncertainty of outcome. Different agencies and actors depend on one another but none can establish the conditions for perfect oversight, let alone control, over the actions of the other. Looking up and down hierarchies, the best that can be hoped for on most occasions is influence. As a result governance, more than ever before, means recognizing that when it comes to collective action, intentions are not always matched in outcomes.

An illustration from the area of Children's Services can be used to illuminate the issues (Emmerich and Stoker, 2002). In principle the aims of service for children should be to: identify a child in need of support and to remove an immediate risk or to deal with an emerging problem; ensure that appropriate services are provided; and monitor the child to ensure that the problems are resolved. However, an internal government review in 2002 found that there were insufficient resources (human if not financial) to provide support to children at risk. The threshold of need required to trigger intervention had increased and only children in immediate danger were tracked (and then not always well, as evidenced by the Victoria Climbié and other such cases). Services to other children were at best patchy and there is no systematic monitoring and tracking.

What explains why such a core service appears to be in such a mess? Some problems reflect issues of funding but many others are governance issues. Children's Services probably have been underfunded over a long period. Councils fund considerably above what is expected of them, yet there have been increasing costs and a sustained rise in the number of cases and range of problems suffered by children. The social work profession at the beginning of the twenty-first century appears to be in a crisis – with lagging morale and poor pay contributing to 30 per cent vacancy rates. The underlying problem is that no one is clearly in charge. Local authorities are at the centre of responsibilities but they have few of the service leads and limited ability to commission services. The NHS, through Child and Adolescent Mental Health and Family Services, has a key role but services for children have not been an NHS priority. Schools have a key role to play both in spotting emerging problems and ensuring continuing educational and other support for excluded children. Teachers have lost faith in the ability of anyone to provide the first and they have been slow to provide the second. The Criminal Justice System has preventive programmes which are at best loosely tied to these other arrangements.

The role of central government does not bring clarity or direction to the system. Each local organization runs to a different set of targets and output measures. There is no coherent picture of what a functioning system of preventive and ameliorative support for children and young people looks like. Even if there was, and despite the volume of inspection undertaken by the different agencies, there is no systematic assessment of what is and is not working. The combination of these different functional allocations creates perverse incentives and inefficient and inequitable outcomes including imbalance between preventive and ameliorative spend, proliferation of intervention, failure to identify emerging problems and to provide suitably escalating support to vulnerable children.

Not getting governance right, as the above case illustrates, can be costly. And getting governance right is a complex business that requires interventions at both the national and local level at a minimum. The result of governance failure means the kind of policy and organizational mess that appears to be present in the case of Children's Services in Britain at the start of the twenty-first century. Few would disagree that governance issues, in the context of the multiple agencies operating at different spatial scales, provide a considerable challenge.

That message of complexity may be one that policy-makers can swallow but it presents some difficulties in the relationship between elected politicians and the public in a democracy. 'Vote for me I can guarantee the delivery of very little because the system is very complex and levers of control don't work', provides a somewhat uncomfortable campaigning platform. Governance brings into focus the complexities of implementation that straightforward constitutional accounts of institutional relationships may overlook. The difficulties in ensuring effective implementation of policies are not new to the governance era but they have gained somewhat in their intractability.

Decline in public trust

It is important to be careful about making connections between changes in practice of governance and changes in the way the practice is perceived. However, there is evidence to support the idea that at least in some of the post-industrial democracies there has been a decline in public trust of government. This decline reflects both senses that government has become less effective (indeed at times part of the problem rather than the solution) and that politicians have lost the advantage of deference. In short, people have become more cynical and more challenging about politics and less convinced that it could achieve collective benefits.

The theme of public disenchantment with politics is certainly a dominant element in commentaries from both Right and Left. The Thatcher and Reagan eras in Britain and the United States respectively led the way from the Right, although many countries proved reluctant to follow. From the Left a strand of anti-state rhetoric can be detected from the 1960s onwards (see Mulgan, 1994), and recognition of the limits and incapacity of the state (as well as its continuing potential) is a core theme of the Third Way debate (see Giddens, 2000).

Fukuyama offers one convincing argument as to why trust in formal politics is in decline. Namely, that the same processes that have generated demand for governance have made achieving governance more challenging. He argues that industrial societies are giving way to globalized information societies. 'A society built around information tends to produce more of the two things people most value in a modern democracy: freedom and equality.' People as a result feel more empowered and more willing to think and do for themselves. In consequence, 'hierarchies of all sorts, whether political or corporate come under pressure and begin to crumble' (Fukuyama, 1999: 4). Information empowers individuals. It facilitates rapid self-organization. People are not only, it appears, more willing to engage in collective action but more capable of making it work effectively, whether through legitimate lobbying or more direct action. The decline in public trust in politics is connected, in turn, to an enhanced sense of the public's capacity to organize and challenge. A related direction of explanation can also be offered: namely that people's general trust in institutions and their environment has declined and politics as a result is operating in a more challenging environment.

Others place the causes of the loss of trust at the door of politicians and public officials (Kelly and Muers, 2002). There are a number of possible candidates to explain declining trust. First, it may be that the task of governance has become more complex and demanding. People as a result have less faith than in the past in the ability of governments to act effectively, at least on their own. People are not as convinced as they were in the 1950s, 60s and 70s that governments can make effective interventions against major social and economic problems. Declining trust might also reflect the way that politicians or officials behave. It may be that in the eyes of the public they have become less trustworthy and more prone to make decisions in their own private interests.

Bromley *et al.* (2001: 221) comment that survey evidence shows 'the decline in confidence in how we are governed that emerged during the last Conservative government has not been reversed during Labour's first term in office'. The evidence in respect to local government in Britain is also partially supportive of the argument that there has been a decline in trust (see Table 10.1). The time series data is not adequate to come to any strong conclusion but it appears that a substantial proportion of the population feel that councillors get quickly out of touch with the public and that councillors do not care about them. What is noteworthy, in particular, is the sense of decline in the efficacy of local politics. In 1998 only a half felt that local elections were a determining factor in local affairs compared to over three-quarters thirty years earlier. Of course we do not know why people appeared to have shifted their views on this issue. It may be that people judge that local government has lost legal and financial powers but it may be that people just have less faith in government in general to make a positive difference in their lives.

There is evidence that people trust the traditional representative decision-making process less than deliberative or direct democracy alternatives that give a stronger say to the public (DETR, 2000). Respondents were given two scenarios in surveys conducted in the late 1990s (Rao and Young, 1999; Bromley *et al.*, 2001: 214). The first involved a decision over a building development. The second required a judgement about a council tax increase

Table 10.1 *Trust in local government through time*

Statements in summary	% Agree/strongly agree in different time periods			
	1965	*1985*	*1994*	*1998*
Voting in local elections is the main thing that decides how things are run in this area	77	60	54	51
Local council elections are so complicated that I do not know which way to vote	29	34	30	32
No point in voting because it makes no difference who gets in	N/A	N/A	26	18
Councillors lose touch with people pretty quickly			47	55
Councillors don't care much what people like me think			36	40

Source: Figures and evidence taken from DETR (2001).

above the national average. Whereas roughly a third considered that councillors would come to the best decision on these issues, just over half felt that a citizens' jury (an experimental public participation technique) would provide a better judgement over the building decision. Moreover, close to two-thirds felt that a referendum would lead to the best decision over the council tax increase.

Other survey findings support the argument that there is public uncertainty about the political system at the local level but suggests that it is the system rather than the individuals within it that are seen as untrustworthy (Miller *et al.*, 2000: ch. 5). A study that was part of the ESRC local governance programme asked split parts of its sample to respond to differently slanted questions and therefore can reveal some of the subtleties of public opinion. It found that four out of ten people agree that councillors are just involved in local politics for their own benefit or just want people to look up to them. Equally it discovered around eight out of ten would agree that councillors have the good of the community at heart and a sense of duty towards their fellow citizens. A similar split emerges when it comes to the public's judgement about businessmen and others who serve on appointed bodies. All this suggests that individual councillors may well be given the benefit of the doubt.

What is clear is that the public are far less trusting of the system of local governance than the elites that run the system (see Table 10.2). Councillors

Table 10.2 *Trust and local governance*

Groups trusted to do the right thing on scale +/−5	By public	By councillors	By DHA/HB members	By businessmen on TEC/LECS
People elected to local councils	0.8	2.8	1.2	1.2
People appointed to DHA/HB boards	0.6	0.8	3.0	1.6
Businessmen appointed to TEC/LECs	0.4	0.6	1.4	2.6
Parliament and Government	−0.7	0.2	0.9	0.6

Source: Adapted from Miller *et al.* (2000) Table 7.25: 169.

and appointed members trust themselves to do the right thing for the area to a substantially greater degree than do the public, although, as Table 10.2 also shows, they are not necessarily as trusting of one another as they are of themselves. The public overall appear to have a barely better than neutral perspective when it comes to trusting the people who are elected to local councils or those chosen for appointed boards to do the right thing. Councillors it appears do trust themselves, giving themselves a nearly plus three rating out of five. Yet they are much less trusting of those appointed to health bodies or businessmen chosen to serve by the Government in the mid-1990s in local Training and Enterprise Councils (TECs) in England and Wales or Local Enterprise Councils (LECs) in Scotland. It can, at least, be noted that the public's trust rating for all local governance bodies was at least marginally positive; the same survey revealed a negative 0.7 rating for Parliament/Government, a reflection perhaps of the particular problems of the Conservatives in the period when the survey was undertaken (1994/5).

There can be little doubt that trust in the political system is modest, although how far it has declined is a more open question (see Mori, 2003). Traditional local councils and new governance arrangements through appointed bodies receive little in the way of positive endorsement. People are more sceptical in their attitudes towards governance leaders and in their assessment of their capacity to make a difference than the governors are themselves. A doubting public in respect of their governors is not an unprecedented historical event but it does create particular challenges for today's local governance.

The presence of flawed institutional legacies

Reforming governance arrangements inevitably involves change, yet the emerging forms of governing associated with that change have not been designed against the backcloth of a clean slate. Early forms of governing have left in place institutions with considerable residual capacity but whose continuing operation, along established lines, is proving a stumbling block for the new governance. As argued in Chapter 1, a key implication of describing a period as post-X is the recognition that the new forms that are emerging are in a sate of flux and may operate in the context of period X or even pre-X forms.

Three institutional forms deserve a mention in any account. First, the role of established central and local bureaucracies designed along functional lines, cut through with further divisions and differentiation, presents an obstacle that has to be overcome (Perri 6 *et al.*, 2002). Organizational divisions, that may have been effective once and still have some residual value, are not necessarily going to be easy to overcome in the search for new forms of governance. Institutional forms with strong roots cannot easily be swept away in the reconfiguration required by governance.

Second, and clearly related, is the role of professional networks which cut across governance patterns at all levels defining career paths, managing information, defining expertise and laying claim to exclusive arenas of control and accountability. The institutional history of the establishment of the welfare state runs parallel with the rise of the state-paid professional (Dunleavy, 1980). Professionals and their networks that define their relationships provided a substantial institutional rock against which the wave of governance has crashed. There are signs that some professionals have had to yield some ground to the forces of managerialism, as discussed in Chapter 1, yet professionalism remains an important feature on the landscape in which governance has to operate.

Third, governance is making new demands on political parties and in turn has had to accommodate itself to their pre-eminence in the organized politics of industrial democracies. Parties in the twentieth century provided a substantial role in delivery of the institutional framework for a mass democracy (Dalton and Wattenberg, 2000). They recruited candidates, organized election campaigns, provided the building blocks for government and defined political career paths. Governance challenges party by moving decision-making into arenas where party disciplines and rules do apply. Yet at the heights of government party reasserts itself in the selection of leaders and control over their careers. Governance allows for the channelling of demands outside the orbit of party control but the commanding heights of governance are occupied by party appointees. Governance has to accommodate itself to a weakened and declining party system and the party system in turn is having to adapt to the new conditions of governance.

Each of these institutional legacies has a substantial role in the British system of local government. The bureaucratic form dominates local government history. Professional influences also abound and from the early 1960s party organization, which for long held sway in urban areas, began to dominate throughout the system. Each of these institutional legacies has provided a barrier to the governance reforms discussed in earlier chapters. New forms of governing can be trapped and to an extent tamed by these historical legacies. As argued in Chapter 7, in both the design and implementation of the governance reforms of local political leadership and management systems the legacies of the past party-based system have loomed large.

Learning the new processes of governance

Reforming governance is concerned with changed forms of management and politics. It therefore follows that a major issue for governance is how institutions and individuals manage the process of change. But more than that new forms of governance often demand that policy-makers are reflexive and adaptable and that they change their governing strategies to meet new changing circumstances.

Meeting the change challenge of organizational change

It is possible to summarize the experience of change associated with British public sector reforms under three broad headings. First, some sense of crisis has often provided the crucial initial stimulus to reform. Second, for reforms to be launched, organizations need leadership, a culture that allows for institutional creativity, a capacity for whole systems thinking and practice and an ability to give reforms legitimacy. Finally, to become embedded reforms have to be institutionalized through diffused and complex networks of learning. Organization innovation, in general, is 'a game of two halves with compulsory extra time' (Perri 6 *et al.*, 2002: 102).

A sense of crisis can provide a crucial stimulus to change in established bureaucratic institutions. As Stoker (1999b: 14) has argued elsewhere:

> The challenge of New Management has produced effective reform not necessarily because of the validity of its prescriptions but because the threat that it posed has unleashed forces of creativity and innovation previously dormant in local authorities and other service providers.

A sense of crisis – or even more graphically a 'near death' experience – can cause previously slow-to-change organizations to become a hive of radical change and generally much more concerned to look to managing their environment.

The sense of crisis in organizations can be stimulated in a variety of ways. It has been at times in Britain a question of immediate reductions in budget or a sense that resource constraint is here for the long term that has encouraged the search for new ways of working. The introduction of Best Value in the late 1990s, for example, reflects a sense that the pressure to get more from less is likely to be sustained for public service providers. On other occasions it has been wider changes in the environment that have provided a stimulus to change. Central government has imposed many changes on local government and government agencies. Best Value and Compulsory Competitive Tendering reforms provide examples of this sort of change. Another stimulant to change can be the arrival of a new challenging leadership at either political or official level that can lead to the search for new solutions. A cadre of local officials and politicians have built their reputations on their capacity to drive through change processes in their organizations (for examples and accounts of such individuals see Goss, 2001). A further source of stimulus has been a crisis of confidence in the fundamental standing of the institution and a search to achieve a new source of legitimacy. Local government in Britain has felt the need to win back public support for its role both in service provision and representation. Finally, change can be stimulated by a fear that critical thresholds in basic performance standards are or will not be met. School league tables or Comprehensive Performance Assessment for councils, where a poor rating is likely to lead in some instances to institutional soul searching, followed by change programmes, illustrates this factor at work.

These 'push' factors in explaining change are matched by many pull factors. Undoubtedly, as suggested already, the emergence of good leadership committed to change can have a major effect. Another important factor is the capacity, somewhere in the organization, to allow space for innovation. Initiatives often require some new organizational framework to be created – a new unit, team or arm – where the right calibre of staff can be attracted and a culture established which allows them to take risks. Innovations depend on the willingness of key individuals to drive change. A further factor in successful change is the capacity to engage in 'systems thinking' so that not only the organizational form of change is specified but the implications for staffing, training, performance arrangements and so on are thought through. Finally, reforms often need to be legitimized through the support of respected figures and leaders, or perhaps more systematically, by the development of evidence and measures to demonstrate that reforms have had a positive impact. The search for feedback mechanisms to demonstrate the value of reforms is often crucial.

The successful launching of change, however, is only the beginning of the challenge facing reformers. A key lesson from British experiments is that reform needs to be embedded through a process of learning and institutionalization. A crucial role in spreading developments in the British reforms has been the role of semi-formal networks of professionals, consultants and practitioners in demonstrating the value of change to others and in enabling them to come alongside to learn lessons. Innovators are often keen to promote their changes. The best and most successful can be offered funding to offer their experience to others. Investors in People and Charter Mark, for example, have institutionalized support mechanisms that provide 'how-to-do-it' guides and opportunities to meet with people in institutions that have been through the process. In a similar manner the national Best Value programme has produced an array of support mechanisms. Finally, centres can be established in universities, government departments or local authority associations which can provide a 'clearing-house' for good ideas and practice. These centres can also provide a focus for training, management development or, for example, the running of websites dedicated to the task of supporting change.

The challenges facing individual managers and politicians in developing the skills of governance are considerable. In part the crucial skill is the management of change (Perri 6 *et al.*, 1999, 2002; Goss, 2001). The task is to know how to create the momentum for change, championing its delivery and sustaining its impact. Perri 6 *et al.* (1999: 77) comment:

> Managers engaged in integration often describe what they are doing as managing 'out of control' ... Managing out of control takes particular

skills. One interviewee explained: 'The work involves battling all the time and we're asking people to work outside their professional training. They need to learn new skills that they haven't been trained for – persuasion, brokering and so on. You need people who can think outside their box.'

There is not necessarily a whole new set of skills that need to be leant to work in the context of governance, although new capacities may have to be developed among both politicians and managers (see Moore, 1995; Bardach, 1998; Kettl, 1993). What is required, above all, is the capacity to manage change. From the perspective of management literature and practice these skills and knowledge are not in the realm of rocket science but they are nevertheless challenging to sustain.

*How to manage the mix: combining governance
strategies and coping with failure*

A core theme of the governance and literature is how far government can learn to work in a new way. The Anglo-Saxon literature is striving hard to find adjectives to describe the new 'light-touch' form of government appropriate to the circumstances of governance. 'Enabler', 'catalytic agent', 'commissioner' have all been offered to capture the new form of governing. Government in the context of governance has to learn an appropriate operating code which challenges past hierarchical modes of thinking. The crucial challenge, however, is how to manage the mix. There is some evidence of success as well as failure in meeting that challenge. As Chapter 8 made clear, central government is finding it hard to establish a clear new operating code in managing its relationship with the local level.

There is a growing literature on network management by the state (see, for example, Kickert *et al.*, 1997) which can range from instrumental incentive-driven top-down approaches, through strategies to encourage co-operation, to institutional reframing to create new spaces for governance. In chapter 1 specific governance mechanisms were identified: regulation inside government, greater use of market forms, the development of new forms of voice and interest articulation for the public and the development of networks of trust and co-operation. Each of the strategies has drawbacks or tensions associated with them and none provides a panacea for achieving effective governance (Rhodes, 2000: 72–6; Stoker, 2000c: 98–104). Indeed the concept of governance failure has fairly quickly entered the literature. As Jessop depressingly reminds us, 'markets, states and governance all fail. This is not surprising.

For failure is a central feature of all social relations' (Jessop, 2000: 30). But what counts as failure in governance? There are at least two possibilities. The first expression of failure may be the absence of a process of engagement and re-engagement among partners. To put it the other way round, when asked for their criteria of success partners often cite the numbers of meetings held and the continuing existence of a process of dialogue and negotiation as a positive measure. So a lower tier of governance failure would be the breakdown of ongoing reflection and negotiation among partners. However, it appears slightly bizarre to leave the issue there. The reflection and negotiation must ultimately be about achieving some social purpose. The higher tier of governance failure must be based on an assessment of its capacity to produce more effective long-term outcomes than could have been produced using markets or imperative co-ordination by the state. It is necessary to consider not only the doing of governance – either by coalition-building or by government steering and pulling policy levers – it is also necessary to consider the impact of governance. How best to undertake the evaluation of governance is one of the most pressing technical challenges faced by policy-makers and practitioners

Governance cannot afford to be a utopian vision but rather has to be a political practice that can cope with conflict. Indeed, conflicts should not automatically be seen as undermining governance (Hirschman, 1995). On the contrary, they provide the energy and drive for governance. A never-ending series of conflicts is characteristic of market societies and these conflicts can be managed as long as they are divisible, that is conflicts over getting more or less. Such conflicts lend themselves to compromise and the art of bargaining. Yet they are never resolved 'once and for all' and so the scene is always set for the next round of negotiation. The cumulative experience of managing numerous such conflicts is at the heart of an effective governance system.

What can be disabling to governance is conflict that is not divisible. Conflicts which are driven by matters of religion, race, language or ideology, which have an 'either-or' character, present considerable difficulties to governance. They are not inherently irresolvable but in so far as they figure strongly they are likely to make the compromise and messiness central to governance appear inadequate.

What does create problems for governance is operating on several different spatial scales which in turn is often linked to differences in the timescales of policy-making seen as appropriate by different actors. Effective action at the local level may depend on decisions taken at a higher level. Some actors may enter the governance relationship with a very localist perspective, for others the boundary is regional, for still others it may be international. Reconciling these different spatial perspectives is complicated. In the same way with respect to timescales, what is short-term to some will appear like an eternity to others. Governance arrangements are in general about encouraging a longer-term time horizon but the perception of 'long-term' for a community group, politician or multinational company is likely to vary to such a degree that governance failure may result.

Finally, a general source of governance failure can be associated with the contingencies of politics. Electoral considerations may encourage politicians to break apart complex governance arrangements for short-term advantage. The trust on which governance arrangements often rely may prove too weak to carry the burden placed on them. Governance fails because the dialogue, bargaining, consensus-seeking and other-regarding perspectives it may demand cannot always be established and made effective.

Emphasizing the 'improbability of success' (Jessop, 2000: 30) for governance should not be read as leading to the conclusion that it is necessary to look elsewhere for the salvation. On the contrary, by recognizing the incompleteness of any particular governance the aim is to encourage continued experimentation and learning. Jessop (2000: 31) argues that those concerned with governance should deliberately cultivate a 'flexible repertoire' of responses. This in turn involves a commitment to review and reassessment, to check that mechanisms are achieving desired outcomes and a 'self-reflexive irony' in which participants 'recognise the likelihood of failure but proceed as if success were possible'. Rhodes (1997b) comes to similar conclusions in his analysis of governance and argues that government needs to keep on picking up the skills of indirect management and learning.

Reforming governance presents a double challenge. The process of establishing a new governing arrangement involves a process of change and, once established, governing strategies need to be reviewed and developed in the light of changed circumstances. In contrast to traditional constitutional rules that set down a set of clear rules about the way things should be done, the governance message is: expect things to change and keep on changing.

Confronting the structural contradictions of governance

With some simplification, it can be argued, that researchers approach governance from two different vantage points. One perspective is to look at governance as those formal or informal processes of co-ordination and the resolution of common problems and challenges. Here, self-governing networks have been suggested as the key instrument of governance and are said to have a predominant role in governance (Marsh and Rhodes, 1992; Rhodes, 1997a). The other perspective looks at governance in a more state-centric perspective and asks questions about how traditional institutions are transforming to meet the challenge of governance (Pierre and Peters, 2000). In this latter perspective, the state is assumed to remain the key actor in governance by virtue of the vast resources, broadly defined, which it still controls and also by the legitimacy it enjoys as the sole actor in society which can properly define the collective interest.

Both literatures reveal structural contradictions at the heart of governance that provide an enduring challenge to its development. Networks – central to so much of governance – are by definition exclusive and closed. As a result issues of accountability and equality of access to decision-making come to the fore in any discussion of the new governance. On the other hand, state management of networks – to reassert the public interest – is by no means a straightforward solution to the problem. It certainly does not resolve accountability dilemmas. The state – defined by its monopoly of legitimate coercion – is prevailed upon to achieve its aims through softer tools, to ensure a 'maximum of compliance with a minimum of coercion' (Pierre and Peters, 2000: 105). An institution designed to impose its will is expected to learn new tools of the trade and to be seen as a plausible and legitimate defender of the public interest by civil society. The former as already noted is a daunting task, the latter may for many societal groups stretch their credulity to breaking point. The state may further not be a neutral referee but tend to favour some interests rather than others.

The dilemmas of governance through networking

Networks in governance are more than just any collection of individuals or organizations that share dependencies (cf. Dowding, 1995). The self-governing networks at the heart of governance find a way of blending their resources together to achieve common purposes. They are involved in taking over the business of government. Ultimately networks develop shared values and norms and define an exclusive arena of operation.

In both the literatures of urban politics and international relations the term regime is used to describe the emergence of governance networks. In international relations (Rittenberger, 1995) regimes are formed between states, although sometimes with the involvement of non-state actors, to provide regulation and order without resort to the overarching authority of a supranational government. In urban studies regimes provide an informal basis for co-ordination without an all-encompassing structure of command. They are primarily created through the bringing together of public and private sector actors each with access to institutional resources but whom when combined in a long-term coalition can pre-empt the leadership role in their community (Stone, 1989; Stoker, 1995; J. Davies, 2001; Mossberger and Stoker, 2001). For Stone, selective incentives provide the initial glue for regime-building and so regimes can be more easily assembled where tangible resources are available for distribution. Ultimately, long-standing regimes develop shared values and a commitment to members.

Ostrom's work (1990) on the management of common-pool resources suggests that networks of self-organization can be constructed in circumstances where people co-operate over the use of finite resources to which they have open access. Incentives combined with sanctions provide the key to building networks. Above all, the availability of information and a capacity to direct on the behaviour in others creates the conditions under which people will seek to main their reputations by behaving in an appropriately co-operative manner.

The regimes and self-organizing networks identified above share common characteristics. They are to a degree exclusive and closed. They bring together actors with at least a formal equal status. Their participants interact frequently. These characteristics provide the basis for building trust, an essential element in making organizational networks operate effectively (Sydow, 1998) but raise major questions about accountability and equal access to decision-making.

Rhodes (2000: 77) states the problem of accountability with his native Yorkshire bluntness: networks 'substitute private government for public accountability' and 'accountability disappears in the interstices of the webs of institutions which make up governance'. Exclusivity and lack of clarity about where responsibility should rest combine to produce a major accountability deficit. Add to this the argument that the resources necessary to build networks, as represented by social capital, are declining (Putnam, 1995; 2000) or in any case unevenly distributed (Maloney *et al.*, 2000) and it would appear that there is a fatal flaw in governance by networks from a democratic perspective.

The defenders of network governance have been able to muster a number of replies to these doubts about accountability and access to decision-making. There are three main forms of accountability to consider and under any circumstances none of these forms is easily established in any system. Day and Klein (1987) offer a split between: (a) fiscal/regularity accountability (or probity); (b) efficiency accountability (or value for money); and (c) programme accountability (or achievement of desired outcomes). They go on to comment that accountability has become 'an ever-more complex and difficult notion to apply in practice' (Day and Klein, 1987: 7). Complicated divisions of labour, the constraining impact of specific expertise and the sheer scale and variety of government intervention make accountability a considerable challenge. In short, we should not exaggerate the accountability achieved in any political system so that the shortfalls of accountability within governance should be put in perspective.

Second, new financial inspection and regulation frameworks which can run alongside the emergence of networks of governance can make for greater rather than reduced accountability, at least in its terms of probity, and a focus on value for money, as the discussion in Chapters 2 and 5 on regulation within government have suggested. It may be that such central interventions make the conditions for networking more problematic (J. Davies, 2001: ch. 8) but at least in Britain it could be argued that greater management accountability has been part of the drift towards governance. More generally, as argued in Chapter 1, the rise of the governance era has seen the increased use of various forms of accountability, from judicial and administrative review through to political accountabilities, that stretch beyond elections to various stakeholder or other forms of participation.

In defending network governance from the charge that it neglects accountability, another argument can be brought into play. In shifting the attention from inputs and processes to the achievement of desired outcomes, the thrust of governance has been to create a more demanding accountability hurdle (Moore, 1995; Perri 6 *et al.*, 1999; 2002). Yet it has to be conceded that accountability for outcomes (programme accountability) is problematic because there is a danger that what is inevitably demanded of leaders is accountability without responsibility. Why? Programmes involve multiple actors. What makes for successful policy is almost always a complex mix of factors and the measuring of outcomes is often uncertain, as the discussion of Children's Services earlier indicates. To quote March and Olsen (1995: 161): 'Democratic political systems have generally insisted on an allocation of personal accountability for political outcomes that most modern students of political history would consider descriptively implausible.' The problem may therefore lie not with network governance but with the inadequacy of our understanding of accountability and democracy.

Yet accountability is central to democratic theory and practice, especially the third form of programme accountability. The democratic emphasis is on informed consent as the basis of governmental authority. Those who hold office in these circumstances have to be active representatives, providing both an account of their (proposed) actions and being subject to enforced accountability for results achieved and outcomes. Accountability therefore involves justification and being held responsible. Democratic theory usually demands that someone takes a leadership role in both functions. 'Leading from the front' and 'the buck stops here' may be myths but they are important ones (March and Olsen, 1995).

Accountability in the context of network governance demands political leadership: people to offer justifications and to be held to account. These leaders are of a new type, organically part of the system not outside it (Wheatley, 1999). Governance is a world where no one is in charge but where leaders at various levels play a key but different role. That understanding of the role of leadership lay behind some of the arguments for elected mayors at the local level as outlined in Chapter 7. But, equally as that chapter showed it to be, a form of leadership that is not easily understood or established.

A final defence of network governance is that it offers a richer form of democracy. It may fail always to deliver a clear-cut accountability framework but it does provide more effective governing by giving scope for learning and the development of shared ownership of the search for solutions. Governance offers new forms of accountability through the direct involvement of users and stakeholders in service delivery and decision-making (Hirst, 2000). Moreover, there are opportunities to engage in the reconstruction or redistribution of the social capital resources necessary to underwrite mobilization, as suggested in Chapter 6.

Democracy in the twentieth century triumphed as an ideology because of two core virtues: democratic arrangements intrinsically treat all as free and equal (one person, one vote) and moreover they help protect the basic rights of citizens by insisting on the popular endorsement of exercises of public power. Democratic theory in this light tended to emphasize the separation of state and society, in part to ensure that the occupants of the latter had some scope to be free from the former. Democracy is justified first and foremost as a protection for the individual. From this perspective the extent and variety of individual involvement in democracy is not inherently an issue of concern. The key is people's right to have a say and the opportunity to use their vote if they choose to express satisfaction or dissatisfaction.

This view of democracy as a protector of our rights can be challenged as inadequate and restrictive for modern society on at least two grounds. First, it might have been appropriate to limit democracy to a protective role when the state itself was restricted to such a role but with the rise of welfare state spending to between a third and a half of the wealth of nations it would appear that the state is not an institution that can be separated off, but is *de facto* a part of every aspect of our lives. We need, therefore, a more extended capacity to exchange than that afforded by the simple act of voting. Second, the state is no longer a local or even a national institution, it also takes a supranational form of which the development of the EU is one of the strongest expressions in the world. Holding the state at bay is an inadequate response in such a globalized world as our lives are affected by global forces and we need a way of influencing those institutions that take decisions for us on that global terrain.

The key question becomes then the appropriate form and role of democracy in this changed setting. The focus in modern democratic theory therefore goes beyond democracy's moral or instrumental value in defending basic human rights to an argument that properly organized democracy increases our capacity to address fundamental social problems. Democracy helps to provide solutions by enabling us to exchange and learn from one another. The appeal that lies behind the networked governance is that it provides a framework for that more expansive vision of democracy to operate.

The conception of democracy that underlies the idea of networked governance is that democracy is a process of continuous exchange between governors and governed. As Hirst (2000: 27) argues, 'democracy in this sense is about government by information exchange and consent, where organized publics have the means to conduct a dialogue with government and thus hold it to account'. The issue is not the subjection of all decisions to majority approval. Elections or even referendums may have a role but they are not what takes centre stage in the construction of a sustained dialogue between governors and governed. What makes democracy work is networked exchange. But what is required to confirm its democratic credentials is a way of extending the rights to consultation to the widest possible range of issues and the construction of a dialogue that allows space for the involvement of the disorganized many as well as the organized few.

In a democratic system the participation of all is not required; rather its defining characteristic is its openness to all. Many people prefer to spend their time on non-political activities or they face social and economic constraints that limit their time for political activity. As Held (1987: 291) argues:

> What is at issue is the provision of a rightful share in the process of 'government' ... [I]t requires that people be recognized as having the right and opportunity to act in public life. However, it is one thing to

recognize that right, quite another to say it follows that everyone must, irrespective of choice, actually participate in public life.

Citizens may well decide on reasonable grounds not to avail themselves of the opportunities to participate, believing that their interests are already well-protected or not threatened. In short, if representative politics is working then on many occasions further public participation may be unnecessary. The value of openness does not require or assume large-scale and continuous direct participation. It rests its case on the richness of democratic practice and the availability of options for extending participation. These options should operate without making overwhelming time demands and in a way that enhances the broad representativeness of those involved. Effective democratic exchange also requires opportunities for deliberation. Judgement requires the sharing of experiences and the give and take of collective deliberation. As Chapter 6 has shown, it is possible to engineer democracy to a degree to enable a wider range of opportunities for public involvement and to build social capital. Establishing the conditions for network governance to meet the democratic challenge is hard and certainly those conditions have not yet been achieved in local politics in Britain, but we cannot assume that the challenge is impossible to meet.

Networked governance offers a challenging perspective to traditional theories of democracy. The protection of individual rights is seen as a necessary but not a sufficient guide to democratic practice in the twenty-first century. We need also to move beyond the still valuable but limited contribution of formal representative democracy driven by occasional elections. Democracy is more than a safety valve to protect our basic rights. It has the potential to provide the basis for learning, to drive the search for collective solutions to complex and shared problems. Networked governance provides the frame on which a more extended exchange between governors and governed can be built. It provides a cutting edge for modern democratic theory.

Managing through the state: tensions and difficulties

For some the tensions around accountability in governance lead to a view that the state can be brought back in as the guarantor of the public interest and the key legitimate democratic institution. This is a mistake since attenuated lines of accountability apply whether the governance structure is in network form or directed by central state. More subtly, the state is called upon to manage governance (Pierre and Peters, 2000). It is plausible to argue that the state can learn new skills in undertaking this task and pursue a new *modus operandi*. In doing so 'state strength will become something contextual and entrepreneurial rather than as previously the case, something derived from the constitutional and legal strength of state institutions' (Pierre and Peters, 2000: 194). New policy instruments that rely on more subtle techniques than simple coercion have emerged and become part of the practice of the state at all levels.

The problem remains, however, that the state is the state: institution defined by its monopoly of institutional coercion. Even in terms of inter-governmental relations the central state finds it hard to work in a new way with other tiers. As Chapter 8 argued, New Labour may be looking for a new governing rhythm but it is clear that it has not yet found it. At the local level a parallel challenge can face local institutions. Even if local authority may learn new techniques of engagement it cannot disguise from citizens its essential core. Accounts of attempts at state steering (see for example Stoker, 2000c) return continually to the difficulties the state has in present-ing itself in a more flexible light-touch mode. But what is at issue is more than failure to learn new tricks. It also reflects a dominant image of the state in the minds of those from business, voluntary and community sectors, namely that it is not only prone to bureaucratic rigidities but that it is an agent of coercion and control. As a result there is a fundamental underlying tension between state steering and the effective engagement of the other stakeholders in the world of governance. The state may seek to steer but stakeholders may fail to engage or bypass the state for fear of its control and coercion.

Governance faces two contradictions: the reconciliation of network governance with democratic accountability and the emergence of a new governing rhythm to guide state steering that can overcome the coercive legacy of the state form.

Conclusions

A key lesson from British public sector change experience is that reform invariably has an uneven impact. As Lowndes (1999a: 28) argues, 'There is no one process of 'management' change, as individual organisational and service sectors respond differently to system-wide triggers for change.' The external pressures for reform are experienced differently by organizations. Some feel the squeeze of financial constraint, for example, sooner than others. In addition, within organizations particular cultures, traditions, incentive systems and personnel filter the demands made on the organization. With these complex of relationships each organization develops its own 'management recipe' to guide its path of change. As a result management change inevitably tends to produce a pattern of path-breakers, followers and laggards. As a result implementation failures and limitations, when examining the whole field of public service organizations, are likely to be characteristic of any reform programme (cf. Stoker and Mossberger, 1995). Moreover, reforms programmes, as noted earlier, have a habit of generating unintended consequences.

Recognizing the inevitability of some implementation failure and the likelihood of some unintended consequences is not a fatal blow to a reform strategy. Rather it suggests the need for strategies to be reflective and flexible. Effective planned change is not impossible but neither is it likely to be easy. Research into managing changes tells us two clear things. The first lesson is that the immediate stimulus for change often comes from a sense of crisis, a challenge or a feeling of having to respond. The second lesson is that for change to be successful and maintained requires there to be ownership among staff expressed through champions, new mindsets and the capacity to gain new skills.

In the light of these factors it would be reasonable to favour a two-fold reform strategy (Peter, 1998). The first element is top-down and accepts there is a need for central direction and intervention. Without the pressure for change and without disciplines imposed from the outside it is difficult to ensure that all organizations will change. The centre must create a dynamic for change to ensure that it has appropriate controls and incentives are present. However, reform also demands a bottom-up development of ownership and commitment by supporting local champions, creating the space for innovation, building capacity through training and development and establishing effective channels for networking and the dissemination of good practice. Above all it requires a recognition that taking an initiative does not guarantee success and so a willingness to tolerate failure is also necessary.

Reform strategy requires a combination of top-down and bottom-up approaches to provide leadership and build ownership. It also requires a capacity to listen and learn from those at the sharp end of change both among the public and officialdom so as to be able to adopt and adjust the reform approach. It is that capacity that has perhaps been too often absent from New Labour's approach. An issue that will be explored further in the final chapter.

11 New Labour and Local Governance: Unfinished Business

Robert Hill was Prime Minister Blair's first-term local government adviser. In an article published in 1996 in *Renewal*, a journal that carries much of New Labour's internal debate, he provided the leitmotif to New Labour's attitude to local government once it achieved power:

> Around half the population, on their own admission, know hardly anything about local government and are confused about what little they do know ... Given this state of affairs, is local government worth bothering with? 'Yes ... but' must be the answer. (Hill, 1996: 22)

Local authorities needed, according to Hill, a new vision of their role built less on providing services alone and more on taking on the challenge of community leadership, identifying and meeting the needs of local areas in partnership with central government, businesses and the voluntary sector. Along with a new vision there was a requirement that local authorities change their ways of working, showing flexibility in the way they ensured that services were delivered, developing political leadership through the adoption of executive councillors and elected mayors, extending their capacity to speak for and protect their communities and reaching out to the public through better consultation and better community planning. Robert Hill's article laid out an agenda that was pursued in government by New Labour, as we have seen in the earlier chapters in this book.

It appears, however, after six years of reform that New Labour and the public are still in 'Yes ...' but' territory. It is probably fair to say that many New Labour ministers remain ambiguous at best about local government and the strategy of reform remains unfinished business.

This chapter initially draws out some conclusions on the reform strategy implemented by New Labour in its first six years in office and identifies some highs and some lows. It does establish that there have been some advances as well as recognizing that a new era of dynamic and engaging local governance has not arrived. The next section explores one key reason for the limited achievements of New Labour in relation to local governance: namely its lack of coherent and consistent faith in localism. But you may ask: does it matter to New Labour that it has not created a renewal of local governance? The next section argues that it does matter because what is at stake is not the future of local government but rather the future of New Labour's whole strategy of reform. Without renewed local governance then the ambition of an enabling state guiding social and economic renewal cannot be realized. The chapter concludes by arguing for a New Localism to become a core feature of New Labour's future strategy.

New Labour's reform of local governance: an assessment

The programme of reform launched by New Labour has made some very real gains (see Stoker, 2003). As noted in Chapter 5, the reform of public services has made some progress. The Audit Commission's (2002) review of those councils responsible for the largest variety of services paints a picture of overall managerial and political competence at leadership levels and quality in service delivery. With roughly half of all councils in the excellent or good category – ranging from leafy Kent to gritty Hartlepool – it can be suggested that New Labour's commitment to inspection, peer review, Best Value and better service delivery has had a positive impact. Various stakeholders in local government appear to regard the Best Value process as helpful (Enticott *et al.*, 2002). As noted in Chapter 7, local authorities have adopted the new executive structures with remarkable speed and that in turn has probably enhanced their capacity for effective political leadership (Stoker *et al.*, 2003). The discussion in Chapter 8 revealed that myriads of new partnerships have been established and that although the system can be a bit confusing and messy there is little doubt that local authorities are better at partnership than they were (Sullivan and Skelcher, 2002). Chapter 6 showed there is also evidence that local authorities have proved adept at developing their participation and consultation strategies (Lowndes *et al.*, 2001a, b). So on much of the modernization agenda set out by New Labour there has been progress.

There is however, you guessed, a 'Yes ... but' waiting in the wings. Local government may be demonstrably less incompetent than it was, it may have learnt several new tricks but it still is not a significant player in our political system nor does it engage local communities in anything other than a fairly shallow way. In a remarkable echo of Robert Hill's comment,

John Williams, a former Executive Director of the New Local Government Network, is moved to comment at the start of his 2002 debate with George Jones:

> Let's be frank about where we are. If I mention the phrase 'local government' there's a good chance that 75% of people who read the first sentence of this letter will suddenly feel a compelling urge to skip a few pages or watch the Parliamentary Channel. (Jones and Williams, 2002: 77)

The public remains largely unengaged in local politics. Turnout rates in local elections have remained very low. But still no one really cares about local government.

There have been limitations to the modernization agenda pursued by New Labour. First, as Chapters 3 and 4 explored, there has been a lack of real trust in local government by central government. Second, the Labour party at national and local levels has ducked the demands of a new politics and preferred to carry on running things pretty much as before with only marginal changes.

The evidence about a lack of trust is to be found in the often confusing messages put out by central government and limits of its commitment to elected local government. The object of desire in terms of decentralization appears at times to be local government but at other times it is regional government, city regions and cities, neighbourhood communities, local strategic partnerships, other partnerships, local trusts, local head teachers and other officials. Central government has been quite promiscuous in its chosen range of partners at the local level. There are good reasons behind each of the centre's initiatives but together they create a general impression that elected local authorities are not particular or special but merely one among a variety of partners that the centre can choose to play with. In education, social services and crime prevention the centre has been quite happy to barge local government out of the way to get what it wants. There has been no great bonfire of unelected quangos, indeed far from it. As Chapter 8 makes clear, New Labour appears content to see Regional Development Agencies, Learning and Skills Councils and Police Authorities make major decisions about localities with only a nod in the direction of co-operation with elected local government. The level of co-ordination represents a step forward from the Conservatives' time in office but it has not created anywhere near an integrated system of local governance. On local government finance, as Chapter 9 notes, despite some useful reforms on the margins and a very welcome boost in funding, there has been no great move to free local authorities to raise more on their own income. Local authorities remain as supplicant children to the parent which is central government.

The Labour Party has in effect ducked the crisis in local politics, as Chapter 7 illustrates in relation to the mayoral issue. Fundamentally, local government remains dominated by party politics and politicians yet the reach of those parties into local communities is weaker than it has ever been before. Local political leaders may be a more competent bunch than before New Labour came to power but there is a huge problem with disengagement from the system by the public. Some political groups have shown themselves able to address the gap that exists and reach out to their communities through consultation and partnership. Research (Lowndes *et al.*, 2002) into levels of local participation show the impact that a long-term commitment to a more inclusive politics can have. Areas of similar socio-economic status show real differences in the levels of public participation they achieve and the difference is driven by how open the political system of the local authority is and how modernized is its management structure.

Yet institutional arrangements that might have addressed the problem more generally, such as the option of directly elected executive mayors, have been blocked and put at the margins of the system. There are only eleven elected mayors in mainstream English local government and one functioning as part of the Greater London Authority but none in our other major cities. There is a base from which to see if the initiative works but an opportunity for a wider change has been missed.

Narrow party concerns about the implications in terms of political control blocked the mayoral initiative at local and national levels. Local party groups have opposed the idea *en masse* and the issue of pushing for referendums in Birmingham and Bradford, where consultation exercises had shown clear support for the idea among local people, was ducked by central government, primarily because it was unclear that if a mayoral election resulted the Labour Party would be able to find a credible candidate. As for the idea of proportional representation, another institutional reform floated in Robert Hill's article, it appears to have disappeared from the radar screen all together with the exception of Scotland. Various forms of stakeholder democracy have been toyed with at neighbourhood, local and regional levels but none has delivered the engagement and legitimacy that would be required for a vibrant sub-national politics to take off in England. Devolution in Scotland and Wales may have delivered a new base for politics in those places but England still waits. No one but a few delusional individuals could think that the option of regional elected assemblies now on offer will solve the problem in the short run, although it may have a longer-term positive impact.

Searching for a new localism: the limits to steering centralism

New Labour was right to put local government on trial using a mix of top-down and bottom approaches. Ultimately, however, there is a limit to what the centre can do through special initiatives, sponsoring partnerships and top-down interventions. Recognizing the limits of central interventions, New Labour has sought instead to set in motion a new dynamic where the centre steers and facilitates rather than commands and controls.

As Chapter 8 indicated, steering centralism has been developed by, among others, the Chancellor's right-hand man Ed Balls, who refers to it as 'constrained discretion' (Balls, 2002). Another phrase that has been used by several government ministers to describe what they are trying to do is 'earned autonomy' for service providers. Those that provide 'better services should get more freedom and flexibility – earned autonomy for schools, hospitals, local government and other public services' (Office of Public Services Reform, 2002: 17). The commitment to national standards alongside local discretion in service delivery is also a key feature in the Prime Minister's principles of public service reform (Office of Public Services Reform, 2002). While there are some differences between these various approaches, in general they are all pushing for the same shift in the centre's thinking.

This is a major change in perspective. It shows that the Government has accepted the validity of the criticisms of its earlier phase of chaotic centralism. Yet ultimately the new steering centralism remains a cousin of the centralist approach. To paraphrase Tony Wright MP, Chair of the Public Administration Select Committee on earned autonomy, 'constrained discretion' is a phrase that would only be understood in a system where the centre calls the shots (Wright, 2002).

The shift in thinking towards steering centralism is certainly a step forward: a recognition and admission that New Labour did not get everything right in the beginning. More than a few critics would allow that it does address some of the ingrained pathologies of centralism. But it does not address them all. The discussion below draws extensively from Corry and Stoker (2002).

All authority-based systems are, as the American economist Charles Lindblom (1977: 665) observes, 'clumsy'. They provide some considerable capacity to get things done but little sensitivity. They provide 'strong thumbs, no fingers'. In terms of inherent weaknesses three immediately stand out: insufficient prospects for the devolution of learning, communication failure and information overload. It is worth looking at each in turn to consider the extent to which they can be addressed by steering centralism.

Lesson learning in a centralized system is deeply problematic. The centre may say it wants to co-ordinate the spread of good practice and give guidance. But if learning is in turn tied to accountability systems and perhaps even the threat of sanctions, the possibility of open learning is undermined. 'Public managers in fear of central sanctions will, understandably, be more concerned to cover up failures than to discuss the lessons learned frankly with colleagues' (Perri 6 *et al.*, 2002: 98). Moreover, the lessons learnt about what works often have a highly specific local flavour. Deciding what works requires local judgement.

Steering centralism might well overcome some of the difficulties of more traditional authority-based systems because it encourages local discretion over defining the detail of policies. What it may be less good at is enabling the spread of best practice, since under this system winners are likely to over-claim their achievements and be unwilling to share lessons with others for fear of ultimately undermining their advantaged position with the centre. Talking honestly about success and failure is not something that comes easily to an authority-based system, even where the authority is benign. If rewards and sanctions are at stake then those on the lower rungs of the hierarchy will present their behaviour in the most advantageous light. They will do so, however, in a manner that is not always of benefit to the system or the public who use it. Because the system packages its incentives around the careful presentation of performance information then the presentation of that information is an art that head teachers and local NHS managers, as well as senior councillors and council officers, have developed with great skill.

Communication failures are endemic in authority systems, a lesson learnt in the extreme from the Soviet Union's era of central planning (Lindblom, 1977: 67). As the centre cannot know the conditions in every locality, it attempts to design policies for average conditions that, in reality, do not exist in any one location. In turn local managers concerned with managing pressures misrepresent their capacities for fear that they may be asked to do too much and overstate their achievements in order to appease those further up the hierarchial management system.

Although steering centralism does address some of these concerns directly, what it perhaps does not allow for is the demands placed on the centre in a system of subtle steering. To be able to judge the performance of local institutions allowing fully for their circumstances and starting point is always going to be tough. Even then, it is based on the rather heroic assumption – indicated above – that you can rely on what you are being told. The result is that judgements about good service providers who need to be rewarded will have a rough-and-ready quality that may ultimately reduce their legitimacy or encourage a general watering down of the performance threshold that has to be reached.

Finally, authority-based systems contain the seeds of their own destruction – a consequence of information overload. Again, in the words of Lindblom (1977: 66), 'the human condition is small brain, big problems'. To cope with complexity authority-based systems divide up tasks and responsibilities. While this helps, it does not solve the gap between the cognitive capacity of the decision-maker and the scale of the problems they face. The total flow of paper or e-mails is always more than they can digest. As a result, people at the centre are always time-challenged, unable to focus for long on a single issue. Managers at the periphery use the space created through information overload to pursue their own schemes, to get on and do their own thing. The space is there both when the centre is not looking and when it is looking but cannot see through the fog of information that surrounds it. In short, failures of internal control are endemic to authority-based systems. The cool efficiency of centralism is always prone to collapse into a disjointed set of competing institutional interests. 'Overlaid on the formal pattern of unilateral pyramidal control, informal controls run in all directions … participants trade favors with each other, exchange current favors for future obligations, and cash in on older obligations' (Lindblom, 1977: 67).

The model of steering centralism is likely to work best when there is a relatively straightforward alignment between the outcome that the centre desires and an output indicator that it can easily measure and monitor. That is the secret of what is demanded of the Bank of England from the Treasury. It is the reason why the literacy hour worked. The key is a clear general outcome, a tool to attack that outcome that is in the grasp of the agency charged with its delivery and a straightforward low-cost way of measuring whether the appropriate effect has occurred.

The trouble is that there are only a limited number of circumstances when the above factors can be aligned. If you want a good local environment or to discourage teenage pregnancy or for a myriad other reasonable objectives of public policy to be achieved then complications multiple. The outcome is not quite so clear-cut as a range of tools and agencies are involved and you are not sure what would be an appropriate surrogate measure for success. For example, in achieving a good local environment, it cannot be right to reduce everything to measures such as the number of bins collected, streets cleaned or trees planted.

Without a simplifying rule of thumb that enables you to judge whether or not progress is being made, steering centralism will be prone to information overload and may degenerate into nothing more than a different version of an oft-repeated bargaining game between the centre and local institutions.

The argument is not that steering centralism does not have any role to play, particularly in the delivery of public services. Setting high national standards for certain key services where national government cannot accept diversity of outcome or objective but giving more freedom to local actors as to how they deliver it is sensible. Indeed, realistically, it is going to be the furthest we get to devolution in these areas. It is only likely to work, however, where the output to be achieved is universally agreed, clear, simple and correlates very closely with the ultimate objective. Where there are complications and disagreements and disjunctures, steering centralism leads one to ever more complex, 'sophisticated' and intrusive targets, inspection and monitoring with the negative consequences outweighing any benefits.

Steering centralism has some advantages but, if pushed too far, will not overcome the pathologies of more traditional authority-based systems. What steering centralism will find near impossible to deliver is the capacity to react to new demands and new circumstances that a localist system can provide. Many of the best innovations of our public services, such as public health services or clean water supply, came about as a result of local municipalities responding to local concerns and developing new services (Szreter, 2002). On a smaller scale that process goes on everyday in Britain's schools, hospitals and local government. It is what a locally based system is good at and replicating this will be a struggle for even most the well-intentioned steering centralism. Designing polices using known tools to meet established problems is only part of the governance challenge. Picking up on issues that are emerging and experimenting with responses that may or may not work is another key element. If local institutions lose that role because they are so atrophied and weakened then steering centralism will be insufficient to fill that gap.

Why new localism matters

At this point it is worth returning to Robert Hill's original question: is local government worth bothering with? However, this time delete the reference to the local. The real question is whether government is worth bothering with. The summary answer to this question is yes, government is worth bothering with but in order to demonstrate that in practice, to an increasingly disengaged public, it needs to have a strong local dimension.

New Labour's investment and reform strategies aimed at public services are trying to demonstrate in practice that government can play a more than minimum role in our lives (this section draws on Stoker, 2003). The liberal right may believe that the market will provide and the role of government is light-touch regulation and protection against internal and external threat but for New Labour the state has a much more engaged and positive role, as Chapter 3 confirmed.

We should value public services for positive reasons. The case for public services should not rest alone on meeting contingencies where markets fail or because the service cannot easily be made a divisible good. Rather the case for public services should be made for two positive reasons. First, public services provide the infrastructure and support mechanisms that we all need to live our lives to the full. Whether it is education, social care or transport, public services at their best enable people to achieve their own goals and fulfil their potential. Second, public services should be celebrated as an expression of our solidarity and community. They are a practical recognition that we live in society together and owe a level of support to each other.

But if government is going to perform more than a minimal role for us in the future we need to place its development and operation in the context of a strong version of the New Localism (Corry and Stoker, 2002). The argument, here, is not for an independent local government as a good thing in itself, but rather our point is that if the governing system of our country is going to deliver the public services and benefits we want it needs to have a strong local dimension to its operation to match a new role for the centre. For the centre there is a need to be a focus of learning about what works, a spreader of good practice and, where appropriate, a legislator to promote high standards. For the local level there is a need beyond local discretion in the administration of public services and to create the space for a genuine local governance.

Community leadership is not an alternative to service delivery; it is *the* point of service delivery. We need a local government that can, through its services, make a real difference to peoples' lives. Equally we need local government to make an impact beyond the services that it delivers. As argued throughout this book, a commitment to networked community governance means that local government's job is to facilitate the achievement of community objectives. Its role is to lead the debate, develop shared visions and help to ensure that appropriate resources – both public and private – are found and blended together to achieve common objectives. As a result, the political processes necessary for local governance involve a subtle mixture of leadership capacity and opportunities for wider participation and involvement. Local government is there to be a community leader but this is not an authority-based model. Rather it is premised on the establishment of a pluralistic and open politics at the local level.

The critique of new localism offered by David Walker (2002) in many ways misses the mark because it fails to recognize that the argument is about our governing system as a whole rather than the role of local government. New Localism does not imply that local government can do everything and that the centre should stop doing everything. Rather it was more subtle. The argument is that local government can do some things better than the centre. Thus New Localism is not against equalization measures to ensure the fair funding of public services or the idea of nationally defined rights to high-quality services.

But effective local governance can do some things far better than the centre. First and foremost local government has the ability to detect new needs and respond to meet them. Many of what we regard as national services were pioneered by local government and that role remains vitally important today. As Sheldrake (1989) shows, municipal socialism has a rich history through the provision of water, electricity, gas, tramways, hospitals and education. David Walker (2002) appears to think that traffic has all been one way from the centre to reluctant local authorities. In fact the cycle of public service advance is more complex than he allows. As Patrick Dunleavy (1980: 105) pointed out over two decades ago, 'central government policy changes of a substantive or innovative kind, such as the introduction of new standards or methods of service provision, are thus most frequently generalisations of existing local government practice or responses to demands produced by local authorities' practical experience, rather than ideas originating with government departments'. It is this vital role that New Labour and others have come close to losing over the last two decades.

The second thing that local governance can deliver is a way of involving people in the definition and solution of the problems that they confront. Just as we have come to accept that the welfare state needs to offer help to individuals but at the same time demand a response from them, the rights and responsibilities formula, so should we apply the same logic to communities. Unless we involve people in the definition of their problems and the choice of solutions, we will produce a thin governing system that produces public services that patch over problems rather than goes to their heart. We need to find governing mechanisms that involve people and the local one provides a key arena for such activity.

Choosing New Localism

The debate about New Localism can have a rather technocratic flavour and as such be reduced to a case for a little more wiggle room for local and regional government and a little less central direction. If that was all the debate was about then all the future would hold would be a variety of compromises struck over the future governance of the UK, driven by evidence-based analysis and pragmatic judgement. Yet what is at stake in the discussion about New Localism is more profound than that. For the Left, New Localism raises to the fore a set of choices which if made would profoundly shift the current direction of policy trajectory, political practice and value judgements. For New Labour it raises central issues about what its legacy should be.

David Walker's polemic against New Localism is to be welcomed precisely because he recognizes there are bigger issues at stake than the shifting around of some administrative responsibilities and public finances. However, his analysis of the dangers of localism and his defence of centralism is flawed not because his concern with equality of opportunity is mistaken but because he ends up defending inadequate and failing methods of achieving that goal.

Walker and many in New Labour believe that the application of rational thought and its key tools of science and technology provide the formula for social and economic advancement. The British Left has framed much of its policy debate and prescription in the context of that understanding from the Fabians, through the foundations of the welfare state in the 1940s and the commitment in the 1960s and 1970s to the white heat of technology and onwards to New Labour's strong preference for targets, performance indicators and regulation in virtually every field of public policy. Modernism has reached a high watermark in much of New Labour's thought processes and approaches, as my colleague Mick Moran has argued (Moran, 2003).

In praising centralism David Walker seeks to defend those parts of New Labour that are fully fledged disciples of High Modernism. According to their gospel the world is capable of being understood through investigation and reason and of being changed through application of the lessons learnt in that process. Nothing too much wrong with that, you might say. The problem comes from the strength and direction of the application of these principles by High Modernists. In their world everything – both need and performance in meeting need – can be measured, best practice can always be identified and spread and the governance arrangements can be driven by top-down regulation matched by one focus of accountability at the centre. Whether it is school achievements, hospital treatments or services to children, parts of New Labour have shown a tendency to adopt a commitment not only to finding out what people are doing but telling them how to do it better and monitoring their subsequent performance. David Walker supports that trend, wants it to continue and sees no practical alternative.

But the point is that the policy trajectory underwritten by High Modernism is self-defeating. If to tackle complex problems of social exclusiveness and inequality all that was required was the simple application of lessons learnt from a clear and given practice the model would make sense. But life is not like that and, like all world views pushed to extremes, High Modernism is a more destructive than productive force. It demotivates precisely those who are essential to driving forward successful change, it fails to recognize the inherent localness of solutions to complex problems and it creates anger where an illusion of progress through improvements in meeting targets is reported but the substance of service delivery on the ground is not, in practice, advanced. It is not simply a case of NHS managers or head teachers occasionally fiddling the figures, it is that the figures cannot tell the whole story. To tie your reform strategy to that approach is shallow and profoundly mistaken.

The suspicion of localism expressed by David Walker and in some parts of New Labour might have made more sense decades ago when Labour faced squirearchies and traditional seats of power in rural areas with shopkeepers, small businessmen and petit bourgeois officials running many of our town and county halls. Local and regional institutions are, however, now run by modernists. These people are just as committed as anyone at the centre to using evidence and reason to solve local problems and improve the lot and opportunity of their fellow citizens. Maybe before there was not a base on which to build an ownership of a social democratic politics but now there is yet a danger that the ultra-centralist vision will neglect or, worse still, denigrate it.

The political world envisaged by New Labour's High Modernists is incredibly thin. Politics is done by a few ministers supported by a few officials who know what is right and direct UK public services plc. This is a world in which disengagement is inbuilt and appears close to celebrated. It just cannot be a viable model for the twenty-first century. People may not want to be involved in politics all their life but they should not be reduced to the consumers of someone else's politics. There is nothing wrong with central steering but it will never be enough. We need vibrant local and regional decision-making in which people can engage.

The challenge for the Left remains as ever how to balance the values of equality, freedom and community. New Localism offers New Labour a route map to chart its way through these values. If New Labour has a legacy so far it is the establishment of devolved institutions in Scotland, Wales and maybe Northern Ireland. That legacy needs to be spread. The world will truly be a different place if, when Labour leaves office, local and regional politics institutions throughout the country are making a vibrant contribution to identifying and solving problems. David Walker warns of the threat from the Right but the greatest danger is leaving a centralized system for it to take charge of, and denuded local and regional institutions for it to drive through a new orgy of marketization.

The New Localist debate is not about a quick patching up of a few administrative failings in order to continue the smooth running of a reform process. It is about a profound choice that has to be made and one that does perhaps require a stepping out of the modernist frame and a leap of faith. In order to get the change, a radical shift of direction is required from the centre. It has to let go and cultivate a new localism. The future lies not in central direction but in releasing and developing the capacity that exists at all levels of our system of governance.

New Labour was right about local government first time. It needs to be challenged to change but it is has a vital role in delivering community leadership. What is required is the political commitment to deliver on that vision. It means providing the scope to local government to take initiatives and encourage within local communities the discretion and capacity to attempt new responses to old problems, as well as developing new responses to emerging issues. This challenge was ducked in New Labour's first years and it remains to be seen if it will now be acted on. Just as important is a return to the issue of how to construct a local politics that is engaging with and capable of reconciling the demands of traditional representative democracy with the possibilities of a stakeholder democracy.

New Labour has offered an unusual mix of rationalist confidence and fatalistic distrust of others in approaching the reforming of the state. It believes that it can make the world a better place but it is not sure how and who to trust, and in particular it is uncertain about the role of community governance in that search for solutions. It needs to abandon its fatalism about the local level and local politicians and officials and its attendant lottery strategy, and take a leap of faith in favour of localism. If it does so it will find both the means and ends of its reform commitment more clearly specified and it will provide a legacy that will set Britain in a positive shift of its governing arrangements that will reverse nearly a century of centralization. Local government needs to be challenged but it needs to be liberated at the same time.

New Labour should abandon its 'Yes ... but' approach and unequivocally commit to a New Localism. That means choosing the local finance option that provides for substantial local choice and it means developing a governing rhythm that accepts the virtues of multiple centres of local power in a system of multi-level governance. For local stakeholders the challenge is to break from past forms of politics and develop a leadership capacity so that communities can feel led and at the same time an openness of style to enable all who want to make their contribution. Britain would be a better place if community governance was stronger and New Labour needs to be braver and bolder if it is to deliver its vision in the local arena.

References

Aldridge, R. and Stoker, G. (2002) *Advancing a Public Service Ethos* (London: New Local Government Network).

Armstrong, H. (2000) 'The Key Themes of Democratic Renewal', in L. Pratchett (ed.) *Renewing Local Democracy?* (London: Frank Cass).

Audit Commission, Best Value Inspectorate (2001) *Another Step Forward* (London: Audit Commission).

Audit Commission (2002) *Comprehensive Performance Assessment: Scores and Analysis for Single Tier and County Councils in England* (London: Audit Commission).

Balls, E. (2002) *The New Localism*, Speech by the Chief Economic Adviser, Ed Balls to the CIPFA Annual Conference, www.hm-treasury.gov.uk, 12 June.

Bardach, E. (1998) *Getting Agencies to Work Together: The Theory and Practice of Managerial Craftsmanship* (Washington, DC: Brookings).

Barnes, M., Harrison, S., Mort, M., Shardlow, P. and Wistow, G. (1999) 'The New Management of Community Care: User Groups, Citizenship and Co-Production', in G. Stoker (ed.) *The New Management of British Local Governance* (London: Macmillan) pp. 112–27.

Barry, B. (1974) 'Review Article: Exit, Voice and Loyalty', *British Journal of Political Science*, 4, pp. 79–107.

Beetham, D. (1987) *Bureaucracy* (Milton Keynes: Open University Press).

Beetham, D. (1991) *The Legitimation of Power* (London: Macmillan).

Beetham, D. (1999) 'Democratic Audit in Comparative Perspective', *Parliamentary Affairs*, 52, 4, pp. 567–81.

Benington, J. and Harvey, J. (1999) 'Networking in Europe', in G. Stoker (ed.) *The New Management of British Local Governance* (London: Macmillan).

Benyon, J. and Edwards, A. (1999) 'Community Governance of Crime Control', in G. Stoker (ed.) *The New Management of British Local Governance* (London: Macmillan) pp. 145–67.

Bernstein, M. (1955) *Regulating Business by Independent Commission* (Princeton: Princeton University Press).

Birch, A. (1975) 'Economic Models in Political Science: The Case of Exit Voice and Loyalty', *British Journal of Political Science*, 5, pp. 69–82.

Birch, A. (2002) *Public Participation in Local Government: A Survey of Local Authorities* (London: ODPM).

Blair, T. (1998a) *The Third Way: New Politics for a New Century* (London: Fabian Society).

Blair, T. (1998b) *Leading the Way: A New Vision for Local Government* (London: IPPR).

Blair, T. (2001) 'Third Way, Phase Two', *Prospect*, March, pp. 10–14.

Blair, T (2002) 'New Labour and Community', *Renewal*, 10, 2.

Blaug, R. (2002) 'Engineering Democracy', *Political Studies*, 50, 1, pp. 102–16.

Boyne, G., Kirkpatrick, I. and Kitchener, M. (2001) 'Introduction to the Symposium on New Labour and the Modernisation of Public Management', *Public Administration*, 79, 1, pp. 1–5.

Brady, H., Verba, S. and Schlozman, S. (1995) 'Beyond SES: A Resource Model for Political Participation', *American Journal of Political Science*, 89, 2, pp. 27–291.

Bromley, C., Curtice, J. and Seyd, B. (2001) 'Political Engagement, Trust and Constitutional Reform', in A. Park, J. Curtice, K. Thomson, L. Jarvis and C. Bromley (eds) *British Social Attitudes: The 18th Report* (London: Sage).

Brown, G. (2001a) *Remarks by Gordon Brown at the Active Community Launch*, 11 January.

Brown, G. (2001b) *Enterprise and the Regions Speech* (UMIST, Manchester, 29 January).

Bulpitt, J. (1996) 'The Discipline of the New Democracy: Mrs Thatcher's Domestic Statecraft', *Political Studies*, 34.

Burns, D., Hambleton, R. and Hoggett, P. (1994) *The Politics of Decentralisation* (London: Macmillan).

Butler, D., Adonis, A. and Travers, T. (1994) *Failure in British Government: The Politics of the Poll Tax* (Oxford: Oxford University Press).

Carter, C. (1986) *Members One of Another: The Problems of Local Corporate Action* (York: Joseph Rowntree Foundation).

Chisholm, M., Hale, R. and Thomas, D. (1997) 'Introduction', in M. Chisholm *et al.* (eds) *A Fresh Start for Local Government* (London: CIPFA).

Chisholm, M. (2002) *Structural Reform of British Local Government: Rhetoric and Reality* (Manchester: Manchester University Press).

Cochrane, A. (1996) 'From Theories to Practices: Looking for Local Democracy in Britain', in D. King and G. Stoker (eds) *Rethinking Local Democracy* (London: Macmillan).

Cockburn, C. (1977) *The Local State* (Southampton: Pluto).

Commission for Local Democracy (1995) *Taking Charge: The Rebirth of Local Democracy* (London: Municipal Journal Books).

Copus, C. (1999) 'The Party Group: A Barrier to Democratic Renewal', *Local Government Studies*, 25, 4, pp. 77–98.

Copus, C., Stoker, G. and Taylor, F. (2000) *New Council Constitutions: Consultation Guidelines for English Local Authorities* (London: Department of the Environment, Transport and the Regions).

Corera, G. (1998) 'More by Default than Design': The Clinton Experience and the Third Way', *Renewal*, 6, 2 April, pp. 6–16.

Corry, D. and Stoker, G. (2002) *New Localism: Refashioning the Centre–Local Relationship* (London: NLGN).

Crouch, C. (2000) *Coping with Post-Democracy* (London: Fabian Society).

Dalton, R.J. and Wattenberg, M.P. (eds) (2000) *Parties without Partisans* (New York: Oxford University Press).

Davies, J. (1972) *The Evangelistic Bureaucrat* (London: Tavistock).

Davies, J. (2001) *Partnerships and Regimes* (Aldershot: Ashgate).

Davies, P. (1998) *The Fifth Miracle* (Harmondsworth: Penguin).

Davis, H. Downe, J. and Martin, S. (2001) *External Inspection of Local Government: Driving Improvement or Drowning in Detail?* (York: Joseph Rowntree Foundation).

Day, P. and Klein, R. (1987) *Accountabilities: Five Public Services* (London: Tavistock).

Day, P. and Klein, R. (1990) *Inspecting the Inspectorates* (York: Joseph Rowntree Memorial Trust).

Dearlove, J. (1973) *The Politics of Policy in Local Government* (Cambridge: Cambridge University Press).

Dearlove, J. (1979) *The Reorganisation of British Local Government* (Cambridge: Cambridge University Press).

Department of the Environment (DoE) (1991) *The Internal Management of Local Authorities in England* (London: HMSO).

DETR (1998) *Modern Local Government: In Touch with the People* (London: Department of the Environment, Transport and Regions).

DETR (1999) *The Beacon Council Scheme: Prospectus* (London: Department of the Environment, Transport and Regions).

DETR (2000) *1998 British Social Attitudes Survey: Secondary Data Analysis of the Local Government Module* (London: DETR).

DETR (2001) *Supporting Strategic Service Delivery Partnerships in Local Government* (London: DETR).

Doogan, K. (1999) 'The Contracting out of Local Government Services: Its Impact on Jobs, Conditions of Service and Labour Markets', in G. Stoker (ed.) *The New Management of British Local Governance* (London: Macmillan) pp. 62–78.

Douglas, M. (1982) 'Cultural Bias', in M. Douglas (ed.) *In the Active Voice* (London: Routledge).

Douglas, M. (1986) *How Institutions Think* (London: Routledge).

Dowding, K. (1995) 'Model or Metaphor: A Critical Review of the Policy Networks Approach', *Political Studies*, 44, pp. 343–57.

DTLR (2001) *Public Attitudes to Directly Elected Mayors* (London: Department, Transport, Local Government and the Regions).

Dunleavy, P. (1980) *Urban Political Analysis* (London: Macmillan).

Dunleavy, P. (1986) 'Explaining the Privatisation Boom: Public Choice Versus Radical Approaches', *Public Administration*, 64, pp. 13–34.

Dunleavy, P. (1991) *Democracy, Bureaucracy and Public Choice: Economic Explanations in Political Science* (New York, London: Harvester).

Dunleavy, P. and Margetts, H. (1999) *Electoral Reform in Local Government: Alternative Systems and Key Issues* (York: Joseph Rowntree Foundation).

Electoral Commission (2002a) *Modernising Elections. A Strategic Evaluation of the 2002 Electoral Pilot Schemes. Executive Summary* (London: EC).

Electoral Commission (2002b) *Public Opinion and the 2002 Local Elections. Findings* (London: EC).

Emmerich, M. and Stoker, G. (2002) 'A Trust Policy for Local Government?' Paper to the Strategy Unit, Cabinet Office.

Enticott, G., Walker, R., Boyne, G., Martin, S. and Ashworth, R. (2002) *Best Value in English Local Government: Summary Results from the Census of Local Authorities in 2001* (London: ODPM).

Fabian Society (2000) *Paying for Progress* (The Commission on Taxation and Citizenship) (London: The Fabian Society).

Filkin, G. (1999) *Achieving Best Value* (London: New Local Government Network).

Filkin, G. (2001) *Local PSAs – Next Steps* (London: Mimeo).

Filkin, G., Dempsey, S., Larner, A. and Wilkinson, G. (2001a) *Winning the E-Revolution in Local Government* (London: New Local Government Network).

Filkin, G., Williams, J. and Allen, E. (2001b) *Can Strategic Partnering Deliver Best Value?* (London: New Local Government Network).

Fukuyama, F. (1999) *The Great Disruption* (London: Profile Books).

Gamble, A. (1984) *The Free Economy and the Strong State: The Politics of Thatcherism* (Basingstoke: Macmillan).

Gamble, A. (1990) 'Theories of British Politics', *Political Studies*, 38, pp. 404–20.

Game, C. and Leach, S. (1996) 'Political Parties and Local Democracy', in L. Pratchett and D. Wilson (eds) *Local Democracy and Local Government* (London: Macmillan).

Geddes, M. and Martin, S. (2000) 'The Policy and Politics of Best Value: Currents, Cross Currents and Undercurrents in the New Regime', *Policy & Politics*, 28, 3, pp. 379–95.

Giddens, A. (1998) *The Third Way: The Renewal of Social Democracy* (Cambridge: Polity).

Giddens, A. (2000) *The Third Way and its Critics* (Cambridge: Polity).

Glennerster, H., Hills, J., and Travers, T. (2000) *Paying for Health, Education and Housing: How does the Centre Pull the Purse Strings* (Oxford: Oxford University Press).

Goodin, R. (1996) 'Institutions and Their Design', in R. Good in (ed.) *The Theory of Institutional Design* (Cambridge: Cambridge University Press).

Goss, S. (2001) *Making Local Governance Work* (London: Macmillan).

Gwyn, W. (1965) *The Meaning of the Separation of Powers* (New Orleans: Tulane Studies in Political Science).

Gwyn, W. (1986) 'The Separation of Powers and Modern Forms of Democratic Government', in R. Goldwin and A. Kaufman (eds) *Separation of Powers – How Does it Work?* (Washington DC: American Enterprise Institute for Policy Research).

Gyford, J. (1976) *Local Politics in Britain* (London: Croom Helm).

Gyford, J. (1991) *Citizens, Consumers and Councils* (London: Macmillan).

Gyford, J. Leach, S. and Game, C. (1989) *The Changing Politics of Local Government* (London: Unwin Hyman).

Hall, D. and Leach, S. (2000) 'The Changing Nature of Local Labour Politics', in G. Stoker (ed.) *The New Politics of British Local Governance* (London: Macmillan).

Held, D. (1987) *Models of Democracy* (Cambridge: Polity).

Hill, R. (1996) 'Mission Possible: A New Role for the Local State', *Renewal*, 4, 2, pp. 21–7.

Hirschman, A. (1970) *Exit, Voice and Loyalty* (Cambridge, MA: Harvard University Press).

Hirschman, A. (1995) *A Propensity to Self-Subversion* (Cambridge, MA: Harvard University Press).

Hirst, P. (2000) 'Democracy and Governance', in J. Pierre (ed.) *Debating Governance* (Oxford: Oxford University Press).

HM Government (1999) *Modernising Government* Cm 4310 (London: HMSO).

Hodge, M., Leach, S. and Stoker, G. (1997) *More Than a Flower Show – Elected Mayors and Local Democracy*, Fabian Paper No. 32 (London: Fabian Society).

Hood, C. (1983) *The Tools of Government* (London: Macmillan).

Hood, C. (1986a) *Administrative Analysis. An Introduction to Rules, Enforcement and Organizations* (Brighton: Wheatsheaf).

Hood, C. (1986b) 'Concepts of Control over Public Bureaucracies: "Comptrol" and "Interpolable" Balance', in G Kaufmann, G. Majone and V. Ostrom (eds) *Guidance, Control and Evaluation in the Public Sector* (Berlin: Walter de Gruyter).

Hood, C. (2000) *The Art of the State* (Oxford: Oxford University Press).

Hood, C., Scott, C., James, O., Jones, G. and Travers, T. (1998) *Regulation Inside Government* (Oxford: Oxford University Press).

House of Commons (2001a) Public Administration Committee, Sixth Report Session 2000–1, *Public Participation: Issues and Innovations* HC 373-I (London: HMSO).

House of Commons (2001b) *Public Administration Committee, Fifth Report Session 2000/01: Mapping the Quango State, HC367* (London: HMSO).

House of Commons (2002a) *How the Local Government Act 2000 is Working* Transport, Local Government and the Regions Committee, Report and Proceedings of the Committee, vol. 1, HC 602-I (London: House of Commons).

House of Commons (2002b) *Draft Local Government Bill*, Transport, Local Government and Regions Committee, Fifteenth Report of Session 2001–02, vol. 1, HC 981-I (London: House of Commons).

House of Commons (2002c) *The Public Service Ethos*, Public Administration Select Committee, Seventh Report of Session 2001–02, vol. 1, HC 263-I (London: House of Commons).

House of Lords (1996) Select Committee on Relations between Central and Local Government, *Rebuilding Trust, Volume 1* Report, HL Paper 97 (London: HMSO).

IDeA (2001) *So Far So Good ... Progress on Delivering Best Value* (London: Improvement and Development Agency).

Ingraham, P., Thompson, J. and Sanders, R. (eds) (1998) *Transforming Government* (San Francisco: Jossey-Bass).

IPPR (2001) *Building Better Partnerships: The Final Report of the Commission on Public Private Partnerships* (London: IPPR).

Jackson, R.M. (1971) *Enforcing the Law* (London: Penguin).

Jenkins, S. (1995) *Accountable to None* (London: Hamish Hamilton).

Jessop, R. (2000) 'Governance Failure', in G. Stoker (ed.) *The New Politics of British Local Governance* (London: Macmillan).

John, P., Stoker, G. and Gains, F. (2003) 'The Challenge of Institutional Design and Re-Design: Changing the Political Management Practices of English Local Government', PSA Annual Conference, 15–17 April.

Jones, B. (1995) 'Bureaucrats and Urban Politics: Who controls? Who Benefits?' in D. Judge, H. Wolman and G. Stoker (eds) *Theories of Urban Politics* (London: Sage).

Jones, G. (1969) *Borough Politics* (London: Macmillan).

Jones, G. and Williams, J. (2002) 'Debating Elected Mayors', *Renewal*, 10, 2, pp. 77–87.

Kagan, R. and Scholtz, J. (1984) 'The Criminology of the Corporation and Regulatory Enforcement Strategies', in K. Hawkins and J. Thomas (eds) *Enforcing Regulation* (Boston, MA: Kluwer-Nijhoff).

Kelly, G. (2000) *The New Partnership Agenda* (London: Institute for Public Policy Research).

234 References

Kelly, G. and Muers, S. (2002) *Creating Public Value: An Analytical Framework for Public Service Reform* (London: Cabinet Office Strategy Unit).

Kettl, D.F. (1993) *Sharing Power: Public Governance and Private Markets* (Washington, DC: The Brookings Institution).

Kettl, D.F., Ingraham, P., Sanders, R. and Horner, C. (1995) *Civil Service Reform. Building a Government that Works* (Washington, DC: The Brookings Institution).

Kickert, W., Klinjin, E. H. and Koppenjm, J. (1997) *Managing Complex Networks: Strategies for the Public Sector* (London: Sage).

Kleinman, M., Burton, P., Croft, J. and Travers, T. (2002) *Links between the Finance and Non-Finance Elements of Local Government: A Literature Review* (London: ODPM).

Laver, M. (1976) 'Exit Voice and Loyalty: The Strategic Production and Consumption of Public and Private Goods', *British Journal of Political Science*, 5, pp. 69–82.

Layfield Committee (1976) *Report of the Committee of Enquiry into Local Government Finance*, Cmnd 6543 (London: HMSO).

Leach, S. (1999) 'Introducing Cabinets into British Local Government', *Parliamentary Affairs*, 52, 1, pp. 77–93.

Leach, S. and Stoker, G. (1997) 'Understanding the Local Government Review: A Retrospective Analysis', *Public Administration*, 75, 1.

Leach, S., Stewart, J. and Walsh, K. (1994) *The Changing Organisation and Management of Local Government* (London: Macmillan).

Leigh, I. (2000) *Law, Politics and Local Democracy* (Oxford: Oxford University Press).

LGA (1999) *Whose Zone is it Anyway? The Guide to Area Based Initiatives* (London: Local Government Association).

LGA (2001) *An Inspector Calls: A Survey of Local Authorities on the Impact of Inspection* – LGA Research Report 18 (London: Local Government Association).

LGA (2003) *The Balance of Funding – The Issues*, Discussion Paper (London: Local Governments Association)

Lindblom, C. (1977) *Politics and Markets* (New York: Basic Books).

Loughlin, M. (1996) 'The Constitutional Status of Local Government', in L. Pratchett and D. Wilson (eds) *Local Democracy and Local Government* (London: Macmillan).

Lowndes, V. (1999a) 'Management Change in Local Governance', in G. Stoker (ed.) *The New Management of British Local Governance* (London: Macmillan).

Lowndes, V. (1999b) 'Rebuilding Trust in Central/Local Relations: Policy or Passion', *Local Government Studies*, 25, 4, pp. 116–36.

Lowndes, V. (2000) 'Rebuilding Trust in Central/Local Relations: Policy or Passion?', in L. Pratchett (ed.) *Renewing Local Democracy?* (London: Frank Cass).

Lowndes, V., Stoker, G., Pratchett, L., Wilson, L., Leach, S. and Wingfield, M. (1998a) *Enhancing Public Participation in Local Government: A Research Report* (London: DETR).

Lowndes, V., Stoker, G., Pratchett, L., Wilson, L., Leach, S. and Wingfield, M. (1998b) *Modern Local Government: Guidance on Enhancing Public Participation* (London: DETR).

Lowndes, V., Pratchett, L. and Stoker, G. (2001a) 'Trends in Public Participation: Part 1 – Local Government Perspectives', *Public Administration*, 79, 1, 0pp. 205–22.

Lowndes, V., Pratchett, L. and Stoker, G. (2001b) 'Trends in Public Participation: Part 2 – Citizens' Perspectives', *Public Administration*, 79, 2, pp. 445–55.

Lowndes, V., Pratchett, L. and Stoker, G. (2002) 'Social Capital and Political Participation: How Do Local Institutions Constrain or Enable the Mobilisation of Social Capital?' Paper for the Robert Putnam Cambridge Social Capital Seminar, 19 November.

Ludlam, S. and Smith, M. (2001) *New Labour in Government* (Basingstoke: Palgrave).

McGarvey, N. and Stoker, G. (1999) *Lessons Learnt from Intervention. The Literature Review* (November) (London: DETR).

McIntosh, N. (1999) *Commission on Local Government and the Scottish Parliament, Report* (Edinburgh: The Scottish Executive).

Maloney, W., Smith, G. and Stoker, G. (2000) 'Social Capital and Urban Governance', *Political Studies*, 48, pp. 823–34.

Mandelson, P. (2000) *Next Steps for New Labour*. The London Young Fabians Herbert Morrison Memorial Lecture, 1 November.

March, J.G. and Olsen, J.P. (1995) *Democratic Governance* (New York: Free Press).

Marquand, D. (1998) *Must Labour Win?* (London: Fabian Society).

Marsh, D. and Rhodes, R. (1992) *Policy Networks in British Government* (Oxford: Oxford University Press).

Martin, S. (1999) 'Learning to Modernise: Creating the Capacity to Improve Local Public Services', *Public Policy and Administration*, 14, 3, pp. 54–66.

Martin, S. (2000) 'Implementing "Best Value": Local Public Services in Transition', *Public Administration*, 78, 1, pp. 209–27.

Martin, S. *et al.* (2001) *Improving Public Services: Evaluation of the Best Value Pilot Programme: Final Report* (London: DETR).

Miller, W. (1980) *Irrelevant Elections* (Oxford: Clarendon Press).

Miller, W., Timpson, A.M. and M. Lessnoff (1995) 'Opinions: Public Support for Equality', in W. Miller (ed.) *Alternatives to Freedom: Arguments and Opinions* (Harlow: Longman).

Miller, W., Dickson, M. and Stoker, G. (2000) *Models of Local Governance: Public Opinion and Political Theory in Britain* (Basingstoke: Palgrave).

Moore, M. (1995) *Creating Public Value* (Cambridge, MA: Harvard University Press).

Moran, M. (2003) 'Regulation and Reform', Paper to Corporate Governance Cluster, IPEG, University of Manchester.

Mori (2003) *Trust in Public Institutions* (London: Audit Commission).

Mossberger, K. and Stoker, G. (2001) 'The Evolution of Regime Theory', *Urban Affairs Review*, 36, 6.

Mulgan, G. (1994) *Politics in an Antipolitcal Age* (Cambridge: Polity).

Mulgan, G. and Perri 6 (1996) 'The Local's Coming Home: Decentralisation by Degrees', *DEMOS Quarterly*, 9, pp. 3–7.

National Audit Office (2001) *Joining Up Public Services* (London: National Audit Office).

Newton, K. (1976) *Second City Politics: Democratic Processes and Decision Making in Birmingham* (Oxford: Oxford University Press).

ODPM (2002a) *Tackling Poor Performance in Local Government: A Consultation Paper* (London: ODPM).

ODPM (2002b) *Your Region, Your Choice: Revitalising the English Regions* (London: ODPM/ DTLR).

ODPM (2003) *Background Papers to the Balance of Funding Review* (London: ODPM).

Office of Public Services Reform (2002) *Reforming Our Public Services: Principles into Practice* (London: The Prime Minister's Office of Public Service Reform).

Ostrom, E. (1990) *Governing the Commons: The Evolution of Institutions for Collective Action* (Cambridges: Cambridge University Press).

Perri, 6. (1997) 'Governing by Cultures', in G. J. Mulgan, *Life After Politics: New Thinking for the 21st Century* (London: HarperCollins).

Perri, 6. (1999) *Neo-Durkeimian Institutional Theory*. Paper presented to University of Strathclyde Conference on Institutional Theory in Political Science, Ross Priory, 18–19 October 1999.

Perri, 6., Leat, D., Seltzer, K. and Stoker, G. (1999) *Governing in the Round* (London: DEMOS).

Perri, 6., Leat, D., Seltzer, K. and Stoker, G. (2002) *Towards Holistic Governance* (Basingstoke: Palgrave).

Perri, 6. and Peck, E. (2003) 'New Labour's Management Signature', unpublished paper.

Peters, G. (1998) 'Tailoring Change Strategies: Alternative Approaches to Reform', in P. Ingraham, J. Thompson and R. Sanders (eds) *Transforming Government* (San Francisco: Jossey-Bass).

Peters, G. and Pierre, J. (2001) *Multi-Level Governance: A Faustian Bargain*, Conference on Multi Level Governance, Sheffield, July.

Pierre, J. (2000) *Debating Governance* (Oxford: Oxford University Press).

Pierre, J. and Peters, G. (2000) *Governance, Politics and the State* (London: Macmillan).

Pierre, J. and Stoker, G. (2000)'Towards Multi-Level Governance', in P. Dunleavy, A. Gamble, I. Holliday and G. Peele (eds) *Developments in British Politics 6* (London: Macmillan).

Pimlott, B. and Rao, N. (2002) *Governing London* (Oxford: Oxford University Press).

PIU (2001) *Better Policy Delivery and Design: A Discussion Paper* (London: Performance and Innovation Unit, March).

Pollitt, C. (1995) 'Justification by Works or by Faith? Evaluating the New Public Management', *Evaluation*, 1, 2 October, pp. 133–54.

Pollitt, C. (1996) 'Managerialism Revisited', Paper presented to the Canadian Centre for Management Development, Taking Stock Project, Ottawa, May.

Pollitt, C., Birchall, J. and Putnam, K. (1998) *Decentralising Public Service Management* (London: Macmillan).

Pollitt, C., Birchall, J. and Putnam, K. (1999) 'Letting Managers Manage: Decentralisation and Opting-Out', in G. Stoker (ed.) *The New Management of British Local Governance* (London: Macmillan).

Purdam, K., Fieldhouse, Kalra, V. and Russell, A. (2002) *Voter and Engagement among Black and Minority Ethnic Communities* (London: Electoral Commission).

Pratchett, L. and Wilson, D. (1996) (eds) *Local Democracy and Local Government* (London: Macmillan).

Putnam, R. (1993) *Making Democracy Work: Civil Traditions in Modern Italy* (Princeton, NJ: Princeton University Press).

Putnam, R. (1995) 'Bowling Alone: America's Declining Social Capital', *Journal of Democracy*, 6, 1, pp. 65–78.

Putnam, R. (2000) *Bowling Alone* (New York: Simon & Schuster).

Rallings, C. and Thrasher, M. (2000) *Turnout at Local Elections: Influences on Levels of Local Registration and Electoral Participation* (London: DETR).

Rallings, C., Thrasher, M. and Temple, M. (1996) 'Participation in Local Elections', in L. Pratchett and D. Wilson (eds) *Local Democracy and Local Government* (London: Macmillan).

Rallings, C., Thrasher, M. and Stoker G. (2000) *Proportional Representation and Local Government: Lessons from Europe* (York: Joseph Rowntree Foundation).

Rallings, C., Thrasher, M. and Cowling, D. (2002) 'Mayoral Referendums and Elections', *Local Government Studies*, 28, 4, Winter.

Rao, N. (2004) 'Mayors, Cabinets or the Status Quo', *Local Governments Studies* (forthcoming).

Rao, N. and Young, K. (1999) 'Revitalising Local Democracy', in R. Jowell, J. Curtice, A. Park and K. Thomson (eds) *British Social Attitudes: The 16th Report* (Aldershot: Gower).

Rashman, L. and Hartley, J. (2002) Leading and Learning? Knowledge Transfer in the Beacon Council Scheme', *Public Administration*, 80, 3, pp. 523–42.

Rhodes, R. (1997a) *Understanding Governance* (Buckingham: Open University Press).

Rhodes, R. (1997b) 'From Marketization to Diplomacy "It's the Mix that Matters"', *Public Policy and Administration*, 12, pp. 31–50.

Rhodes, R. (1988) *Beyond Westminster and Whitehall* (London: Unwin Hyman).

Rhodes, R. (2000) 'Governance and Public Administration', in J. Pierre (ed.), *Debating Governance* (Oxford: Oxford University Press).

Riddell, P. (2001) 'Review of The Control Freaks by N. Jones', *The Stakeholder*, 5, 2, pp. 36–7.

Russell, A., Fieldhouse, E., Purdam, K. and Kalra, V. (2002) *Voter Engagement and Young People* (London: Electoral Commission).

Savas, E. (2000) *Privatisation and Public–Private Partnerships* (London: Chatham House).

Seldon, A. (ed.) (2001) *The Blair Effect: The Blair Government 1997–2001* (London: Little, Brown & Company).

Sharpe, L.J. (1970) 'Theories and Values of Local Government', *Political Studies*, 18, 2, pp. 153–74.

Sheldrake, J. (1989) *Municipal Socialism* (Aldershot: Avebury).

Skelcher, C. (1992) *Managing for Service Quality* (Harlow: Longman).

Skelcher, C. (1998) *The Appointed State. Quasi-government Organisations and Democracy* (Buckingham: Open University Press).

Smith, G. and Wales, C. (2000) 'Citizens' Juries and Deliberative Democracy', *Political Studies*, 48, 1, pp. 51–65.

Social Exclusion Unit (2001) *A New Commitment to Neighbourhood Renewal* (London: Cabinet Office).

Spencer, L., Elam, G. and Turner, R. (2000) *'It is Our money Anyway...' Lessons Learnt from Giving the Public a Voice in Local Authority Spending Decisions* (London: DETR).

References

5) 'The Internal Management of Local Authorities', in J. Stewart and
s) *Local Government in the 1990s* (London: Macmillan).

7) 'The Local Authority as Regulator', *Local Government Policy*

Stewart, J. (2000) *The Nature of British Local Government* (London: Macmillan).

Stewart, J. and Stoker, G. (1988) *From Local Administration to Community Government*, Research Series, 351 (London: Fabian Society).

Stewart, J. and Stoker, G. (eds) (1989) *The Future of Local Government* (London: Macmillan).

Stewart, J. and Stoker, G. (1995) 'Fifteen Years of Local Government Restructuring 1979–1994', in J. Stewart and G. Stoker (eds) *Local Government in the 1990s* (London: Macmillan).

Stoker, G. (1989) 'Creating a Local Government for a Post-Fordist Society: The Thatcherite Project', in J. Stewart and G. Stoker (eds) *The Future of Local Government* (London: Macmillan) pp. 141–71.

Stoker, G. (1990) 'Regulation Theory, Local Government and the Transition from Fordism', in D. King and J. Pierre (eds) *Challenges to Local Government* (London: Sage).

Stoker, G. (1991) *The Politics of Local Government* (London: Macmillan).

Stoker, G. (1993) *Cities in the 1990s: Local Choice for a Balanced Strategy* (Harlow: Longman).

Stoker, G. (1995) 'Regime Theory and Urban Politics', in D. Judge, G. Stoker, and H. Wolman (eds) *Theories of Urban Politics* (London: Sage).

Stoker, G. (1996) 'Redefining Local Democracy' in L. Pratchett and D. Wilson (ed.) *Local Democracy and Local Government* (London: Macmillan).

Stoker, G. (1997a) 'Local Political Participation', in *New Perspectives in Local Governance* (York: Joseph Rowntree Foundation).

Stoker, G. (1997b) 'The Privatisation of Urban Services in the United Kingdom', in D. Lorrain and G. Stoker (eds) *The Privatisation of Urban Services in Europe* (London: Pinter).

Stoker, G. (1998) 'Governance as Theory: Five Propositions', *International Social Science Journal*, 155, pp. 17–28.

Stoker, G. (1999a) 'Quangos and Local Democracy', in M. Flinders and M. Smith (eds) *Quangos, Accountability and Reform* (London: Macmillan).

Stoker, G. (1999b) 'Introduction: The Unintended Costs and Benefits of New Management Reform for British Local Government', in G. Stoker (ed.) *The New Management of British Local Governance* (London: Macmillan) pp. 1–21.

Stoker, G. (ed.) (1999c) *The New Management of British Local Governance* (London: Macmillan).

Stoker, G. (1999d) 'The Moderniser's Guide to Local Government', in G. Hassan and C. Warhurst (eds) *A Moderniser's Guide to Scotland: A Different Future* (Edinburgh: The Big issue/Centre for Public Policy) pp. 241–8.

Stoker, G. (2000a) 'The Three Projects of New Labour', *Renewal*, 8, 3, pp. 7–15.

Stoker, G. (2000b) 'Learning from Social Experiments?', *Municipal Journal*, December.

Stoker, G. (2000c) 'Urban Political Science and the Challenge of Urban Governance', in J. Pierre (ed.) *Debating Governance* (Oxford: Oxford University Press).

Stoker, G. (2001) *Money talks: Creating a Dialogue Between Taxpayers and Local Government* (London: New Local Government Network).

Stoker, G. (2002a) 'Life is Lottery: New Labour's Strategy for the Reform of Devolved Governance', *Public Administration*, 80(3), pp. 417–34.

Stoker, G. (2002b) 'Introduction', in I. Parker and A. Randle (eds) *Beyond SW1. Elected Mayors and the Renewal of Civic Leadership* (London: New Local Government Network).

Stoker, G. (2003) 'New Labour needs local government', *Renewal*, 11(1), pp. 61–7.

Stoker, G. and Mossberger, K. (1995) 'The Post-Fordist Local State: The Dynamics of its Development', in J. Stewart and G. Stoker (eds) *Local Government in the 1990s* (London: Macmillan).

Stoker, G. and Travers, T. (1998) *A Tale of Two Cities. The Government of New York: Lessons for London* (London: Association of London Government).

Stoker, G. and Travers, T. (1999) *Barcelona: Lessons from its Mayor-Council Model* (London: Deloitte & Touche).

Stoker, G. and Travers, T. (2001) *A New Account? Choices in Local Government Finance* (York: Joseph Rowntree Foundation).

Stoker, G. and Wolman, H. (1992) 'Drawing Lessons from US Experience: An Elected Mayor for British Local Government', *Public Administration*, 70, 2, pp. 241–67.

Stoker, G., Hatter, W. and Gilby, N. (2002) *Council Tax Consultation – Guidelines for Local Authorities* (London: Office of the Deputy Prime Minister).

Stoker, G., Smith, G., Maloney, W. and Young, S. (2003) 'Voluntary Organisations and the Generation of Social Capital', in M. Boddy and M. Parkinson (eds) *City Matters: Competitiveness, Cohesion and Urban Governance* (Bristol: The Policy Press).

Stone, C. (1989) *Regime Politics* (Lawrence: University of Kansas Press).

Sullivan, H. (2001) 'Modernisation, Democratisation and Community Governance', *Local Governance Studies*, 27, 3, pp. 1–24.

Sullivan, H. and Skelcher, C. (2002) *Working Across Boundaries* (Basingstoke: Palgrave).

Sydow, J. (1998) 'Understanding the Constitution of Interorganizational Trust', in C. Lane and R. Bachmann (eds) *Trust Within and Between Organizations* (Oxford: Oxford University Press).

Szreter, S. (2002) 'A Central Role for Local Government? The Example of late Victorian Britain', *History and Policy*, May.

Talbot, C. (1994) *Reinventing Public Management: A Survey of Public Sector Managers' Reaction to Change* (Corby: Institute of Management).

Temple, M. (2000) 'New Labour's Third Way: Pragmatism and Governance', *The British Journal of Politics*, 2, 3, pp. 302–25.

Thompson, G., Frances, J., Levacic, R. and Mitchell, J. (1991) *Markets, Hierarchies and Networks: The Co-ordination of Social Life* (Buckingham: Open University Press).

Thompson, M., Ellis, R. and Wildavsky, A. (1990) *Cultural Theory* (Boulder: Westview).

Travers, A. (2001) 'Local Government', in A. Seldon (ed.) *The Blair Effect* (London: Little, Brown and Company).

Waldegrave, W. (1993) *The Reality of Reform and Accountability in Today's Public Service* (London: Public Finance Foundation).

Walker, R. (2000) Policy Evaluation of Welfare to Work Schemes in the UK: Learning without Social Experiments? Paper presented to ESRC Conference, November 2000.

Walker, D. (2002) *In Praise of Centralism. A Critique of New Localism* (London: Catalyst).

Watt, P. and Fender, J. (1999) 'Feasible Changes in the UK Controls on Local Government Expenditure', *Public Money and Management*, 19, 3, September pp. 17–22.

Wheatley, M. (1999) *Leadership and the New Science* (San Francisco: Berrett-Koehler).

White, S. (1998) 'Interpreting the Third Way: Not One Road but Many', *Renewal*, 6, 2, pp. 17–30.

Widdicombe Committee (1986) *The Report of the Inquiry into the Conduct of Local Authority Business* (London: HMSO).

Wilson, D. and Game, C. (1998) *Local Government in the United Kingdom*, 2nd edn (London: Macmillan).

Wilson, D. and Game, C. (2002) *Local Government in the United Kingdom*, 3rd edn (Basingstoke: Palgrave).

Wright, A. (2002) 'The Curse of Centralism', in *Public Finance*, June 28–July 4.

Young, K. and Davies, M. (1990) *The Politics of Local Government since Widdicombe* (York: Joseph Rowntree Foundation).

Young, K. and Mills, L. (1993) *A Portrait of Change* (Luton: Local Government Management Board).

Young, S. (2000) 'Participation Strategies and Local Environmental Politic: Local Agenda 21', in G. Stoker (ed.) *The New Politics of Local Governance* (London: Macmillan).

Index

accountability 75, 180–1, 191;
administrative 17–18, 20; and
local quangos 43; and network
governance 208–10; state
212–13
Armstrong, H. 50, 78, 108, 149
Audit Commission 92, 95–6, 98, 216
authority-based systems 221

Balance of Funding Review (2003)
68, 175
Balls, E. 167–8
Beacon status 64, 79, 89
Beecham, J. 149
Benefit Fraud Inspectorate 95
Bernstein, M. 103
Best Value Inspectorate 88, 92
Best Value policy 5, 55, 63–4, 74, 80,
81, 86, 114, 145, 203;
audit/inspection process 89; and
bureau-shaping 93–4;
collaborative 90; and
commitment to group values/
tight-knit social relations 93; and
compliance culture 92–3;
development of 88; difference
with CCT 87; effect of fatalistic
outlook on 90, 92; establishment
of 87; fatalistic attitude 94;
funding issues 64; hierarchical
90, 92, 94; and in-house services
90; and individualism 93;
introduction of 202; market 90;
and outsourcing 90; and
performance management 63–4;
positive view of 216; and re-
engineering services 90;
response of local authorities to
89–94; star system 88–9; support
for local government 89; as top-
down approach 86, 87–8; and use

of control/compliance techniques
88; virtue of 88
Birch, A. 119, 120
Blair, T. 57, 108, 127, 135
Blaug, R. 122
Bogdanor, V. 45
Brady, H. 123
Bromley, C. 197
Brown, G. 75, 167
Burke, E. 53

Campaign for English Regions 83
central-local relationship 18–20, 193,
204; and disharmony 80–1; and
education 176–7; egalitarian
aspect 75; fatalist 75–6; and
finance 177–8; finance 184–6;
government interventions 60, 63,
101; hierarchist framework
74–5; and non-compliance
102–6; plethora of initiatives
79–80; and shared responsibility
181; and social services 177;
steering centralism model
219–22; taxation 178–9
challenge culture, and client/producer
separation 80; and governance
192–214; and
inspection/regulation processes
80; and institutions 200–1; and
mayoral model 147; and
modernization 49; and
multi-level governance 193; and
networked governance 24,
136–9; and New Labour 7; and
peer review 80; and public trust
197; and regulation 37; support
for 80
Charter Mark 203
Child and Adolescent Mental Health
and Family Services 195

241